SOUTH ASIA INSTITUTE, NEW DELHI BRANCH

HEIDELBERG UNIVERSITY

SOUTH ASIAN STUDIES NO. XXVIII

Maharashtra: Culture and Society

Folk Culture, Folk Religion and Oral Traditions as a Component in Maharashtrian Culture

Edited by

GÜNTHER-DIETZ SONTHEIMER

MANOHAR

2026

First published 1995
Reprinted 2021, 2022, 2023, 2024, 2025, 2026

ISBN 978-81-7304-087-0

Published by
Ajay Kumar Jain *for*
Manohar Publishers & Distributors
4753/23 Ansari Road, Daryaganj
New Delhi 110 002

Printed at
Replika Press Pvt. Ltd.

TABLE OF CONTENTS

PREFACE

One of the most challenging aspects of Indian culture is its variety and complexity. The multiplicity of groups and traditions in India and the manifold character of their interrelations provide much of the richness of the tapestry of Indian life and thought. Günther Sontheimer was fascinated by this aspect of Indian culture. He sought to understand Indian culture, and especially Hindu religion, in all its wealth and variety. In his article "Hinduism: The Five Components and their Interaction",[1] Sontheimer distinguished the following five elements of the dominant religious tradition of India: the work and teachings of Brāhmans, asceticism and renunciation, tribal religion, folk religion, and *bhakti*. In distinguishing these five "components", Sontheimer considered it important that they "not be viewed as watertight compartments, but rather as presenting a continuum and as interacting among themselves in a fluctuating process over thousands of years."[2]

Although Sontheimer's early work dealt with Indian religious law *(dharmaśāstra)*, one of the learned disciplines of Brāhmans, it was folk religion and tribal religion that he studied in the greatest depth from the late 1960's until his death in 1992. Focusing on the cult of the folk god Khaṇḍobā and on the traditions of the Dhangar shepherds of Maharashtra, Sontheimer's studies also extended to other groups, deities and traditional cults in the pastoral and forest areas of Maharashtra, Karnataka and Andhra Pradesh. His interest was

---

[1] In *Hinduism Reconsidered*, edited by Günther D. Sontheimer and Hermann Kulke (Manohar, 1989), pp. 197-212.

[2] Ibid, p. 197.

not confined to religion, nor his methods to those of either philology or ethnology. Like his teacher D. D. Kosambi, Sontheimer aimed "to combine armchair philology with archeological, ethnological, linguistic, and other investigations."[3]

It was thus extremely appropriate that, when Günther Sontheimer convened the Third International Conference on Maharashtra: Culture and Society in Heidelberg in June of 1988, one of the two principal themes of the conference was "The Folk Element in Maharashtrian Culture". In inviting scholars of Maharashtra to the conference, he stated this theme as follows:

> By "folk" we do not mean fashionable contributions to folk festivals for tourists and to "India Festivals" or the study of phenomena at the most considered worthy only of footnotes in subjects kept separate, like history, Indology, philosophy, politics etc., but an integral part of Maharashtrian (and, for that matter, Indian) culture and ethos. "Folk" means the direct accessibility of living *(jāgṛt)* deities, rituals connected with them—whether, e.g. *divya* or *kaul, jatrā* or *kheḷ*, or local or regional traditions—as well as oral literature such as the oral epics, *povāḍās, lāvaṇīs* and folk performances such as *tamāśā*, or—to cite only one more example of oral literature—women's songs about Ambedkar. Though folk culture has preserved its own identity, it has played its important role while *interacting* with other components of Maharashtrian culture, like the *bhakti* of the *sants*, or

[3] Günther-Dietz Sontheimer, *Pastoral Deities in Western India*, translated by Anne Feldhaus (New York: Oxford University Press, 1989), p. vi. Cf. D. D. Kosambi, "Combined Methods in Indology", *Indo Iranian Journal* 6 (1963): 177-202.

> with the śāstric tradition and with modern reductionism, which tends to assign the folk beliefs and customs of traditional culture to the realm of "superstition".

All but one of the papers collected in this volume were originally presented at the Third International Conference on Maharashtra: Culture and Society in Heidelberg in June, 1988. R. C. Dhere, who, although invited to the conference, was not able to attend, submitted his paper later as a sign of his interest in the subject of the conference and of his respect for Professor Sontheimer and his work. The paper was translated from the Marathi by S. G. Tulpule. Hugh van Skyhawk, who had been charged before Sontheimer's death with the technical aspects of editing the volume, continued this work in Sontheimer's absence. The manuscript was computerized and the corrections entered by Michael Martinec, Klaus-Werner Müller, Sibylle Zerr, and Christine Walter-Mendy, whose untimely death occurred on 6 June 1992. Hugh van Skyhawk and Anne Feldhaus copyedited the manuscript and, together with Parasnath Chaudhary, corrected the proofs.

Scholars at the Fifth International Conference on Maharashtra: Culture and Society (Bombay, December, 1992), many of whom had also been present at the Heidelberg conference and had submitted papers for this volume, agreed that it should be brought out in Sontheimer's name, but without the substantial introduction he would have contributed had he lived to write one.

Anne Feldhaus
Heidelberg, July, 1993

James W. Laine

ŚIVĀJĪ AS EPIC HERO*

The Himālayas are yours and mine
and the Sahyādris are mine alone

The Mahābhārata and Rāmāyaṇa
are yours and mine
The heroic tales of King Śivājī
are my delight alone.

(Kavi Vasant Bapat in
Kulkarni and Atre 1960: 158-60)

The turning point where the sacral nexus of conflict, violence and death was cut through can perhaps best be characterized as an 'axial breakthrough.' The once unitary world of agonistic sacrifice was definitively broken and thrown open by the rift between uncompromising transcendence and mundane reality. The axial breakthrough did not, however, restructure the world. It posed a transcendent order that, like the renouncer, turned its back on the world. Having no other meaning than its internal 'rational' order, it left

* The author wishes to thank Professor S. G. Tulpule, Mr. V. L. Manjul, Dr. S. Bahulkar and Mrs. Sucheta Paranjpe for invaluable assistance in the research of this article.

the world to its age-old devices of magic and meaning, to ambivalence and conflict.

(Heesterman 1985: 4-5)

Vasant Bapat, in the modern Marathi ballad, or *povāḍā*, quoted above, makes a number of comparisons between things of pan-Indian cultural significance (*e.g.*, the Himālayas) and their regional counterparts (*e.g.*, the Sahyādris). His respect is for the national, but his special affection is for the local. When he turns to the great classical epics, the *Mahābhārata* and the *Rāmāyaṇa*, he compares them to the heroic tales *(vīra-kahāṇi)* of the Maratha King Śivājī. We may take Bapat's verses as a point of departure for two paths of inquiry and reflection. Firstly, how are we to understand the regional and folk culture of Mahārāṣṭra in its relation to classical, Sanskritic or pan-Indian culture? And secondly, how are the heroic legends of Śivājī continuations of the classical epic tradition of the *Mahābhārata* and *Rāmāyaṇa?*

Along the first line of inquiry, we can take the *povāḍā*, the Marathi ballad, as an expression of regional culture. The *povāḍā* is composed by a *śāhīr*, and traditionally sung in the context of a folk drama *(tamāśā)* or in the popular ritual known as the *gondhaḷ* by devotees of the goddess Bhavānī. Traditional *povāḍās* have been collected and published and thousands of modern popular ballads are printed in pamphlets, but the tradition was originally a predominantly oral one.

The *povāḍā* is meant to express the heroic sentiment *(vīra-rasa)*, just as the love song, a sister genre known as the *lāvaṇī*, should express the erotic *(śṛṅgāra-rasa)*. The earliest *povāḍā* that we have is *The Killing of Afzal Khān*, described internally as a *bīr māla* (heroic song) by its author Agrindās (Ajñāndās).[1] It appears to be a

---

[1] Ajñāndās, *Afzal Khān Vadh* in Kelkar 1928: 1-23. This ballad was loosely trans-

panegyric praising Śivājī directly after the great Maratha victory at Javli in 1659. Thus the *povāḍā* as we know it is intimately related to the legendary biography of Śivājī—*The Killing of Afzal Khan* is the earliest expression of praise for the king, and is related to the praise of the hero's favorite deity, the goddess Bhavānī of Tuljapur.

To the present day, Śivājī—whose daring adventures and political successes as an independent Hindu ruler have made him the Mahārāṣṭrian hero *par excellence*—remains a favorite subject of the balladeer. Other Mahārāṣṭrian heroes and heroines[2] (Tānājī, Bājī Prabhu, Rāma Bāī *et al.*) were also celebrated from an early period. In the last hundred years, the *povāḍā* has often become more overtly ideological, whether reformist or reactionary, while celebrating less the sentiment of heroism than a more abstract patriotism, in the process growing more pan-Indian in ideology and turning to non-Mahārāṣṭrians—e.g. Mahatma Gandhi—as subjects.[3] At this point, although the *povāḍā* is a regional literary form wedded to the Marathi language, the dividing line between folk and classical, regional and pan-Indian is no longer clear. Thus, while we need to be alert to the distinctiveness of regional and folk themes and ideologies and class-interests, we must always remain aware of the interaction between folk and classical, regional and pan-Indian spheres. Imposing such categories as "folk" or "classic" can obscure the organic relations between them. If a pan-Indian classic like the *Mahābhārata* is rich in folkloric material, and is informed by submerged, encompassed, even totally forgotten themes and ideolo-

lated by Acworth 1894: 1-13.

[2] See *Tānājīcā Povāḍā* in Kelkar 1928: 24-63 and Acworth 1894: 14-55. See *Bājī Pasalkarācā Povāḍa* in Kelkar 1961: 8f. See *Thorle Mādhavarāvāñcī Patnī Rāmabāī Satī Gelī* in Acworth and Shaligram 1891: 114-118.

[3] For example, I was given a *povāḍā* published in a pamphlet in 1973 about Indira Gandhi by Śāhīr Anna Maralikar. Also see O'Hanlon 1985: 168-186, which discusses Jyotiba Phule's anti-brahmin *povāḍā* about Śivājī.

gies,[4] certainly the regional ballad and related folklore and legend may contain ideological features which reveal themes and structures of a classical, or even pre-classical, pan-Indian nature.

Regarding the second point—the continuation of classical epic themes in the heroic legends of Śivājī—we may state that while the extant *Mahābhārata* and *Rāmāyaṇa* have been structured, read and encompassed by a Purāṇic ideology—a mythic structure which Madeleine Biardeau has termed "the universe of *bhakti*" (Biardeau 1981, *passim)*[5] —both epics retain an underlying ideology of heroism and tragedy that is kṣatriyan and pre-classical and perhaps orginally Indo-European. Thus, while the classical epics have been redacted and mythologized from a Vaiṣṇava, brahmanical, philosophical and atemporal-mystical point of view, the more truly *epic* voice of legend, conflict, tragedy and dharmic ambiguity, a voice echoing from the pre-classical world Heesterman has described as the world of the unreformed sacrifice (Heesterman 1985: 1-4, *passim*)—remains secondary but nontheless audible. The voice which declares war to be a blood-sacrifice is, moreover, heard not only by listening intently to the classical epics where it survives but is covered by the dominant voices of brahmin reformers. In one sense the classical epics are succeeded by the *Purāṇas* and devotional poetry of the medieval period, but in another sense they were succeeded by the truly heroic poetry of regional ballads and epics. Songs of heroism from Tamil Nadu and Andhra Pradesh and Rajasthan[6] and, of course, Mahārāṣṭra, celebrate the deeds of legendary and historic warriors and heroines and, though here too the otherwordly transcendentalism of brahmins, ascetics and saints retained its profound cultural authority, a martial religious spirit served as a perhaps nec-

---

[4] See my discussion of competing ideologies in the *Mahābhārata*, Laine (forthcoming).

[5] For reviews of Biardeau's program, see Laine 1986 and Hiltebeitel 1983.

[6] For studies of regional heroic literatures see Beck 1982, Blackburn 1978, Roghair 1982, Wadley 1983 and Blackburn and Ramanujan 1986.

essary worldly counterpoint.

Now let us turn to the Mahārāṣṭrian memories of the epic king Śivājī.

The sources for the study of the legendary hero Śivājī are many and varied, far more numerous than for the "historical Śivājī." There are countless *povāḍās,*[7] Hindi poems,[8] texts for *kīrtans,*[9] a score of chronicles *(bakhars),*[10] Sanskrit *mahākāvyas*[11] and modern Marathi novels[12] and modern political and historical studies in Marathi and English. Moreover, every Mahārāṣṭrian with a mental image is a possible source for the study of the heroic Śivājī. As I have neither the ability nor the space to discuss even the written sources nor examine even the main legendary events in the life of Śivājī, I must limit myself to a few sources and two parts of Śivājī's epic biography. In what follows, I will discuss (1) the killing of Afzal Khān and (2) Śivājī's relationship to the poet-saint Rāmdās. I will examine a Sanskrit epic poem, the *Śivabhārata* of Paramānanda, a few *povāḍās,* a few *bakhars* and Mahīpati's *Santavijaya* (a hagiography of Rāmdās).[13]

---

[7] The most thorough collection of *povāḍās* is Kelkar 1928-1961.

[8] Śivājī's court poet Bhūṣan composed several Brajbhāṣā poems. See Sardesai 1927: 12-26.

[9] On *kīrtans* in Mahārāṣṭra, see Damle 1960.

[10] For translated selections from the earliest *bakhars,* see Sen 1920 and Patwardhan and Rawlinson 1929. Also see K. T. Telang, *Gleanings from Maratha Chronicles,* in Ranade 1961: 117-146.

[11] For a discussion of the historical sources for Śivājī's life, see Sarkar 1961: 391.

[12] H. N. Apte's famous novel *Gaḍ Ālā Paṇ Siṃha Gelā* (twenty-second printing, 1972) is a good example of the use of heroic narrative by a novelist.

[13] See Abbott 1932.

The Killing of Afzal Khān

In 1659, the court of the Adil Shahi Sultanate in Bijapur sent a force of some 12,000 cavalry under the general Afzal Khān to confront the rebellious son of Shahji. Though Shahji was himself an Adil Shahi *sardar*, his son Śivājī, while responsible for Puṇe, had captured several more forts within the Sultanate's territory. Through envoys, Afzal Khān and Śivājī agreed to a diplomatic meeting at Javli, at the foot of Pratapgad (near Mahabaleshwar). Each agreed to have only a few guards in attendance. During the meeting, Śivājī killed the Muslim captain, a pre-arranged signal was given and the Adil Shahi troops were routed by the surprise attack of Maratha soldiers. It was a stunning military victory and quickly became the stuff of legends. Muslim and later British historians (*e.g.* Khafi Khān, James Grant Duff) treated the event as a victory won through a treacherous murder. In the eyes of the Hindu Marathas, it was, at the very least, an act of highest heroism.[14]

The killing of Afzal Khān is the subject of the earliest extant *povāḍā*, the *Afzal Khān Vadh Povāḍā* of Ajñāndās.[15] In the *povāḍā* tradition, this event is primarily one of religious rather than military significance.

According to Ajñāndās, prior to coming to Javli, Afzal Khān desecrated several temples, including the temple to Viṭhobā in Pandharpur and, more importantly, the shrine of Śivājī's favorite deity, the goddess Bhavānī of Tuljapur. The ballad says

> Tulja Bhavānī was smashed
> And above (the image) a mosque was built.
> After the mosque was built

---

[14] On the Afzal Khān incident as an historical event, see Sardesai 1946: 124ff.; Sarkar 1961: 58ff.; also see Duff 1971: 87ff.

[15] See Kelkar 1928: 1-23 and id. 1961: 321-328.

A cow was slaughtered.

Then Afzal Khān taunted Bhavānī:

Show me some miracle (now)!

Angered, the goddess appeared to Śivājī in a dream to inform him that she was delivering the Khān into his hands "in a neat bundle" *(bāndhunī...dilā)* or, as we might put it, "on a silver platter." She declared:

A goat of thirty-two teeth
has come for the killing.

Afzal marched on to Wāī, a town on the Kṛṣṇā River in the valley below Panchgani and Mahabaleshwar. According to a later tradition, the Khān's men so molested the women of the town that a group of brahmin men entered the river and resolved to fast to death as a plea to the goddess. She responded to them by giving Śivājī victory. This event is commemorated as part of the annual Kṛṣṇā River festival in Wāī (January/February)[16] and reinforces the image of the Muslim invaders as demonic men of passion and violence.

The *povāḍā* treats the negotiations between Śivājī and Afzal Khān at some length. Both men sent messages of good will while harboring intentions to the contrary. By expressing great fear and feigning respect, the crafty Śivājī lured the overconfident Khān into a dangerously unguarded situation. Warned by the goddess, the king, however, kept his wits and went to the meeting with concealed armor and weapons (including the *wāgh nakh,* "tiger claws" and the Bhavānī sword either given him by the goddess or possessed by her;

---

[16] On the relation of Afzal Khān to the Kṛṣṇabāī festival of Wāī, see Joglekar, n.d. I thank Anne Feldhaus for this reference.

Ajñāndās uses the epithet *khandeśvarī* or "sword goddess" for Bhavānī). The ballad continues:

> Bhavānī and Śaṅkar were pleased.
> Tuljā gave her help to Śivājī.
> The Khān's fate was sealed.
> He came weaponless, empty-handed to the meeting tent.

Once inside the tent, the pretense of politeness was dropped and the two men traded insulting slurs on each others' birth:

> [Afzal:]
> "You are the son of a peasant *(kuṇbī)*
> but (you are vain enough) to decorate your
> tent in a royal style!"
>
> [Śivājī:]
> "I know *your* caste
> You're the son of a cook.
> Does a cook's son put on
> airs before Śivājī the Lion?"

Angered, the Khān grasped Śivājī and attempted to stab him, but his knife was blunted by the chain-mail hidden beneath Śivājī's clothes. The much smaller, agile Śivājī reacted quickly, stabbed the Khān and tore out his intestines with his "tiger claws". A fight broke out. The Khān managed one more blow, striking the King on his head. But again, though his turban was cut, his head was protected by a metal cap. When bearers came running to bear the dying Khān away in a palanquin, they were cut down and Śivājī decapitated the Khān. The signal was sounded and the Marathas made their successful surprise attack. The *povāḍā* concludes with a stanza in praise of Śivājī, the "avatāra of the Kali Yuga", the devotee of the goddess Bhavānī "who used to speak with him". Finally, reference is made to the gifts the poet received for composing the ballad.

This earliest ballad of Ajñāndās established the basic structure for the popular legend of Śivājī's killing of Afzal Khān. It was a David and Goliath affair, the smaller, savvy king overcoming a huge and conceited opponent.[17] The Khān was seen as a demonic iconoclast, threatening the gods, despising brahmins and—as the story of the molestation of the good women of Wāī suggests—a man of passion and violence. One tradition claims that, fearful of failure and impending death, Afzal Khān slaughtered the women of his huge harem lest any of his widows be touched by another man.[18] (The demonically lustful Muslim is always contrasted with the chivalry of Śivājī, who always demonstrated utmost respect to Muslim as well as Hindu ladies).

A few more interesting details can be gleaned from later *povāḍās*. Writing shortly after Śivājī's death, Śāhīr Phatanji[19] has Śivājī going to the meeting tent with the words:

> I will truly be Lord Śiva's servant
> (Only) if I take his (Afzal Khān's) life!

The killing of the Khān is usually seen as a sacrificial offering to the Goddess Bhavānī, but Phatanji never mentions her. In a modern *povāḍā* by one Nanivdekar,[20] Śivājī offers the Khān's head not to

---

[17] In his humorous novel about King David, *God Knows*, Joseph Heller has an elderly David reflect on his killing of Goliath: "Saviors who capture the imagination traditionally arrive unheralded from obscure or pedestrian origins. That was true of me. Where would the climax be if I were merely one famed fighter who'd triumphed over another? Achilles' defeat of Hector is the weakest part of the *Iliad*—he was the odds on favorite going in." (1984: 166).

[18] On the legend of Afzal murdering his wives, see Sarkar 1961: 70ff.

[19] Phatanji's ballad *Afzalkhānvadhācā Povāḍā* is found in Kelkar 1961: 1-7 and discussed in relation to Ajñāndās' poem, Kelkar 1961: 321-328.

[20] I recorded Nanivdekar's *povāḍā* in Pune in 1987 as performed by Śāhīr Hinge. I was helped by Mssrs. Bhaskar Chandavakar, V. L. Manjul and B. M. Joshi. See Nanivdekar 1959.

the goddess, but first to his mother Jījābāī's feet.

The *Śivabhārata* of Paramānanda

The basic structure of the story of the killing of Afzal Khān is maintained in the *Śivabhārata,* the unfinished Sanskrit *Mahākāvya* of Kavirājā Paramānanda, a court poet of Śivājī. As one would expect, there are, however, certain ideological shifts. In the *Śivabhārata,* (which means the *Bhārata* of Śivājī) Śivājī is presented as an *avatāra* of Viṣṇu, born to turn the tide against the Muslims (here called *yavanas),* who are incarnate *asuras* (18.37-38). Having described Afzal Khān as a man "wanting to kill every brahmin he sees" (18.20), "an increaser of the evil of the Kali Yuga" (18.18) and "a mountain of sin...determined to obstruct the path of *varṇāśrama-dharma*" (18.32), Śivājī reveals himself to be the incarnate Lord:

> I am that Lord Viṣṇu
> Essence of all the gods,
> Manifest now on earth
> to remove the world's burden!
>
> The Muslims are demons incarnate
> Arisen to flood the earth
> with their own religion.
> Therefore, I will destroy these demons
> Who have taken the form of Muslims
> And I will spread the way of *dharma* fearlessly!
>
> (18.36-38)

Thus, the text follows the same outline of the *povāḍā* tradition, but has shifted the emphasis from the sacrificial offering of a human *bali* to the goddess by her devotee, to the classical theme of the

Vaiṣṇava *avatāra* descending to earth to defend brahmanic orthodoxy—an orthodoxy described in most brahmanic, conservative terms:

> Earth is supported by *dharma,*
> *dharma* by the gods,
> and the gods by the brahmins.
> Thus they (the brahmins)
> should be protected and worshipped
>
> (18.25-26)

In this view, the battle of Śivājī and Afzal Khān was not a unique historical incident, but a mythic recurrence of the *deva-asura* struggle between good and evil *in illo tempore,* the cosmic battle of *dharma* and *adharma.* Echoing the *Gītā* (4.8), Śivājī declares, "Verily, having been born in age after age *(yuge yuge)* I give protection to the gods, brahmins and cows" (18.27). Within such a Vaiṣṇavization, Śivājī is described rather like Arjuna, as "the archer who has never bowed his head to anyone except Śiva" (19.28).

Śivājī is still the devotee of the goddess, for it is Bhavānī who grants him a vision of her divine person and warns him that Afzal Khān is a "second Rāvaṇa" (20.14). She assures Śivājī that the Khān is "deluded by me (Bhavānī) as *Māyā*" and that he should "consider him already killed" (20.12-15). Much of this discussion is reminiscent of the *Bhagavadgītā,* and the sacrificial element, though encompassed as it is in the classical epic, is expressed in a vividly grisly fashion. Bhavānī commands Śivājī to kill the Khān:

> Let the gods see him,
> headless, wet with oozing
> blood, arms and legs

akimbo, his guts drawn out
by foxes, crows and dogs.

(20.17-18)

Comparing Śivājī to Indra (and Afzal Khān to Vṛtra, 21.24), the text portrays the hero as an impure sacrificer, his sword a sacrificial implement possessed by the goddess (20.22). The ensuing battle is itself described as a cosmic sacrifice.[21] Afzal and his soldiers are not just killed but decapitated and dismembered in scenes evoking the sense of dissolution or *pralaya*. Śivājī is described as symbolically moving throughout the cosmos, crossing the triple world:

Though not confused himself
he caused his enemies' eyes
to spin as he moved in
circles against the sky.

Like the protective rings around
the cardinal points, he made
circles with his sword black
as Death ....

One second sitting on the earth,
the next leaping in the sky,
the next hanging in between,
he was not still for a second.

(21.63-67)

The end of the *pralaya*-like battle is described thus:

---

[21] On the theme of battle as sacrifice, evoking *pralaya* symbolism, see Hiltebeitel 1976: 299ff.

> All around (the enemies') bodies were scattered, their shoulders and hands hacked off, their feet and heads and trunks dismembered and smeared with blood ....
>
> In 1581 of the Śalivāhana or Śaka era, in the year known as "Change" *(Vikārī)*, on Thursday the 7th of Mārgaśīrṣa, during the bright fortnight, Afzal, the enemy of the gods, was killed by Śivājī.
>
> When the mighty Afzal was killed by the mighty King, cool breezes blew, soft and cheerful, with many blossoms; the rivers began to flow with pure water and the earth was steady. Each of the gods found his own place and was content.
>
> Having defeated his enemy in battle and while King Śivājī looked splendid, his weapons in hand, loud drums praising the victory resounded from the mountain peaks, filling the triple world.
>
> (21.81-86)

The world has been purified and steadied by this blood sacrifice and the protector of gods, brahmins and cows has triumphed in order to maintain the borders of *varṇāśrama-dharma,* of orthodox Hinduism. While cows, brahmins and saints are symbols for the ideals of Hinduism, of non-violence, renunciation, tolerance and transcendence, they are synonymous with Hinduism only *within* the borders of the realm. At the boundary there must be the protector, *(go-brāhmaṇa-pratipālak)*. Within the realm, even Śivājī must be the proponent of a kind of tolerant, pacific Hinduism, and it is often noted that he patronized a Muslim saint or respected the sanctity of the *Qur'ān*.[22] But at the boundaries of the realm, he must have the

[22] *Sabhāsad Bakhar* portrays Śivājī as religiously tolerant and supportive of Islam;

role of sacrificer.

Rāmdās

Whatever his military successes, in order to obtain legitimate authority, Śivājī had to turn to brahmins for confirmation, thus following the pattern described by Heesterman in several places. And yet, as Heesterman asks, why should the brahmin confer legitimacy on the violent, mundane world he has renounced? In the abstract, and many times in reality, the brahmin could just as easily accept the political order of the Muslim Sultan as he could the Hindu Rājā, for both rulers functioned within the mundane sphere from which the pure brahmin had divorced himself. (Heesterman 1985: 1-25).

Nevertheless, Śivājī did hold out the possibility of support for the borders of status-quo Hinduism, in which the separate roles and values of king and brahmin allowed the brahmin's position to remain intact and yet protected. These separate roles were justified by the *varṇāśrama-dharma* ideology and the quasi-universalism of the *Gītā,* in which everyone, king included, could retain essentially brahmanic values *in spirit,* internally, while nonetheless carrying out necessary deeds of impurity and protection.

Historically, Śivājī sought legitimacy through a coronation ceremony and the declaration of his kṣatriyan status by a respected brahmin pundit. *But in the legend,* his legitimacy was established in another way. As a truly *Hindu* king, he could not be unequivocally a warrior-sacrificer, even a warrior-sacrificer with some hidden and

---

see Sen 1920: 38-39. This is also the image conveyed by school books: "Shivaji made no distinction between Hindus and Muslims. He honoured the saints of all religions and sanctioned yearly grants for them" (*Shivacchatrapati,* Pune: Maharashtra State Bureau of Textbook Production and Curriculum Research, 1985, p. 5)

intangible *spirit* of renunciation. There had to be a tangible sign of his Hinduness, some cross-over link to transcendental authority. That legitimacy and link to the transcendental could not be provided by a simple relationship to Tulja Bhavānī, whose sacrificial cult remained, as it were, "unreformed" (in Heesterman's sense) and "worldly". Śivājī had to be related to the realm of the renouncer. This is the reason for the profusion of stories which not only make him a pupil of the poet-saint Rāmdās, but ascribe to him a strong yearning for the renouncer's life itself. Although the historical evidence on the relationship of Śivājī and Rāmdās is sketchy and inconclusive, what matters is the ideological significance of their legendary linkage.

It does seem that portions of Rāmdās' *Dās Bodh* were written with Śivājī in mind. This text articulates a theory of kingship which is consonant with the teachings of the *Bhagavadgītā*. Indeed, it has been called the *Marāṭhī Gītā* and Rāmdās and Śivājī have been compared to Kṛṣṇa and Arjuna.[23] The *Dās Bodh* (10.7.22) states: "God can bring any fruits to us whatsoever, but a desire for fruits stands between ourselves and God" (quoted in Ranade, 1983: 400-401), in addition to a passage directly advising Śivājī (18.6.9-20), in which he is warned to have faith in Bhavānī but be on guard, resist the Muslims and discriminate carefully between this-worldly and other-worldly matters. He concludes the passage in saying

> To spread the cause of God, to protect the Brahmins, to help one's subjects, are all of them the gifts of God. Those [men], in fact, who re-establish the king-

---

[23] For an explicit comparison Arjuna and Kṛṣṇa to Śivājī and Rāmdās, see Nanalal Dalpatram Kavi's "A saviour of Hinduism" in Sardesai 1927: 114-122. Note also *Sabhāsad* in Sen 1920: 25 and B. G. Tilak's commentary on the *Bhagavadgītā* (Tilak 1935: I, 611). Sardesai (1946: 100) quotes a letter in which Śivājī refers to himself as *nimitta-mātra* ("only an instrument"), surely evoking the *Gītā*'s ideology.

dom of God are all of them the incarnations of God.
(Ranade 1983: 375)

The earliest chronicle, *Sabhāsad Bakhar*, does not, however, mention Rāmdās at all, nor does the *Śivabhārata*. Certain letters do suggest that Śivājī did undergo an initiation at Rāmdās's hands in 1672, just following his coronation. Popular traditions push their relationship back to a much earlier date, so that even before his fateful meeting with Afzal Khān, Śivājī is portrayed as the advisee of Rāmdās (cf. Ranade 1983: 361-369).

The fully developed legend of Śivājī in his relation to Rāmdās is contained in Mahīpati's *Santavijaya*, an eighteenth century hagiography of Rāmdās.[24] This text fills in the story concerning the writing of the "Duties of a King" in the *Dās Bodh*. According to Mahīpati, Śivājī first met Rāmdās while on a hunting expedition where he sees all the animals of the forest going to the protection of the peaceful saint. Having witnessed this miracle, the king finds leaves of the *Dās Bodh* floating in the Kṛṣṇā River and is delighted and, we may say, "converted" by reading them (Abbott 1932: 50ff.). The ultimate conclusion of Śivājī's devotion to Rāmdās is his decision to renounce his kingdom and worldly life to follow him. Rāmdās accepts him as a disciple and they live the life of ascetics together for several days. Satisfied with the king's sincerity, Rāmdās orders his pupil to return to his *dharma* as king, but in *Gītā* fashion, carrying out his duties detached from worldly desires, marching into battle under the saffron banner *(bhagvā zeṇḍā)*. Nonetheless, the king is induced to become a vegetarian and give up hunting (Abbott 1932: 58-59).

---

[24] See Abbott 1932 for a translation of the *Santavijaya*. Śivājī has also been associated with Tukārām, especially by those who resist the idea of a Maratha hero submitting to the brahmin Rāmdās' authority. For a discussion of Śivājī and Tukārām, see Ranade 1983: 266-267, Abbott 1980: 229ff., 278ff. Śivājī is depicted as touching Tukārām's feet on a mural on the side of a new temple on Fergusson College Road, Pune.

It is interesting that Mahīpati does not leave the matter at that, but continues to return to the tension between martial-royal values and brahmanic-ascetic ones. In other words, it is not sufficient to have Śivājī reach a sort of abstract compromise as the result of one experience of real ascetic life. He must again and again lose interest in the world, even falling into trance-like states of meditation and total disinterest in worldly wealth and power, thus terrifying his political counsellors (Abbott 1932: 205, 230). In other words, the tension cannot be resolved but must be repeatedly expressed without resolution. The Lion, who like Nṛsimha ripped open the belly of the demon Afzal Khān, has become, in Mahīpati's portrayal, the Lamb. Here the fragility of the *varṇāśrama-dharma* ideology is showing and manifestly unravelling. We may note that elsewhere in Mahīpati, one finds not merely tigerlike kings becoming saintly under the influence of Rāmdās' teachings, but actual tigers adopting a vegetarian diet (Abbott 1932: 32). He also tells of another pious king who discovers the inferiority of the goddess Bhavānī and shifts his allegiance to the Supreme God Viṣṇu (Abbott and Godbole 1933: 406-414). An adherence to Hindu inclusivism and acceptance of differently ranked but accepted roles and duties is here crumbling under the weight of a universalistic Vaiṣṇava *bhakti*.

Conclusion

The hero, as hero, must cross boundaries: he must be rich and poor, noble but humble, a lover and an ascetic, violent but peaceful. He captures the imagination precisely in being a larger than life image of humanity in which antinomies are held in tension, held by the attractive idea that perhaps humans need not be bound by "either-or" choices. In the case of Śivājī, I have sketched but one of these antinomies, that of the violent sacrificer *vs.* the peaceful renouncer. The values of the latter have had to be emphasized—especially in the accounts of brahmin writers going all the way back to Paramānanda—in order to buttress the *Hindu-ness* of the protector of Hinduism. The emphasis on Śivājī's ideal values, his saintliness, went along with other mythic ideals—*e.g.* the ideal of a noble family in which cooperative harmony reigned supreme. We find the hero having to surrender egoistic, violent-aggressive and erotic traits and hanker after the ascetic life.[25] In so doing, folkloric themes like sibling rivalry, oedipal conflict and challenge to authority and entrenched class-interests are muted. In this we seem to find a pattern found already in the mythicized classical epics.

Today the legend of Śivājī remains primarily a regional cultural expression without being truly "folk". The folk or folkloric dimension was muffled, almost from the beginning, under the impulse of legitimizing the Hindu ruler by making him a truly good Hindu. And "making him a truly good Hindu" meant making him a quasi-brahmin, a saint, an ascetic. I would conclude with the observation that the best-known modern popularizer of the Śivājī legend is himself a brahmin, Babasaheb Purandare, whose writings always emphasize Śivājī's high birth, respect for brahmins, and devotion to orthodox Hinduism (Purandare 1984). Moreover he downplays the less-than-ideal relationships Śivājī had with his father, half-brother and son. One now hears the rumor that Purandare is the reincarnation of Śivājī; not only has the Śivājī of popular legend adopted brahmanic values, he has been transmogrified into a nativistic brahmin popularizer. But perhaps Purandare himself recognizes the sogginess of a mythic ideal without folkloric complexity. In his novel *Śelār Khind* (Purandare 1986), now made into a popular film ("Sarjā"), we find Śivājī in the background, with a low caste acrobat as hero using the earliest epithet ever applied to Śivājī—Sarjā, the "Lion". If, according to the conscious values of the culture, the ruler must be a saintly lamb, the unconscious desire for a fighter summons the Lion to the frontier, the impure, violent border of the

[25] Goldman (1980: 149-189) has noted that the portrayal of Rāma as anerotic, non-egoistic and non-aggressive is balanced in the *Rāmāyaṇa* by his more impetuous brother Lakṣmaṇa.

peaceful realm of brahmins and cows. However regional the legend of Śivājī may be, this frontier and interior are bound together by a structure that is surely ancient and pan-Indian.

REFERENCES

Abbott, Justin E. (trans.) 1932. *Rāmdās; translation of Mahīpati's Santavijaya.* The poet-saints of Maharashtra, No. 8. Poona: Aryabhushan Press.

Id. (trans.) 1980. *Life of Tukaram.* Translation from Mahīpati's Bhaktalīlāmrta. Delhi: Motilal Banarsidass.

Abott, Justin E. and Godbole (trans.). 1933. *Stories of the Indian saints,* vol. I. The poet-saints of Maharashtra, No. 9. Poona: Aryabhushan Press.

Acworth, H. A. 1894. *Ballads of the Marathas.* London: Longmans, Green & Co.

Acworth, H. A. and Shaligram, S. T. 1891. *Powadas or historical ballads of the Marathas.* Bombay: Nirnaya Sagar Press.

Apte, H. N. 1972. *Gaḍ Ālā paṇ Siṃha Gelā!* Puṇe: Ramyakathā Prakāśan.

Atre, P. K. and Kulkarni, K. P. (eds.). 1960. *Mahārāṣṭra Gāthā.* Bombay: Bhāratī Prakāśan.

Beck, Brenda. 1982. *The three twins: The telling of a South Indian folk epic.* Bloomington.

Biardeau, Madeleine. 1981. *Études de mythologie hindoue.* I. Paris: École Française d'Extrême-Orient.

Blackburn, Stuart. 1978. The folk hero and class interests in Tamil heroic ballads. *Asian Folklore Studies* 37.1: 131-149.

Blackburn, Stuart H. and Ramanujan, A. K. (eds.). 1986. *Another harmony.* University of California Press.

Damle, Y. B. 1960. Harikathā: A study in communication. *Bulletin of the Deccan College Research Institute* 20: 63-107.

Duff, James Grant. 1971. *History of the Mahrattas,* vol. I. New Delhi: Associated Publishing House.

Elliott, H. M. and Dowson, J. 1952. *The history of India as told by its own historians* (vol. VII: *Muntakhabu-l Lubab* of Khafi Khan). Calcutta: Susil Gupta.

Goldman, R. P. 1980. Rāmaḥ Sahalakṣmaṇaḥ: Psychological and literary aspects of the composite hero of Valmīki's Ramayana. *Journal of Indian Philosophy* 8: 149-189.

Heesterman, J. D. 1985. *The inner conflict of tradition.* University of Chicago Press.

Heller, Joseph. 1984. *God knows.* New York: Knopf.

Hiltebeitel, Alf. 1976. *The ritual of battle*. Ithaca: Cornell University Press.

Id. 1983. Toward a coherent study of Hinduism. *Religious Studies Review* 9: 206-212.

Joglekar, S. A. n.d. *Sahyādri*. Pune: Prasād Prakāśan Kāryālaya.

Kelkar, Y. N. 1928-1961. *Aitihāsika Povāḍe*, 3 vols. Puṇe: Tilak Mahārāṣṭra Vidyāpīṭh.

Laine, James W. 1986. Hinduism and the *Mahābhārata*. *Wiener Zeitschrift für die Kunde Südasiens* XXX: 73-81.

Id. (forthcoming). *Visions of God: Narratives of theophany in the Mahabharata*. Vienna: Publications of the De Nobili Research Institute, vol. XVI.

Nanivdekar, Śāhīr M. N. 1959. *Chatrapati Śivājī Mahārāj yāṃcā povāḍā*. Bombay: Nanivdekar Shahiri Sangam.

O'Hanlon, Rosalind. 1985. *Caste, conflict and ideology*. Cambridge University Press.

Śivabhārata of Paramānanda. Ed. by D. V. Apte and S. M. Divekar. 1927. Poona: Bhāratīya Itihās Saṃśodhak Maṇḍaḷ.

Patwardhan, R. P. and Rawlinson, H. G. (eds.). 1929. *Source book of Maratha history*, vol. I. Bombay: Government Central press.

Purandare, Babasaheb. 1984. *Maharaj*. Pune: Purandare Prakāśan.

Id. 1986. *Śelār Khind*. Pune: Purandare Prakāśan.

Ranade, M. G. 1961. *Rise of the Maratha power*. Delhi: Ministry of Information and Broadcasting.

Ranade, R. D. 1983. *Mysticism in India: The poet saints of Maharashtra*. Albany: State University of New York.

Roghair, Gene H. 1982. *The epic of Palnāḍu*. Oxford: Clarendon Press.

Sardesai, G. S. 1946. *New history of the Marathas*, vol. I. Bombay: Phoenix Publications.

Sardesai, G. S. (ed.). 1927. *Shivaji souvenir*. Bombay: Tercentenary Celebration.

Sarkar, Jadunath. 1961. *Shivaji and his times*, 6th edition. Calcutta: Orient, Longman Ltd.

Sen, Surendranath (ed.). 1920. *Śiva Chhatrapati*. University of Calcutta Press.

Shivacchatrapati. 1985. Maharashtra State Bureau of Textbook Production and Curriculum Research.

Tilak, B. G. 1935. *Śrī Bhagavadgītā rahasya or karma*

yoga śāstra, trans. B. S. Sukthankar, 2 vols. Poona: Tilak Bros.

Wadley, Susan S. 1983. *Dhoḷā:* A folk genre of North India. *Asian Folklore Studies* 42,1: 1-25.

Dilip Chitre

MUMBAICHI LAVNI:
The First Marathi Poem on Industrial Civilization

While a social scientist among poets could be regarded as a cat among pigeons, a poet among social scientists is without doubt a pigeon among cats. His chances of survival depend on how much the cats fight over him.

Alas! Social scientists are such disinterested cats when it comes to poetry. But the kind of poetry this essay (one dares not call it a paper) deals with is doubly unfortunate. It is not considered poetry proper by proper literary critics either. It belongs to the underworld, in the sense of literary caste, of *tamasha.* It is from folk theatre and it shares with sensuous dancing and ribald comedy the ethos of theatre of audience participation that is a world apart from the ambience of scholarly pursuit of difficult texts.

We are dealing here with what I shall loosely call a ballad; for *The Ballad of Bombay* is the nearest translation one can think of for *Mumbaichi Lavni.* It was composed, presumably around the year 1910, by Patthe Bapoorao Kulkarni, probably the last distinguished *lavni*-composer in the traditional mould. Patthe Bapoorao, incidentally, was a Brahman working in the *tamasha* theatre that was dominated by Mahars and Mangs, and, as such, he was a double outcaste. This *lavni,* at least in part, is dedicated by him to his beloved dancing girl Pavla, herself a Mahar woman of great grace and glamour. The importance of *Mumbaichi Lavni,* however, need not be sought in its creator's romantic life or in the ambience of his colourful profession. If one reads this *lavni* in the context of the arrival of modern industrial and commercial culture into Maharashtra (and India) it appears to have captured a crucial change in the world-view and sensibility of its author and his audience. It marks a change in their perception of themselves in an emerging modern urban environment and shows how they were still able to link this new experience with certain vital continuities of their tradition.

Central to this *lavni* is the myth of the big new city, its energy and intensity and articulation of a complex form of life. Thematically, it has global aspects and parallels the world over and yet it is unique because in its apparently naive or seemingly light-hearted way it touches the deepest apprehension of the machine age.

Patthe Bapoorao's audience in the city of Bombay consisted of the immigrant working class, still psychologically rooted in their own villages in Maharashtra but now working in shipyards, textile mills, factories, railway workshops and similar other non-traditional occupations. Patthe Bapoorao s audience in Bombay, where his ballad was sung and presumably composed, was not only multi-caste but also multi-religious and multi-ethnic, for it included Muslims and Parsees. It was an industrial city audience and the first such audience in Maharashtra or perhaps in India as a whole. This ballad about Bombay was sung in Bombay to a live audience participating in the event of its performance, and the meaning of this ballad cannot therefore be reduced to its text. However, since the text is all that survives of its premiere and perhaps only performance (for Bapoorao never repeated any *lavni* that he composed and presented), we must extend the text imaginatively to include the live audience to whom it made a special kind of sense. It is the implicit participation of a live audience that makes a *lavni* (as much as an *abhang*) a dramatic event, a kind of participatory theatre of simultaneous and multiple interactions within a collective performing awareness, that is distinct from written and printed poetry as such.

Mumbaichi Lavni

Mumbaichi Lavni, in 1910, could not have made the same sense outside the city of Bombay as it did to its audience within the city. It is a ballad of the new city itself: the ballad of a thriving modern seaport connected with foreign lands—especially with Europe—and the ballad of a new industrial-commercial civilisation. It describes the city from within and its meaning is meant to be shared by insiders, residents and immigrants to the city. This audience is the special 'inner circle' for whom the poem makes immediate sense. In fact, the poem invites them to share the creation of its meaning by evoking images of specific city neighbourhoods and landmarks which would be a mere string of proper nouns to outsiders. The poem conveys, for the first time ever in Marathi creative literature, a perception of the special quality of urban-industrial time and space and the interaction of human and mechanical forces, of a man-made, hyperactive and closed universe. It is a cynical song of a city beneath whose glamourous veneer human values are destroyed by purely commercial logic.

Academic literary critics have not so far given Patthe Bapoorao Kulkarni his due credit for being the first Marathi poet of the industrial modern city. They have neatly compartmentalized literature into written and oral sections and would take cognizance only of written and/or printed texts that can be surrounded by written and/ or printed discussion. Thus, the 'inner circle' of academic literature excludes from its sanctum the sort of performed oral poetry that Patthe Bapoorao wrote, along with its supposedly 'non-literate' audience at the 'tamasha'. This schism between 'literary' literature and 'performed' literature persists throughout post-British Maharashtra and right up to the emergence of Dalit literature in the early 1970s. One of the major sources of the Dalit literary sensibility is oral and performed traditions such as the tamasha. That Bapoorao was a brahman by birth makes no difference. The literary form he chose was supposedly a 'Mahar form', a 'non-text'. A detailed critique of this conflict between 'text' and 'non-text' as a contest for literary *status,* with its caste-like and class-like implications, needs to be worked out separately. It appears to be a post-Macauleyan conflict that has no precedent in the Marathi literary tradition. From its very beginning, 'modern' Marathi literary criticism makes a clear division between 'academic' and 'non-academic', 'text' and 'non-text', 'object of study' and 'subject of participatory performance'. Underlying this is a deeper cultural division between the literate and the non-literate that has subsequently de-democratized the entire literary-cultural process in Maharashtra, cutting off its prime sources of energy rooted in living speech. As far as the poetry of urban-industrial time-space is concerned, Patthe Bapoorao is the direct precursor of Mardhekar, Arun Kolatkar, Narayan Surve, Namdev Dhasal, Tulsi Parab, Prakash Jadhav and Vivek Mohan Rajapure. That distinction can hardly go to academically recognized modern 'literary' poets such as Keshavsut, Bee, Balkavi, Tilak or Govindagraj. If Mardhekar modernized the Varkari tradition of poetry then it is as clear that Patthe Bapoorao—much earlier—modernized the tradition of Shahiri poetry. It is also significant that because Shahiri poetry is ostensibly this-worldly, it is secular in nature and therefore could make a smoother transition to modernity. However, this too must be set aside as a subject for future discussion.

All this has resulted, I suspect, in the dwarfing of the identity of Marathi literature and culture in modern times. One tragic consequence of this is the separate status sought for and accorded to Dalit literature in our time. The structural continuities of literary culture are being obscured and blocked by imposing upon them a model alien to the traditional genius of Marathi literature. This traditional genius has been far more open-ended than the modern academic model. Perhaps a new, post-modern model is needed to illuminate the inclusiveness of the literary-cultural process as against the exclusiveness of academic-literary constructions of topology and typology.

With these introductory remarks, whatever they are worth, I shall now turn to the poem itself. I warn you that mine is a very rough translation that attempts to retain the literal flavour of the original but is a rather unhappy blend of slang and standard lexical levels, whereas the original bristles with masterly sarcasm in an inspired colloquial music-hall style. Here is how the poem opens:

Oh the city of Bombay is so hard to win
Of Ravana's Lanka it is next of kin
The drumbeat of its fame is heard loud and clear
In all four corners of the world
'It's a bed of roses', they say of Bombay
And I have been there!

Boy! What a city! Bombay bursts with youth!
It buys and sells as it pleases, that's the truth.
All ships cross the ocean to and fro
But it's a steamship that does it in a terrific style!

Oh the city of Bombay, it s got style!
To pilgrims it's like Benares every sacred mile!
Each day a new convict is hanged in Bombay
A fresh one arrives in his place every day!
Meanwhile more money is minted there
Boy! Have I seen Bombay!

Oh the city of Bombay is a real ambush!
Twelve square *kos* under armed guard
And armoured ships going abroad
Bringing back orders from England!

Oh the city of Bombay by the edge of the sea
It's a place full of hoods, a mad mob
Only a real sharp one can make a hit here
The rest are sure to starve.

Oh the city of Bombay, its ways are so strange
Each streetcorner is policed by roving cops
Up and down they cover their beat
Day and night and down every street
Yet murders take place even on a train
Boy! What a city is Bombay!

Oh yeah, honey! I've seen Bombay!
How cool is the English Empire's rule!
But I'm a smart poet, smart as the state of Shindé!
Therefore Patthe Bapoorao only sings its praise!
Hey, no touching! Give me a flying kiss!
I'll buy you the whole of Bombay, now!

Honey, look! This port of Bombay
Is the prettiest of the whole world
In our beautiful time! Look!
It shines like a light in the evening
And the air becomes yellow as gold!

What fun! Come, let's go to the Play House!
Let's stay near the Play House and visit the theatre!
Let's watch the *tamasha* of the world there
Till we can take it no more!

These are the first nine stanzas that set the pitch, the tone and the pace of the poem. This is followed by a grand poetic tour of the city, capturing its images neighbourhood after neighbourhood, picturing its ethnic diversity, its trades and its traffic and its transactions, its sites and monuments, its temples and bazaars and its brothels. Through these images, Patthe Bapoorao creates a vivid and tumultous montage that becomes progressively sarcastic and sinister. The description is rich with multiple meanings and significances that will require a detailed analysis of the Marathi text. Any translation, at whatever remove from the original text, will fail to serve such a purpose.

Anne Feldhaus

TYPES OF RIVER GODDESSES IN MAHARASHTRA

Rivers provide the focus for a wide variety of religious expressions in Maharashtra. Many local temples, as well as many of the major pilgrimage places of Maharashtra, are located at the sources or along the banks of rivers. Numerous Brāhmaṇical rituals–from *sandhyā* to *śrāddha,* from the bath before worship to the immersion of the festival image of a god–are ideally to be performed at a river; and many primarily non-Brāhmaṇ festivals involve either a palanquin procession in which a god is carried to a river, or a carrying-pole *(kāvaḍ)* journey in which river water is carried–sometimes great distances–to a god. There are Sanskrit and Marathi *māhātmya* texts praising, and narrating Purāṇic stories associated with, the major rivers of Maharashtra: the Godāvarī, the Bhīmā, the Kṛṣṇā, the Tāpī, and the Pūrṇā. Many of the major holy places of the sects of Maharashtra are located along these rivers. And finally, besides the gods like Śiva and Dattātreya whose temples are often found along the rivers, there are a number of deities who are specifically associated or identified with rivers.

It is this last element of the religious significance of the rivers of Maharashtra–deities *of* the rivers–which I plan to discuss in the present paper.[1] I will first discuss the cults of two predominantly

[1] The fieldwork on which this paper is based was carried out over a total of about two and a half years between 1984 and 1988. I am grateful to the American Institute of Indian Studies, the United States Educational Foundation in India, and Arizona

non-Brāhmaṇ deities of different types: the Sātī Āsarā and Bhivāī. Next I will describe the modern, urban, predominantly Brāhmaṇ worship of a type of deity who embodies one or another particular river. And finally, having pointed out some major differences between the non-Brāhmaṇ deities and the modern Brāhmaṇ deities of the rivers, I will attempt to point out some basic similarities among these river deities which can serve to distinguish them as a class from other kinds of deities worshipped or known of in Maharashtra. These similarities will serve to suggest that, in the case of river deities, at least, the differences between those that could be called "folk" and those that could not are more significantly matters of style of worship than of theological substance.

The Sātī Āsarā

The Sātī Āsarā are found all over Maharashtra. How far beyond Maharashtra their cult extends I do not know. Within Maharashtra I have learned about the Sātī Āsarā from people from the districts of Sāṅglī, Kolhāpūr, Sātārā, Puṇe, Ahmadnagar, Auraṅgābād, Buldhāṇā, Akolā, Amrāvatī, Vardhā, Yavatmāḷ, Nānded, Parbhaṇī, Bīḍ, Usmānābād, and Solāpūr. In all of these areas there are locally important sites of Sātī Āsarā worship, but there are no major pilgrimage sites of the Sātī Āsarā which draw pilgrims from all over Maharashtra or even from any large subregion of the state.

Although geographically widespread, the Sātī Āsarā are not universally known in Maharashtrian society. Generally speaking, women are more aware of the Āsarā than are men; the people who,

State University for support during the fieldwork period. For helpful comments on this paper, I am particularly grateful to Dilip Chitre, James Fitzgerald, Mark Woodward, and a number of participants in the Third International Conference on Maharashtra: Culture and Society. For help with field work I am particularly grateful to the Kothavale and Waghmare families, and to M. B. Gaikwad. The present paper is intended as a preliminary report; I plan to present elsewhere a more substantial and detailed discussion of the religious meanings of rivers in Maharashtra.

as a class, are the most uniformly ignorant about the Sātī Āsarā are Brāhmaṇ men. At a major confluence *(saṅgam)* near Puṇe, a Brāhmaṇ man who was showing me the place and explaining its historical and Purāṇic significance was certain that some distinctive red markings on the rocky bank of the river had to do with the *daśakriyā vidhi,* a funeral ritual, and were related to the fact that cremations are performed nearby. When I asked if the Sātī Āsarā are to be found at the place, the man said no. Later I talked with some women who were washing clothes a little ways upstream from the red markings on the rocks. The women knew perfectly well that the marks on the rocks were those of the Sātī Āsarā, and they pointed out two more Sātī Āsarā places nearby. At another *saṅgam,* farther east, a Brāhmaṇ temple trustee gave me wonderfully detailed and precise information about his temple and the rivers which meet at the *saṅgam.* When I asked about the Sātī Āsarā, he looked blank. A Koḷī peon who was standing nearby explained about the Āsarā and informed us that indeed they are found at the place. The Trustee said, in wonder, "I've heard this term 'Āsarā' for the first time today" (*"āsarā hā śabda ājac aikalā"*).

Iconographically the Sātī Āsarā are quite simple. Usually they are represented by seven (or more) red marks made with *kuṅkūṃ* powder or red lead *(śendūr)* on a *ghāṭ,* at the side of a well, on pebbles at the edge of a river, or—most often—on a *khaḍak,* rocky ground at the side of a river or ravine. Sometimes the Āsarā are invisible—that is, not marked or represented at all—but always they have a particular location: *inside* the *khaḍak* at a particular spot, or at *this* place rather than *that* in the water.

The Sātī Āsarā are said to be one another's sisters; quite often they are accompanied by Mhasobā, who is called their "brother," or "protector" *(rākhaṇdār)*. In Deuḷvāḍā, Vardhā District, this role was said to be played by "Bahirām Buvā," or Bhairava, and around Kolhāpūr the protector-brother figure is called Joting. The brother is represented by a somewhat larger red lead mark, or by a stone covered with red lead set somewhat apart from the others. In *ṭāks*, small metal plaques, of the Sātī Āsarā, Mhasobā is sometimes represented by a buffalo, while the Sātī Āsarā appear as uniform standing female figures, each with two hands and one head, and dressed in a sari.

In very few places have I seen *mūrtis* of the Sātī Āsarā or a roofed temple to house them. One such place is the village of Bendrī near Tāsgāv in Sāṅglī District. In the temple at Bendrī there is no Mhasobā; here the Āsarā are represented by seven separate *mūrtis*, each with two arms and dressed in a sari. The *mūrtis* have brass face-masks *(mukhavaṭās)* and are molded over round stones which were found in the clay bank of the nearby ravine.

Another source for the "iconography" of the Sātī Āsarā is to be found in dreams that people report having about them. Several people have told me spontaneously—and several more have affirmed when I asked them—that they dream about the Āsarā. In these dreams the Āsarā appear as seven female figures: young girls, or lovely young women dressed in green or white saris.

Even scantier than iconographic details about the Sātī Āsarā are mythological details about them. I have been told three different stories about the origin of the Āsarā; and two further stories, from the Gond tribe, are narrated in an article by Durgā Bhāgvat (Bhāgvat 1959: 26). Unfortunately, I have been unable to find a second person to tell me any of the three stories which I have heard, nor have I so far found the Gond stories to be known by non-tribals in Maharashtra. Some of the people who gave me the most precise, detailed information about the Āsarā in other respects stated that there *are not* stories about them. For most Maharashtrians, this may, in fact, be the case.

Thus, the Sātī Āsarā do not have a very complex iconography or a very widely known mythology. What they do have, however, everyone who knows about them agrees, is *effects*. The Sātī Āsarā *do* things to people. They cause trouble, especially to women, and the trouble they are best known for causing is trouble with having children: infertility, miscarriages, and the death of infants. Some women who are afflicted with these problems are said to "have" the Sātī Āsarā *(tyānā sātī āsarā [ā]het)*, or the Āsarā are said to have "gotten" such a woman *(tyānā lāgalelyā āhet)*. The Sātī Āsarā, it is explained, are Brāhmaṇs, or one of them is, and they can quite easily get offended–most typically when a girl or a young woman, usually quite unintentionally, goes too close to their place while she is menstruating.

After her marriage, when such a woman has gone for some years without concieving a child, or when she has had a number of miscarriages or a series of children die young, she and her family consult a religious specialist known for an ability to divine the causes of such symptoms. The specialist tells her that she "has" the Sātī Āsarā, and prescribes a set of offerings to be made to the same Sātī Āsarā whom she has offended. The offerings consist of seven each of a variety of items. The most elaborate list I have been given includes seven coconuts, seven lemons, seven bangles, seven (?) combs, seven pinches of bright yellow turmeric powder *(haḷdī)* and bright red *kuṅkūṃ* powder, seven each of seven different kinds of fruit, seven betel nuts, seven dried dates, seven cardamoms, seven nose rings (?), seven bits of coconut, one green blouse piece, seven *āvaḷā* fruits, seven earrings (?), seven lamps, seven chili peppers, seven *roṭī*-breads, seven flowers of seven different colors, toe rings, seven plates *(tāṭs)* made of *jvārī* millet (i.e., *bhākrī*-bread), and seven betel leaf rolls. All of this is to be put into seven new baskets and placed in a water hole in the river. In addition, said the person who listed these items, a chicken, eggs, and tobacco are required; these are presumably for Mhasobā.

After these offerings have been made, a woman's childbearing difficulties should be over. She may still, however, be subject to possession by the Āsarā well past her child-bearing years, and she remains throughout her lifetime someone who "has" the Sātī Āsarā. Whether "having" the Āsarā is on the whole a good thing or a bad one is a question to which I have not yet found a satisfying answer. The unsatisfying answer I have found is roughly that "having" the Āsarā is a good thing, once one "has" them; but it is not something one should intentionally bring onto oneself. The question needs to be investigated in the context of the whole set of disease goddesses and people's attitudes toward them.

For the Sātī Āsarā are essentially a type of disease goddess, a deity[2] of the most widely worshipped but least formally institutionalized sort. With only a few exceptions, the Sātī Āsarā have no *mūrtis,* no temples, no priests, no festivals, and no pilgrimage places. They seem to have little—or, at least, no widely known—mythology. They are regarded with awe rather than affection. The offerings which are made to them are not made in fulfilment of a "vow" *(navas),* but as a placation, to persuade them to remove an unwanted condition which they themselves have brought about.

Bhivāī

Closely related to the Sātī Āsarā is a second type of river deity of which the example I know the most about is Bhivāī. Bhivāī is a goddess found at Kāmbaḷeśvar, near Phalṭaṇ, on the Nīrā river. She is the object of a full-blown cult including regular *pūjārīs,* a pilgrimage festival *(jatrā),* a developed mythology, temples, possession, the

---

[2] It is questionable whether the Āsarā should be called "deities" or "goddesses" at all. People talking about making offerings to them frequently refer to them as *"dev"*—that is, "god" or "deity"—but people asked explicitly about exactly what type of being the Āsarā are either confess ignorance on this point or identify them as "fairies," *"paryā"* (sing. *parī,* possibly cognate with English "fairy"). It is my impression that the feminine form, *"devī,"* "goddess," is used less often for the Sātī Āsarā than is the unmarked, masculine form *"dev."*

practice of "vow"-making *(navas)*, and so on. Bhivāī is particularly associated with the Dhangar shepherds; she is the sister of the Dhangar god Dhuḷoba of Phalṭaṇ; at her festival, Dhangars toss sheep into the water hole next to her temple.

Bhivāī is also called the Seven Bhivayyā: she is a set of seven goddesses who are said to be one another's sisters. She is identified by some with the Sātī Āsarā, and the same metal plaques which are used to represent the Sātī Āsarā are also used for Bhivāī. In many ways, Bhivāī could simply be included in the same category with the Sātī Āsarā. But there is one major difference: Bhivāī is not a disease goddess. She is closely associated with the birth of babies, but she does not prevent conception, nor does she bring about miscarriages or the death of infants. Infertile couples make "vows" *(navases)* to her; they do so not in order that she will stop depriving them of children, but so that she will be of positive help in enabling them to have children.

At Bhivāī's *jatrā*, as well as at the *jatrās* of Gaṅgāmāī on the Pūrṇā river in Amrāvatī District, babies and children are floated on rafts in the river next to the goddess's temple. Some of the children are floated on the rafts in fulfilment of a promise *(navas)* made by their parents as a prayer for offspring. But many Dhangars at Bhivāī's festival say that *all* Dhangar children, whether born as the result of a *navas* or not, *must* be floated on the raft once in their lifetime, and only afterwards are they allowed to marry. Sontheimer has published a story about a woman who became frightened when her baby was floated on Bhivāī's raft. The child drowned because of his mother's lack of trust in the goddess (Sontheimer 1976: 77-78).

Modern Urban River Goddesses

When we turn to the third type of river deities, modern, urban river goddesses, we have entered a quite different religious and social milieu from that of the Āsarā and Bhivāī. The modern, urban river goddesses are found in towns and large villages along the banks of rivers. They are named for, and embody, the rivers along which they are found. Sometimes such a goddess is housed in a small shrine on the riverbank or on a *ghāṭ*. Sometimes she has only a festival image, which is kept in storage for most of the year and is brought out at the time of the annual festival, called not a *jatrā* but an *utsav,* which is the typical form of worship of these goddesses. Examples of such goddesses are the goddess of the Godāvarī, who has three shrines at Tryambakeśvar, three at Nāsik, and one at Nāndeḍ; the goddess of the Karhā, whose only shrine, as far as I know, is found at Sāsvaḍ; the goddess of the Koynā, with a shrine at Karāḍ; and Kṛṣṇābāī, the goddess of the Kṛṣṇā, who is worshipped at Mahābaḷeśvar, Wāī, Bāvdhan, Gove, Limb, Saṅgam Māhulī, Kṣetra Māhulī, Vaḍuth, Pācvaḍ, Karāḍ, Kuḍāḷ, Audumbar, Sāṅglī, and Narsobācī Vāḍī.

Most of the images *(mūrtis)* of these river goddesses are iconographically quite similar to one another. The major exception is found in Nāndeḍ, where the *mūrti* of the goddess of the Godāvarī is an old *satī* stone which has been covered with red lead. Otherwise the river goddess *mūrtis* are usually four-armed, standing female figures. Their hands hold Vaiṣṇava attributes—*cakras,* conches, lotuses, sometimes a water pot—or are held in gestures of reassurance *(abhaya),* blessing *(āśīrvād),* or donation *(dāna).*

In Wāī, the location of the most elaborate of the festivals of this type of goddess, there are eight major Kṛṣṇābāī shrines: one of them is permanent, and seven are temporary. The permanent Kṛṣṇābāī shrine, although centrally located, is relatively small and insignificant in comparison to many of Wāī's temples; but the Kṛṣṇābāī festival, in the course of which the seven temporary shrines are erected, is the major event in Wāī's annual cultural calendar.

The Kṛṣṇābāī festival is celebrated for three to seven days each at seven different locations in Wāī, one following the other on specific days *(tithis)* stretching from the first day of the bright half of the month of Māgh through the twelfth day of the bright half of Phālgun (usually in January and February). The seven festivals of Wāī are each located in and proper to a different "Ghāṭ," that is, a neighborhood defined by its approach to the river. All of the Ghāṭs are on the left, or north, bank of the Kṛṣṇā, that is, on the side of the river on which almost all the Brāhmaṇs of the town live. Each of the festivals includes, with some variation, the same basic features: a temporary shrine and canopy *(maṇḍap)*, a communal meal, devotional songs *(bhajans)* and song-sermon performances *(kīrtans)*, cultural events (a music recital, perhaps, or even a movie), and a procession in which an image of the goddess is carried in a palanquin—or, in one case, a chariot—from door to door through the streets and lanes of the neighborhood. There is no possession, and what crowds there are consist entirely of townspeople and their relatives, not of pilgrims from outside. Each of the festivals has an organizing committee which makes the arrangements for the festival, including printing and issuing receipts for donations, tickets for the meal, and a program of festival events.

The worship of Kṛṣṇābāī at Wāī is dominated by Brāhmaṇs, as is the worship of this sort of river goddess in the other places I am aware of. The priests of these goddesses are Brāhmaṇs; the organizing committees of their festivals are composed of Brāhmaṇs; and the overwhelming majority of their worshippers appear to be Brāhmaṇs as well.

The origin of the Kṛṣṇābāī festival at Wāī is traced to the time of Śivājī, and is explicitly related to Śivājī's encounter with Afjhal Khān. In the words of a citizen of Wāī:[3]

[3] Reminiscent of some of the materials discussed by Laine elsewhere in this volume.

It was at the time of the killing of Afjhal Khān. He was in the service of Alī Ādilśāh of Bijāpūr. [Afjhal Khān] came with a huge army, about 12,000 soldiers, to defeat Śivājī. He set up his army's camp here at Wāī, on the far side of the ravine, to the east of the town. [Wāī] was a settlement of Brāhmaṇs, and there were a number of Māḷīs living here as well.

All of [Afjhal Khān's] soldiers were Arabian Hapśīs. They had come from Arabasthān and places like that. After he had set up his camp here, they began to carry off the young women of the town. They carried off some people's daughters-in-law; they carried off other people's wives. After this had become a daily occurrence, the Brāhmaṇs said, "The whole town's domestic life *(saṃsār)* is being destroyed. What point is there now in living?"

Down below here there's a place called Rāmḍoh. This side of Rāmḍoh there is a pool called Maṇikarṇikā Kuṇḍ, just like the *kuṇḍ* [of that name] at Kāśī. It's a place in the water built up on four sides for bathing. The people undertook to starve themselves to death *(prāyopaveśan surū keleṃ)* in that Maṇikarṇikā Kuṇḍ. They had decided to take *jalasamādhi* [i.e., to stay in the water until they died]. "There's no point now in living," [they said]. And they prayed to Kṛṣṇā Mātā, this Kṛṣṇā, this water deity. They prayed to her, and they began a public recitation of Vedic hymns *(mantras)*....Their leader was an ancestor of the Śeṇḍe whose house is in Rāmḍohāḷī, behind the big chariot....He became the leader, and at that time some Brāhmaṇs began to stand in the water until they would die.

> Just ten or fifteen days later, it happened that Śivājī Mahārāj defeated Afjhal Khān near Pratāpgaḍ....At that same time, Śivājī sent his soldiers here. They destroyed the whole army of 12,000 soldiers. And the people here, the people who were going to end their lives, were saved. Our Kṛṣṇā Māī, this water deity *(jaladevatā)*, did us a great kindness. She was gracious *(prasanna)* to us. So what we call her Gaṅgā *pūjan*, her worship, her festival, was begun. And the festival was held at that place [i.e., Rāmḍoh] from the beginning....

The communalistic overtones of this origin story are resonant with communal tensions and minor incidents of friction in the present-day celebration of the festival. Such tensions and friction are particularly apparent when the goddess's palanquin is carried into Muslim neighborhoods and past some of Wāī's several mosques. However, despite the Brāhmaṇ dominance of the festival's organization, and despite a certain degree of communal tension, the Brāhmaṇ participants understand their festival to promote and renew the *unity* of each of the neighborhoods, and of the town as a whole. People explaining the festival express an almost Durkheimian idea of it as serving to bind together and make conscious of their unity people who merely live *near* one another the rest of the year.

Besides the communal meals, the palanquin processions which form part of each of the seven festivals are the clearest expressions of the unity of each of the Ghāṭs. In the processions, the palanquin stops at doorway after doorway along its route, resting on cloth mats or on rectangular *rāṅgoḷī* designs which have been specially laid out to receive it. While the palanquin is stopped at their doorway, the women of each household do *ovāḷaṇī* to the goddess, waving small oil lamps on metal trays, and "fill the lap" *(oṭī bharaṇeṃ)* of the goddess with coconuts, grain, blouse pieces, turmeric powder *(haḷdī)*, and red *kuṅkūṃ* powder.

Kṛṣṇābāī's worshippers identify her very closely with the water of the river itself. In the festival ritual this is expressed by the presence of a silver water vessel, or *gindī*, next to the images of the goddess. The identity is also expressed verbally, when people describe the necessity of the goddess—that is, the river—for the very existence of their town, and her importance for the general welfare: the physical and economic necessity of water for drinking and washing and cooking and farming. More personal, domestic needs, such as the desire for children, are seldom mentioned in connection with Kṛṣṇābāī, although babies are presented to her palanquin during the festival processions—as well as on her banks, I have been told, when they first leave home at the age of one and a quarter months. The "vow" *(navas)* does not seem to be a prominent aspect of the cult, although it is not unknown in connection with Kṛṣṇābāī. When asked about the practice of floating babies on rafts as is done at Bhivāī's *jatrā*, a priestess of the permanent Kṛṣṇābāī temple at Wāī was horrified. The practice sounded sinful to her, and reminded her of a story from the *Mahābhārata* about Kuntī abandoning her premarital son, Karṇa, to float down a river.

Also seldom mentioned—on the Brāhmaṇ side of the river, at least—is the destructive potential of the river's water. Brāhmaṇs in Wāī, like riverside people elsewhere in Maharashtra, do recall, from the days before dams made flood control possible, the custom of "filling the lap" of the river when it would be swollen in flood: the wife of the village headman—or, in the case of Wāī, the eldest married woman *(suvāsinī)* of the Rāste household, the former Sardārs of the town—would toss into the water a coconut, a blouse piece, and other articles used in the rite of *"oṭī bharaṇeṃ."* This gesture, while ostensibly greeting the goddess, also seems to imply a desire to appease her and to urge her to depart. But it is on the other side of the river in Wāī, the non-Brāhmaṇ side, that the dangerous aspect of the river goddess is explicitly recognized. There I was told, "She needs a man once every three years" *(tīlā tīn varṣānī ek māṇus pāhije)*—the river claims a victim, by drowning, once every three years.

Comparison

The differences between the Sātī Āsarā and Bhivāī on the one hand and Kṛṣṇābāī on the other provide an illustration of the degree and kinds of contrast between cults in Maharashtra. While the cult of Kṛṣṇābāī is dominated by Brāhmaṇs, Brāhmaṇs are by and large absent from—as well as ignorant of—the cults of Bhivāī and the Sātī Āsarā. Possession is a prominent element of the cults of Bhivāī and the Āsarā, whereas it does not seem to occur in connection with Kṛṣṇābāī. The practice of the *navas*, which is prominent in the cult of Bhivāī, is less so in that of Kṛṣṇābāī. The *navas* is also largely absent from the worship of the Sātī Āsarā; as disease deities, they must be placated to prevent them from doing harm, rather than worshipped to encourage them to do good.

Whether objects of *navas* or not, both the Sātī Āsarā and Bhivāī are closely connected with the desire for children which motivates so much of Maharashtrian religious practice. Kṛṣṇābāī, by contrast, has more to do with the general welfare and social solidarity; the birth and well-being of children are of secondary importance in her cult. Whereas the Sātī Āsarā are understood to prevent the birth or to cause the death of children whose mothers should but do not placate the Āsarā, and Bhivāī is liable to drown children whose mothers are afraid to float them on her raft, Kṛṣṇābāī is seen almost entirely as benevolent. She is viewed by her worshippers with a kind of familiar affection.

Finally, whereas Bhivāī has a developed mythology, and the Āsarā, as disease goddesses, have what might be called case histories, Kṛṣṇābāī has a history in a more strict sense. Her modern worship can be traced to a particular series of events, however mythologized, of 300 years ago.

On the other hand, cutting across the social differences between their worshippers and the differences in style of their worship, there are also some basic similarities among these deities. For one thing, whether they have a history or a mythology or only "case histories," none of these deities has a particularly significant textual component to her cult. None of them has a Purāṇic-style *māhātmya*, and none of them is mentioned in the *māhātmyas* of the rivers along which they are found. Their locus is ritual and experience, not texts.

Nevertheless, all of these deities resemble in some important respects a type of figure who does appear in the *māhātmyas* of these rivers: the Apsaras. Like Apsarases, all of these deities are female, all of them are "auspicious," and none of them has a husband in evidence. The marital status of these goddesses is something that most of their worshippers seem not to have thought about until they are asked. The images of Kṛṣṇābāī are adorned with the wedding necklace *(maṅgaḷasūtra)* and bangles of a married, unwidowed woman, and are called *"suvāsinīs"*—a term generally reserved for married women whose husbands are alive—but very few people in Wāī seem to know that Kṛṣṇābāī's husband, and that of other major rivers, is supposed to be the ocean. Mhasobā and the other male deities associated with the Āsarā are their brother, never their husband; and Dhuḷobā is the brother, not the husband, of Bhivāī. Sometimes the Āsarā are called *kumārikās*, virgin girls; sometimes they are said to be *suvāsinīs*, married women; and sometimes they are said to be both *suvāsinīs* and *kumārikās;* a statement like this last one is elucidated by the concept of *"korī suvāsinī"*—a pre-pubescent, virginal, married girl (cf. Dāte and Karve 1942: s.v. *korī savāśīṇa)*. But who the Āsarās' husband is or should be, no one seems to know.

Furthermore, unlike some other husbandless goddesses, none of these goddesses is a demon killer.[4] None of them is identified with Pārvatī, or Kālī, or Durgā, as many goddesses would be at least in some contexts and by some of their worshippers. And the Gondhaḷ

---

[4] One exception is the goddess of the Koynā at Karāḍ, who in many contexts is called Daityanivāriṇī, "She Who Wards Off Demons."

is not performed for any of them,[5] as it is for a whole array of other husbandless goddesses (Ḍhere 1988: 174-189).

And finally, the notion of sisterhood and the persistent recurrence of the number seven—the seven Āsarā, the seven Bhivayyā, and the seven Ghāṭs of Wāī—suggest a link between these goddesses and other, better known sets of seven female deities: the Saptamātṛkā of classical temple iconography, for example (Goetz 1974: 70-71; Plate XXIX, 85), and the "seven sisters," a set of primarily non-Brāhmaṇical deities, variously named, who are widely worshipped in Maharashtra and South India (Whitehead 1921: 29-32, 39; Sontheimer 1976: 38-44; Shulman 1980: 243-267).

Thus, despite important differences among their cults, a theological definition of the Sātī Āsarā, Bhivāī, and Kṛṣṇābāī reveals some remarkable similarities among the goddesses themselves. These similarities suggest a conception of riverine divinity that transcends the caste divisions of Indian society and perhaps also the dichotomy between "folk" and "classical" elements of Indian culture.

---

[5] Again the goddess of the Koynā is an exception, as the Gondhaḷ *is* performed for her.

REFERENCES

Bhāgvat, Durgā. 1959. Dharma āṇī lokasāhitya—abhicāra kiṃvā jāduṭoṇā: 2. *Navabhārata* 13.2: 19-27.

Dāte, Yaśavant Rāmakṛṣṇa, and Cintāmaṇ Gaṇeś Karve. 1942. *Mahārāṣṭra vāksaṃpradāya kośa*, 2 vols. Puṇeṃ: Mahārāṣṭra Kośamaṇḍaḷa Ltd.

Ḍhere, R. C. 1988. The Gondhali: Singers for the Devi. In *The experience of Hinduism: Essays on religion in Maharashtra*. Ed. by Eleanor Zelliot and Maxine Berntsen. Albany: State University of New York Press.

Goetz, Hermann. 1970. *Studies in the history, religion and art of classical and mediaeval India*. Ed. by Hermann Kulke. Wiesbaden: Franz Steiner Verlag GmbH.

Shulman, David Dean. 1980. *Tamil temple myths: sacrifice and divine marriage in the South Indian Śaiva tradition*. Princeton: Princeton University Press.

Sontheimer, Günther-Dietz. 1976. *Birobā, Mhaskobā und Khaṇḍobā: Ursprung, Geschichte und Umwelt von pastoralen Gottheiten in Mahārāṣṭra*. Wiesbaden: Franz Steiner Verlag GmbH.

Whitehead, Henry. 1921. *The village gods of South India.* Second edition, revised and enlarged. Reprint, Delhi: Sumit Publications, 1976.

Traude Pillai-Vetschera

THE IMPACT OF CHRISTIANITY ON THE MAHARS OF AHMEDNAGAR DISTRICT

In a recent article on inculturation[1] Stephen Fuchs says: "The dissemination of the Christian Message results in the presentation of Christian values—values which are bound to create radical cultural changes when accepted by a group of converts....As history teaches, the Christianization of other countries and people all over the world has brought profound social changes in its wake." (Fuchs 1988: 134).

Whether this holds true also for the Mahar community of Ahmadnagar District in the Indian State of Maharashtra is the topic to be discussed in this paper:

Let me start with a few general remarks on "Christian work" in India: It began with the advent of the Portuguese, who arrived in 1498 "with massacres and sacking of Goa, when for three days the

[1] "The inculturation of the Church is the integration of the Christian experience of a local Church into the culture of the people, in such a way that the experience not only expresses itself in elements of this culture, but becomes a force that animates, orients and innovates this culture so as to create a new unity and communion, not only within the culture in question, but also as an enrichment of the Church universal" (A. Roest Crollius 1978, quoted in Fuchs 1988: 141). Fuchs himself understands inculturation as "...a dialogal encounter process that comes from the salvific movement...a discovery of the seeds of the Word which lie hidden in the given cultures and living traditions" (ibid., p. 142).

citizens were subjected to every atrocity," as reports Bishop Badley in *Visions and Victories in Hindustan* (1931: 238). In 1542 Francis Xavier came to Goa "and brought a new vision of what the term Christian stood for" (ibid.). In the course of the years thousands of people were converted, mainly in areas along the western coast of India. Those converts belonged sometimes to the highest but more often to the lowest strata in society, while the core of society was not much influenced. It seems to be the common thing to happen that culture interchange is largely confined to the fringes of society. Especially in the case of Hindus we can usually see that, instead of permitting themselves to be converted, they accept new ideas and values and assimilate them into their own religion. The Christian element may become one more component of their multiple and heterogeneous religious and philosophical systems. This happens more or less in all the highly syncretistic religions of the Asian high cultures, which harbour without much mental or religious difficulties many heterogeneous elements (Fuchs 1988: 145). In a religion like Hinduism only those people on the fringe remain would-be converts, who want to embrace Christianity as an escape from economic exploitation and social degradation. "Their real purpose of religious conversion is not the change to a better religion, but the improvement of their economic or social situation," says Fuchs (ibid., p. 147). He gives the example of Oceania and Africa, where people change their religion to Islam or Christianity because adherence to their old tribal religion makes them appear backward and old-fashioned. Of India he mentions tribes in Chotanagpur and Assam, who embraced Christianity in great numbers because they found their tribal religions inadequate, and also because they desired to benefit by the education and general cultural progress which the Christian missionaries offered them if they turned Christian.

Much of this holds true also for the Mahars, who are the largest caste of untouchables in the Indian State of Maharashtra. Mahars, like all other untouchables in India, have been depressed and suppressed by the higher orders of the Hindu caste system for uncountable centuries. They were regarded as so lowly that even their shadow—let alone their touch—polluted a high-caste Hindu. They were not permitted to enter into the temples or offer sacrifices. They had no possibility to study the sacred scriptures of the Hindus, as this was the privilege of the higher orders, who kept the lowest deliberately ignorant and believed that it was not intended by God that untouchables should learn to read. It is alleged that in former times molten tin or lac was poured into the ears of untouchables who ventured to go too close to the temples in order to hear the holy texts being recited by the Brahmans.

In spite of all that, the Mahars regard themselves as Hindus, as do also other untouchable communities. Their religious ideas however often seem confused. This is nothing special with the Mahars, but seems to be common also with other communities in comparable conditions. Briggs writes about the Chamars (leatherworkers) that the great mass of them knows very little about their own religious beliefs and social customs, and that this ignorance concerning their religion leads many of them to say that they have no religion at all (Briggs 1920: 236). Fuchs reports of the untouchable Balahis (a caste of weavers) of Nimar District that their present religion seemed a strange mixture of remnants of their own and various other creeds the Balahis have adopted without any attempt at a logical systematization. (Fuchs 1950: 223)

However, history shows that the Mahars have often been more open to new ideas than other untouchable castes. Within the fold of Hinduism they tried to find new ways to communicate with God by developing a personal relationship with Him, according to the teachings of the 14th century poet-saint Chokhamela or Chokha Mahar (see Robertson 1938: 15). In more recent times the Mahars were exposed not only to new ideas within the Hindu faith itself, but to altogether different religions, viz. Christianity and Buddhism, and it seems that they reacted more strongly to them than other communities.

Mission Work among the Mahars

Today Christians are the third major religious community in the order of numerical strength in India, comprising about 2.6% of the total population. The strongholds of the Christians are in the states of Kerala, Tamil Nadu and Andhra Pradesh, where we find more than 60% of the total Christian population. Maharashtra has only 5.04% of the Christians living in India.

Mission work in Maharashtra started in 1813, when a group of missionaries of the American Board of Foreign Missions, America's oldest Protestant Missionary Society, landed at Bombay. In Ahmadnagar District and many other parts of Maharashtra, the missionaries of the American Marathi Mission were the first to start work. In 1873 a missionary of the Society for the Propagation of the Gospel (S.P.G.), one of the overseas agencies of the Church of England, started his work in the same area, "and naturally created problems in the beginning," until the area where each one was to work was clearly defined (Moulton 1967: 19). In about 1900 the Methodists turned up, adding to the confusion, which had already increased considerably by the time the Catholics arrived.

The Catholics came to the Deccan after the Protestants, in the second half of the nineteenth century.[2] The opening of the Catholic Marathi Mission near Ahmadnagar occured in 1878 (Hull 1930: 451). Nowadays we find different Christian denominations represented in this district: above all the American Marathi Mission, the Salvation Army, Presbyterians, and Catholics. In former times the Church of England was the strongest, nowadays the Catholic Church also has many followers. Thus in Shevgaon—a town of about 16,000 inhabitants, where I spent most of my time during

---

[2] "Except for one pioneer visit of Matthaeus de Castro to Bijapur in 1639, no Vicar-Apostolic ever set foot on the Deccan plateau down to the year 1851 or 1852, when Bishop Hartmann made his first visitation." (Hull 1930: 451).

several visits to Maharashtra—and in surrounding villages the number of Catholics has increased from about 1500 some 30 years ago, to more or less 6000 at present.

The missionaries certainly had good intentions when they started their work among the downtrodden of Maharashtra, among whom the Mahars were not only the most numerous but in many ways the most interesting. Ernest Hull, author of the *Bombay Mission History,* considered the conversion to Christianity as the Mahars' only way to free themselves of a traditional system of suppression from which they could escape by no efforts of their own; he thought that "their pitiable and hopeless condition called for some effectual measures from outside to ameliorate and raise them" (Hull 1930: 463). He of course was not the only one who thought that the Mahars would have to reject Hinduism openly, if they wanted to free themselves from their bondage. The same idea caused Dr. Ambedkar and his followers to embrace Buddhism and publicly burn the sacred books of the Hindus as a protest against the age-long suppression within the Hindu caste system. In both cases it was implied that getting rid of the "detested name" Mahar and calling themselves "Christians" or "Buddhist" would also finally improve their social status.

However, such positive results were not easily obtained and mission work did not proceed as smoothly as the first missionaries may have hoped it would. One of the greatest calamities of the Christians in India is the fact that they are not a homogeneous, closely knit group, but that they are split up into different denominations, which from the beginning "hampered each other's success by unfortunate and needless competition, especially among village congregations" (Moulton 1967: 18).

In his *Bombay Mission History* Hull describes at length events that took place in 1878 and afterwards which show clearly how some Mahars managed to extract large sums of money from different missionaries, by playing them cleverly one against the other. According to Hull, "...much harm was done by the missionaries helping them (the Mahars) too much with money—thus depriving them of the stimulant necessity of helping themselves. They will prey on the mission as far as they can; and where rival missions exist, will make trade on both parties in turn, offering themselves as converts to the highest bidder" (Hull 1930: 440).

Even today the Mahars often do not hide the fact that for them being Christian is very much connected with the idea of receiving material help from the missionaries. Sometimes Mahar Protestants in the villages told me that they would not mind becoming Catholics if this in one way or the other would help to improve their economic situation.

This attitude should not be simply ascribed to the Mahars' "beggar mentality," but it has to be understood in its historical context: in the traditional socio-economic system, the Mahars, like all other castes, had their rather complex specific duties. Apart from those, they had but little chance to take independent decisions. The low castes worked for those who owned the land, and the landlords told them what to do and how. In times of need a Mahar approached the landlord to whom his family was attached, and requested him with folded hands for help, which very often was granted.

When in a time of transition the landlords refused in increasing number their assistance, the missionaries appeared on the scene, with inexhaustible resources of money, as it must have seemed to those poorest classes of society. And the missionaries—full of Christian ideas of charity and love—expected to solve their problems by feeding the poor, paying their debts, giving them clothes and money for their fields, and filing their court-cases.

Now many missionaries have changed their attitude, showing more interest in the spiritual than the economic conditions of their congregations, and the Mahars say: "The missionaries have deceived us. They made us Christians, and then they went away. Now nobody is there to look after us and the government does not help us any more either."

This point is very true, and it leads us to the discussion of some problems that arose in the wake of mission work among the Mahars.

1. Loss of the Advantages of Scheduled Castes

The Indian Government provides certain facilities for those communities which fall under the definition of Scheduled Castes. Those Mahars who call themselves Hindus are free to enjoy all those facilities, but Christians are not. For the "Constitution (Scheduled Castes) Order 1950" holds under point 3 that "... no person who professes a religion different from the Hindu or Sikh religion shall be deemed to be a member of a Scheduled Caste." Thus the Mahar Christians enjoy none of the benefits of the "backward" classes, like educational concessions (scholarships and free coaching classes, a large number of free places in boarding schools, reserved places in colleges), reserved government jobs and seats in State and Central Government Institutions (for details see Sharma 1975: 133).

Also in day-to-day life men who enter their names as Joseph, Andrew, Michael, etc. in an application form for a job have much less chance to be accepted than people with common Hindu names. Capable and well educated men often remain without work, when the names given in their school-leaving certificates identify them clearly as Christians. To make life at least easier for their children, many young parents give them common, traditional names which do not reveal their true religion.

These drawbacks may on the other hand also be a challenge, which in the long run might have a positive effect on the Mahar Christians. Already ten years ago I met people who did not lament their losses, but reacted very differently. I clearly remember a man of about 50 years of age who told me: "We should be proud that they do not count us among the Scheduled Castes any more. We must prove to them that we don't need their help and that we can stand on our own feet." In a few places in Bombay I could talk to Mahars who had started "action movements": instead of fighting for the right of Mahar Christians to be counted among the Scheduled Castes, participants in those movements strive for economic independence and better education for their children; they regularly discuss their problems, they help each other to find work, all children go to school and get coaching classes by older students; for the sake of the common welfare each earning member of the group parts with a few rupees each month; the money is collected and used to get electricity and water pumps installed, or it is saved for cases of emergency. All huts looked neat and clean; the people who lived in them were in good conditions and proud of their achievements.

The situation in the villages is different, but there are priests and nuns (like the Mary-Sisters) who visit the Christian communities regularly even in remote places and try to help them to solve their problems and to develop higher self-esteem.

In the long run becoming Christian may bring about social and economic changes. This can be seen from many examples from South India: there especially the Christians venture to leave their villages and even go abroad; young Christians more than others in Tamil Nadu join the Indian Army, earning thus a decent regular income; Christian girls more than others venture to become teachers or nurses, earning their own living and often supporting their families.

Compared to those groups, the lives of converted Mahars have not changed much, but it is too early yet to state whether changes on a larger scale will take place or not.

2. Promotion of "Beggar Mentality"

Sometimes people say that the missionaries promoted the "beggar-mentality" of the Mahars. This is true to some extent, and it has been discussed above that for many Mahars being Christian is connected with the idea of receiving material help from the missionaries. The idea that the poor had to be given material help was maintained for a long time by the missionaries. The main reason may have been that almost all missionaries were foreigners, who were imperfectly acquainted with the local conditions of the places in which they were put to work. They may have had the best intentions, but they made many mistakes paying too high salaries and trying to solve many problems with money, which of course spoilt the new Christians.

In the outlook of the Catholic Church major changes started to take place after the Second Vatican Council more than 20 years ago. The clergy became aware of the role of local cultures, traditions and practices and of the importance of studying them thoroughly and objectively. This has two effects:

- Better knowledge leads to a deeper understanding of the people; mistakes can be avoided, and new approaches to solving the problems of the community members can be found apart from material help.

- Local elements, like tunes or even rituals, are being introduced into the Christian liturgical celebrations. Thus it becomes easier for the converts to identify themselves with their new faith.

3. Loss of Ancient Traditions

Mahars in general are losing many of their ancient traditions. Within the Christian community this becomes perhaps more obvious. Thus a young Mahar Christian, watching a Hindu woman who carried turmeric roots to the temple of Maruti, accompanied by a drummer, told me: "Look, all this we do not do any more. We have lost so many of our old things. I would feel bad to become a Hindu again, but I think the Hindus have a more colorful life with more things to enjoy, while our life is duller."

This holds true to some extent. But it has to be repeated that the loss of ancient traditions is not limited to the Christian community. Taking the example of the festivals, it can be seen that the one festival which had a specific meaning for the Mahars—the festival of Bhavai, the tutelary goddess of the Veskar—has not been celebrated in Shevgaon for more than 25 years. Festivals which are celebrated now seem to a large extent "simplified versions" of festivals celebrated by higher castes. This does not mean that the Mahars strive to imitate the high castes at any cost; they rather take over from them customs and practices which seem meaningful to them, and which fit into their own pattern of concepts.

4. Denying the Origin

Mahar converts who received a good education and are economically better off do not want to have anything to do with their less fortunate caste-fellows and often keep aloof from them.

Once I talked with two priests who worked in the Mahar community of Shevgaon about some Mahar customs and ceremonies. One of them—an old man from Switzerland—had a profound knowledge due to his keen interest in the people among whom he had spent many years of his life. The other one pretended not to know anything even about the most common beliefs and practices. He was himself a Mahar.

I had a similar experience with a nice Mahar girl who was a nurse and wanted to become a Catholic nun. Whenever I brought up the topic "Mahar," she became less communicative and obviously felt ill at ease.

Such reactions may seem strange, but they can be explained. I was told that in the case of a priest who comes from an untouchable community, Christian converts from higher castes may even refuse to accept Communion from his hands. Thus it may sometimes definitely be easier to deny one's Mahar origin.

Other people, who do not have such specific problems, nevertheless may have good reasons to keep as great a distance as possible between themselves and their caste-fellows, many of whom are their relatives: very often—and not only among Mahars—poor relatives will soon turn up and try to live comfortably on their fortunate family-member's income.

Conclusion

Let us go back to the question asked at the beginning of the paper—whether Christianization has brought about profound social changes for the Mahars—and sum up:

The old socio-economic system, in which every caste had its prescribed position, its rights and duties, has largely broken down. Today none of the higher castes feel responsible for the untouchables any more, or are prepared to part with a substantial amount of grain for the latters' benefit. They do not feel any obligation towards the low castes, as these to a large extent have given up their traditional jobs. Thus, for example, carcasses of dead animals may be seen lying in the villages for quite some time because neither the Mahars nor anybody else is prepared to remove them.

Mahars in general are undergoing transformations. Alterations take place in many spheres of their lives. The traditional ways are changing, and so are the religious beliefs and the ways of expressing them. Like the Neo-Buddhists, the Mahar Christians also desire a complete break with the past. According to my own observations they have—with a few exceptions, as, e.g., among the so-called "action movements"—not yet succeeded as a group in finding a new identity as a "new" and "different" kind of people, and in being accepted as such by the higher orders. The foreign missionaries often used a wrong approach, the conversion remaining a superficial one, with the emphasis on material benefits, and with permanent jealousies among the converts. Now, with a change in the outlook of the priests themselves, striving for a better understanding of the local cultures and trying to help the people organize themselves, there seem to be good prospects for a positive change in the social conditions of the Mahar Christians as well.

REFERENCES

Badley, Brenton T. (Bishop) 1931. *Visions and victories in Hindustan—A story of the mission stations of the Methodist Episcopal Church in Southern Asia.* Madras.

Briggs, G. W. 1920. *The Chamars.* Oxford.

Fuchs, Stephen. 1950. *The children of Hari.* Wien-Horn.

Id. 1988. Inculturation: An anthropological and theological perspective. In *Dialogue in action.* Ed. by Thunberg and Pandit. New Delhi.

Hull, E. R. 1930. *Bombay mission-history,* vol. II. Bombay.

Moulton, J. L. 1967. *Faith for the future (the America Marathi Mission - India Sesquicentennial 1963).* New York.

Robertson, A. 1938. *The Mahar folk.* Oxford.

Sharma, G. S. 1975. *Legislation and cases on untouchability and Scheduled Castes in India.* New Delhi.

Eleanor Zelliot

THE FOLKLORE OF PRIDE:
Three Components of Contemporary Dalit Belief

> The Hindus wanted the Vedas and they sent for
> Vyasa who was not a caste Hindu.
> The Hindus wanted an Epic and they sent for
> Valmiki who was an Untouchable.
> The Hindus wanted a Constitution,
> and they sent for me.
>
> Dr. B. R. Ambedkar
> (Mathai 1978: 25)

Do Dalits have a culture of their own, a counter culture or a parallel culture to the "Great Tradition"? Is their culture a "Little Tradition" waiting to be absorbed into the Sanskritic tradition of India, a concept defined by Redford (1956) and applied to India by Singer (1958)? Or is their culture a pale reflection of high caste culture (Moffatt 1979)? Dr. Ambedkar's startling claim, quoted above, could be read several ways, but it seems to suggest most boldly a claim to a tradition, a culture, which is in itself both Great *and* a creative, contributing, essential factor in the all-Indian culture. This is perhaps a fourth way of looking at the culture of the Dalits, a word I use because ex-Untouchables and other low castes involved in a contemporary cultural movement identify themselves as *dalit*—ground-down, downtrodden, oppressed—not as Untouchables, Scheduled Castes, or Harijans.

An early challenge to the Little-Great Tradition theory came in Robert J. Miller's "Button Button..." article (Miller 1966), a provocative essay based on the folklore of the Mahars, the caste at the heart of the Dalit movement. Other work supporting this idea of a different set of cultural attitudes among low status groups is to be found in Juergensmeyer (1980) and most recently has appeared in the Ph.D. thesis of Vincentnathan (1988). The case for a widespread counter culture has been carried farthest in David Lorenzen's *Traditions of Non-Caste Hinduism: The Kabir Panth* (Lorenzen 1987). He also summaries the opposing view "from the top down" found in the influential work of Dumont (1972). Another dimension of Untouchable cultural creativity is encountered in the new research on the songs and epics of the Untouchables themselves, a genre well represented by the "crying songs" of an Untouchable caste described for the first time in a recent article by Egnor (1986).

In this essay, rather than entering directly into this debate, I want to examine the folklore of the Dalits through the current "folklore of pride", i.e. some of the beliefs of the Dalits in Maharashtra, who come chiefly from the Mahar caste, and are now by and large converts to Buddhism. It is now virtually impossible to re-create the older folk culture of the Mahars. Bhimrao Ramji Ambedkar (1891-1956) not only served as Chairman of the Drafting Committee for the Constitution of Independent India, as he notes in the quotation above, he also changed the lives of many Untouchables in India in the realms of religion, education, politics and cultural life. The movement he led from 1920 until his death brought about increased education, political representation, a widespread conversion to Buddhism and a literary flowering (Zelliot 1977). It also created a new Dalit folklore which has in many ways replaced or adapted the traditional folklore of the Untouchables who were influenced by his movement. Since I am dealing with the folklore of a self-conscious group, the Dalits, rather than a traditional caste, I will simply state that Dalits feel they do have and have had a culture of their own, in no way inferior to anyone else's tradition.

The folk beliefs of today's Dalits center around three ideas:

(1) the idea that they are and were creators of culture, an idea expressed graphically in the Ambedkar quotation which begins this article.
(2) the idea that they were "Lords of the Earth," the original inhabitants of their areas shunted aside by the Aryan invaders; corollary with this is a disbelief in hereditary pollution and purity, a disbelief in karmic rebirth.
(3) the idea that they were and are a militant people, with heroes who used their strength in a self-sacrificial way for their people.

While my chief references for these beliefs are current in the area of Maharashtra, similar ideas may be found in the folklore of other ex-Untouchable groups in other areas of India, and I will explore those when relevant. Not much is left of the traditional system of beliefs among the Mahars, but those past beliefs will be referred to as they can be reconstructed from older people's memories and such sources as the Gazetteers and the Tribes and Castes volumes of Bombay and the Central Provinces which deal at length with Mahars.

Dalits as Creators of Culture

The Dalits of Maharashtra have in the past twenty years created a school of literature, Dalit Sahitya (Zelliot 1976; id. 1978a; id. 1978b; *A Marathi Sampler* 1982: 93-101; Dharwadker 1989), which has changed the face of Marathi literature and inspired similar literary creativity in Gujarat and Karnataka. Among their many themes is an occasional reference to the epics, often identifying the creators as low caste, even Dalit, as does Ambedkar in the quotation above. Along with this belief is a sense that Mahars have *always* been contributors to culture. Daya Pawar, an important contemporary Dalit writer, in particular holds this opinion, and quotes a Marathi proverb to show acceptance of the idea of Mahar gifts:

In the Brahman house—writing
In the Kunbi house—grain
In the Mahar house—singing

(Pawar 1974: 2)

Pawar mourns the loss of the "great cultural treasure" the Mahars could have had if the kind of music his father and those who visited his home made had not been considered "debased" by other castes.

It is clear that Mahars did have a place in the cultural life of traditional Maharashtra. Even though it is the Untouchable Mang caste which most often is described as "village musicians" in the Gazetteers, Mahars seem to have been the chief musicians and actors in *tamasha,* the folk drama of Maharashtra. We do not know if Mahars had a part in creating *tamasha,* which was a recognized form by the 16th century and at its height under the Peshwas of the 18th century, but we know they dominated the field. The revival of *tamasha* in the late 19th century is credited to a Brahman, Patthe Bapu Rao, together with his "beautiful Mahar consort," Pawala (Abrams 1974). *Tamasha,* however, was considered vulgar by the 20th century Mahar reformers, and the low status of *tamasha* women countered an image of progress, so that village drama was frowned upon by Dr. Ambedkar. Nevertheless, Dadu Indurikar, also known as Indu Mahar, was until very recently a sterling example of *tamasha* art (Paranjpye 1971). And some of the skills of *tamasha,* although not its earthy, even vulgar humor, were continued in *jalsa* groups which travelled the countryside singing the message of Ambedkar's movement in the 1930's.

There are other suggestions that Mahars may have had special musical gifts. The *Thana Gazetteer* notes that Mahars refused to play music for the Muslim Muharram procession since the Muslims refused to let the image of Vithoba be carried through the streets at the same time (1882: 524), which implies a public music tradition.

Converted Christian Mahars had special music duties during the feast of Mount Mary in Bandra and played the reed pipes and drum at weddings (Fernandes 1927: 53). The *Khandesh Gazetteer* reports that the Mahars are "fond of music, playing a one-stringed instrument *tuntune*, a lute *vina*, a tambourine *daf*, and a small drum *dhol*" (1880: 119). However, Mahars had no such overweening musical duty as the *pariah* of Madras, whose very name means drum.

Other Untouchable groups have claims to cultural achievement. Many of the Bhangi caste of the North call themselves "Valmiki," tracing their lineage to the author of the *Ramayana*, supposedly an outcaste and a criminal before his conversion by the inadvertent repetition of the name of Ram. There seems to have been no building of literary tradition based on this claim, but an effort of the much-scorned Bhangi sweepers to elicit pride for self-improvement (Kolenda 1960). (The recognition of Vyasa, son of a Brahman sage and a fisher-girl, supposed author of the Vedas and of the epic, the *Mahabharata*, as a fellow Dalit is found, however, only among the contemporary Dalit intellectuals and seems to not be traditional). A poem by Daya Pawar illustrates the way in which a modern poet thinks of Valmiki as a betrayer of his low caste identity. His reference to Shambuk relates to the story of Rama's punishing the Shudra Shambuk for hearing the Vedas:

Oh Great Poet

Oh Valmiki
Should you sing the praises of Ramarajya
Because you're the great poet of poets?
Seeing the heron's wounded wing
Your compassionate heart broke out in
  lament.
You were born outside the village
In a shunned neighbourhood...
  where misery itself was born
Never festooned with fruit or flower...

The dejected faces...furrowed with care...
Is it true you never heard
Their lament as they cried for liberation?
One Shambuk of your own blood
Caught fire, rose in anger.
Oh great poet,
Singing the praises of Ramarajya,
Even there the icy cliff of inhumanity towered up.
Oh great poet,
How then should we call you a great poet?

(Pawar 1976: 34-35)

"Dalit culture" has now become something of a fashionable article of faith. The *Dalit Voice,* an English weekly from Bangalore, claims from time to time that Devadasi culture, which includes the classical dance form Bharata Natya, is a Dalit form of creativity. The June 1986 issue of *Religion and Society,* a scholarly journal published in Banglalore by the Christian Society for the Study of Society, is entirely devoted to Dalit culture, Hindu as well as Christian. Even more striking, however, are the ways in which today's Dalits encourage cultural creativity. The poem by Daya Pawar on Valmiki both indicates a belief in the Dalit creative past and is itself an act of creation. Since the early 1970's, short stories, a few novels, much poetry and most recently autobiography have flowed from Dalit pens in great quantity.

Dalit theater followed close on the heels of Dalit poetry and short stories, and Dalit Rangabhumi, the first Dalit theater, which was based in Pune, has been followed by dozens of others, both in Maharashtra and outside the state. The Delhi-based Ahwan Theatre, Cinema and Mass media group has "definite plans to provide extensive exposure to the rich cultural heritage and traditional Dalit and folk arts of the country" (Ahwan brochure 1987). The first two plays of the Ahwan Theatre were a Hindi play entitled *Devadasi* and a Hindi translation of Langston Hughes' *Mulatto*. The Ahwan group has also attempted to help the Bhats, puppeteers originally from Rajasthan who are counted among the Scheduled Castes. The Bhat puppeteers travelled to Washington D.C. during the Festival of India celebrations, but are now back in their Delhi slum, trunks filled with magnificant puppets, but with no change in their economic or social status.

Several Dalit drama conferences have been held, and it is said that there are now more than forty Dalit theatre groups. Many write their own plays, a few adapt plays from the American Black theater, some revive the arts of *tamasha*. B. S. Shinde of Pune, founding father of Dalit Rangabhumi, has written plays based on Buddhist themes and a drama built around the legendary Mahar hero Amrutnak who is featured in the third section of this paper.

There seems to be no end to new Dalit cultural creativity. Dalit women in Bombay organized the Dalit Stri Samwadini (Dalit Women's Dialogue) in 1986, probably the first women's literary conference in Maharashtra. A Dalit art exhibition was held in Nagpur in connection with the Asmitadarsh literary conference in 1979, and an all-India art conference was called in Hyderabad in 1987. Some Dalits believe that the sculptors of the classic period of Indian art were an Untouchable caste!

The current interest in creativity is fully within the modern structures of Indian cultural activity, and critical recognition of Dalit accomplishments by the moderators of culture, who are generally high caste, is expected by Dalits. Dalit culture is no longer a separate culture, if it ever was. But although it seeks to contribute to general Indian culture, and maintains that it always has been a contributor, the Dalit cultural movement stresses Dalit themes, the Dalit past, and Dalit traditional ways.

The Lords of the Earth / The Sons of the Soil

One of the most common beliefs among Untouchables all over India is that they were the original inhabitants of the land. The Ad-Dharm movement of the North rose and fell in the 1920's and 1930's as it attempted to list Untouchables as those of the "original religion," separate (and pure), in the Punjab and United Provinces Censuses (Juergensmeyer 1982); and in the Adi-Dravida movement of Tamilnadu (Pandian 1899; Barnett 1976; Kamalanathan 1985), the claim to "original Dravidian" status is still somewhat important as the designation of some groups of Untouchables in the South.

In Maharashtra, the idea that the Mahar was the original settler is one of the most persistent images among Mahars, Dalits *and* Buddhists. The Mahar was called *dharnice put* or *bhumiputra,* Marathi and Sanskritized Marathi terms for "sons of the soil." Many educated Mahars know that scholars such as John Wilson (1857: xxiii) and R. E. Enthoven (1922: 401) believed that the very word Maharashtra was derived from "the country of the Mahars," although most Indian scholars denied the claim vehemently. Irawati Karve stressed the identification of the Mahar with all areas of Maharashtra, reporting that on the eastern edge of Vidarbha where Hindi speakers are mixed with Marathi, a Mahar told her proudly, "Wherever you find Mahars, there is Maharashtra" (Karve 1959). A rather unflattering folk saying implying that nothing is perfect, "Wherever there is a village, there is a *maharwada,*" is also a recognition that Mahars were probably the only caste to be found in every village in the entire Marathi-speaking area. Some of the traditional duties of the Mahars also lend credence to this belief, especially their position as "authorities in all boundary matters" (Enthoven 1922: 416).

What is most interesting about the Mahar case is that Dr. B. R. Ambedkar, the still all-important Mahar leader, opposed any idea that Untouchables were a separate race from other Indians. In his earliest testimony to a governmental commission, that to the Southborough committee gathering evidence in 1918 for the Montagu-Chelmsford Reforms, he argued in a most sophisticated manner that Untouchables deserved a low franchise and a large communal representation in the popular assemblies because there was no "like-mindedness," no "endosmosis" between Touchables and Untouchables (The Reforms Committee (Franchise) 1919: 729-739). Other Untouchable petitioners argued for separate electorates, pre-Aryan status, recognition as non-Hindu. But Ambedkar's words are somewhat ambiguous; they recall his student days at Columbia University where he wrote for a sociology seminar that caste divisions were "an unconscious growth in the life of a human society under peculiar circumstances," not a command of a Supreme Authority (Ambedkar 1917). The implication seems to be that separation caused by human society could be replaced by unity and fellow-feeling if that human society so chose. Ambedkar's hesitancy to use any "original people" or "pre-Aryan" formula was not shared by his followers; the idea of the "Lords of the Land" persisted. In the end the ambiguity of ideas about Mahar origins was resolved by the conversion to Buddhism.

Maharashtrian Dalits (and some caste Hindus) accept wholeheartedly Ambedkar's final solution to the problems of origins and the relationship of Untouchables to the Hindu religion. Untouchables had been Buddhists, he claimed, loyal to their religion, and pushed to the outskirts of the village when Brahmanism won out over Buddhism well over a millennium ago (Ambedkar 1948). The Mahars had been proud Buddhist Nagas, said Ambedkar at the 1956 conversion ceremony to Buddhism in Nagpur, a city chosen for the event as not only an active center of the Mahar movement but as the "city of the Nag people" (Ambedkar 1969). The status of Buddhist, past and present, links the ex-Mahar to a rich heritage, one which encompasses art and egalitarianism, rationality and humanism, and is also part and parcel of the all-India past. The Buddhist identiy encompasses the "Lords of the Earth claim," the idea of past creativity, and the disbelief in pollution or *karma* as the cause of Untouchability.

Just as Ambedkar's final message to his people, the 1956 Buddhist conversion speech, stated a belief of origin that was both a proud claim to a past and a denial of the whole theory of pollution, so the earliest Mahar document of the modern period propounded a belief in origins which inherently denied hereditary untouchability. The petition for re-admission into the army prepared by Gopal Baba Walangkar in 1894, now in manuscript form in the Khairmode Collection of the Bombay University Library, is from the "Non-Aryan group for the removal of wrongs," but claims Kshatriya status in the body of the document. This ambiguity is resolved by a sweeping and scornful history of everyone's origins: high caste people from the South were "Australo-semitic non-Aryans" and African Negroes; Chitpavan Brahmans were "Barbary Jews;" the high caste Marathas' forebears were "Turks" (Walangkar 1894). In other words, almost everybody was "non-Aryan;" most Indians were something else at one time! Clearly belief in a hereditary hierarchy based on pollution is denied in this account. It should be added that Kshatriya status claims never became a serious Mahar plea, possibly because the Marathas had pre-empted that claim, possibly because the whole system of caste hierarchy was under attack from the earliest days of the movement.

The need to be recognized as a separate (and separated) yet not inherently inferior people has been met in many ways by various Untouchable and low-caste groups. A idea first promulgated by Mahatma Phule in 19th century Maharashtra (O'Hanlon 1986: 136ff.) was that the low castes possessed a king, Bali, who represented pre-Aryan religion and culture brought low by the Aryan invasion. The Bali theme seems to have been dropped very early on by Phule's own Shudra groups, Malis and Marathas. Ambedkar never referred to such a myth at all. However, Bali is still a current theme in the re-creation of some Dalits' cultural past. A recent article tells how "the Great Dalit Emperor" Bali out of misplaced faithfulness to his oath lost the land of the Untouchables to the wily Aryan dwarf Waman (Rai 1989: 15-16, 18).

A natural part of the "Lords of the Earth" theme, but also independent of it, is a total rejection of the idea of hereditary pollution. The myths of origin of Untouchable castes almost always refer to a sort of cosmic (or comic) accident or some mistaken act of good will, not a polluting occupation or a sinful past life. One such myth from the past will serve to illustrate the hundreds that have been recorded.

> ...Mahars are descended from one of the four sons of the cow. The mother asked her sons how they proposed to honour her after her death. Three of them said that they would give her divine honours. The fourth answered her that as she had born him in her body, so would he carry her in his. The other sons were astounded at his impiety, and they exclaimed *mahā āhar,* that is, great appetite. The name, Mahār, thus clung to him and his descendants; for he and they have kept the vow until this day in their eating of beef.
>
> (Robertson 1939: 74)

Although the origin myths differ, the attitude that pollution is not a hereditary factor has been found among Untouchables by almost all those who have studied an Untouchable community closely, beginning with Kolenda's pioneering work on Untouchable Sweepers in a North Indian village (1964). One of the most thorough and most recent is Vincentnathan's study of a group that calls itself Harijan in the South (1988). The rejection of the idea of pollution may be much older than the modern period. A classic statement was made in the 14th century by the Mahar saint-poet Cokhamela, who asked:

In the beginning, at the end,
There is nothing but pollution.
No one knows anyone who is born pure.
Cokha says, in wonder, who is pure?

Abhang 11

In this *abhang,* Cokhamela speaks the mind of the modern Dalit, seeming to suggest a coherent tradition of belief, or disbelief, over six centuries.

Dalits as Militant; The Hero as Sacrificer

Buddhists though they may be, contemporary descendents of the Mahars are very proud of their military record. Mahars had guard duties in the days of Shivaji's 17th century kingdom. They were in the British army and marines almost from the initial days of any British military force. The cancellation of Mahar recruitment in the late 19th century as the British leaned more and more on "martial" races brought the first Mahar protest, Gopal Baba Walangkar's petition for reinstatement. The return of the Mahars to the army came in an impressive way during World War II when the Mahar Machine Gun Regiment was formed in 1942 at Kampti near Nagpur, and three battalions later in the year at Belgaum, Kampti and Nowshera (Thorat 1954). The creation of these units in the name of the Mahar caste was Ambedkar's doing, possibly since he served on the National Defence Council and then as Labour Member of the Viceroy's Council. It seems to me clear that army recruitment was not the only reason for the creation of the Mahar Regiment. Surely the building of pride in the past, and hence the present, was part of the motive. The Regiment still exists, still bears the name Mahar, although members of other castes and religions serve and have been part of the unit from the beginning.

The Folklore of Pride

The cap of the Mahar Regiment when it was founded bore the word "Koregaon" and a symbol of a pillar. The final battle of the British with the Marathas was fought at Koregaon, a village near the Marathas' capital of Pune in 1818. In commemoration of that historic event, a pillar was erected, and the names of those who died in the battle engraved upon it. Many of those names end in *nak*, the designation of a Mahar. There is no agreement on the meaning of the suffix *nak*. Some derive it from *naik*—leader. Others believe it is a derivation of *nag*—the Naga people. Either definition is satisfactory to the Mahars; either supports an origin of distinction and militancy.

Since Independence, identifications with the British army such as the Koregaon pillar insignia have been abandoned. However, the mythic quality of the Mahar military past is seen in the fact that the Dalit Panthers, a militant group formed in the early 1970's to fight injustice and protest atrocities, meets every year at the Koregaon pillar. Dalit Panthers from Pune ride bicycles to Koregaon village and gather at the pillar to pay their respects to past heroes and to gain inspiration from the Mahar military past.

In his article on the Mahar tradition (Miller 1966), Robert Miller uses the legend of the Mahar hero Amrutnak as an example of a tradition which is one of many unrelated to the Brahmanical system, as a denial of the idea of *one* Great Tradition. The story of Amrutnak is one of heroism and self-sacrifice. The handsome warrior volunteered to rescue the Queen of Bedar, lost during an attack on a hunting expedition. Before going on his long journey, all the way to Kabul on his wondrous Ablakha horse, Amrutnak gave a small box into the hands of the Sultan for safe-keeping. After many adventures, he brought back the Begum, but was met with hostility as well as gratitude because of the days and nights he had spent alone with the Queen. Then "Amrut laughed and reminded the king about the small box," which contained proof of the Queen's chastity and Amrutnak's ultimate sacrifice. In return for his self-castration and his bravery, Amrutnak requested fifty-two rights for his people, the Mahars. The poem celebrates not only Amrutnak but his people: "Great Great are the Mahars...Mahars are known for their bravery during wars, protecting their empire, keeping their sword always active" (Khairmode 1961).

The Amrutnak story was published in 1929 by an educated Mahar, C. B. Khairmode, and reprinted in 1961 after the Buddhist conversion by S. T. Savant, who was a Buddhist convert. There is no reference to it in any Gazetteer, not does it seem to have been sung by any group preserving Mahar epic literature. Whatever its provenance, the Amrutnak story enlarges on themes of militancy and self-sacrifice which *are* documented in the Mahar tradition. Robertson tells a similar story of an unnamed watchman who castrated himself lest a Moslem king doubt his Queen's chastity, adding that the Mahar received not only fifty-two rights but the name *mahavira*, great hero, which in time became "Mahar" (Robertson 1938: 72-73).

The idea that the fifty-two rights of the Mahar, a traditional number involving such perquisites as the clothes of the corpse and grain at certain times, were won by a Mahar for his people is present in a number of myths. The *Akola Gazetteer* tells of Dego Mego, who had the power of commanding rain, and so he secured "definite and enforced payment" of rights of Mahars when he brought a grievous famine to an end (Gazetteer 1910: 119). The *Tribes and Castes of the Central Provinces* volume tells the story of Mayo, beheaded while singing the praises of Vishnu so that a tank of water stopped leaking, and so winning the reward that his people should not be compelled to live at a distance from the towns nor to wear a distinctive dress (Russell 1916: 144).

Along with the Dego Mego story in the Vidarbha area is a common myth of five brothers, or a reference directly to the Pandavas, an association repeated in the apparatus and speech of the *potraj,* the servant of the epidemic goddess Mariai, who was almost always a Mahar and who seems to have been a village phenomenon all over the Marathi-speaking area. This Pandava connection, however, was not appropriated for use in the modern period, and no reference appears in the work of those who strove for greater unity and militancy. The Mahar seems to have had a variety of myths from which to choose, but in the contemporary period preferred to base his idea of a militant past either on the historic record or a quasi-historic figure, rather than on legendary ancestors or an origin myth of great antiquity.

What seems to be missing in Maharashtra is the quantity of poems, ballads, even epics in other language areas which are associated in some way with Untouchables. Blackburn has recorded astonishing tales of Untouchable as heroes, Brahmans becoming Untouchables (Blackburn 1978). Welbon has recorded the touching Candala's song of devotion (Welbon 1982). Rogair found a group of Untouchables in Andhra who had preserved the oral tradition of a major epic (Roghair 1982). There is an ever increasing record of tales, most of them from the South, in which Untouchables figure prominently. We are left with questions: are there unexplored areas in which traditions are shared? in which caste epics interpenetrate each other? in which both Untouchables and caste Hindus act in heroic ways? The folk literature of the Maharashtra area has barely been scratched; no one has yet explored the creative connections of Untouchables with other castes as Shulman has in the Tamil tradition (Shulman 1984; id. 1985).

However partial this view of Dalit folklore in contemporary Maharashtra, it at least can be said that the folkways of the past persist into the present. The current folklore of the Dalits, self-conscious and changed though it is, seems clearly related to much of the past, and seems to relate a timeless need. In the person of Dr. B. R. Ambedkar, whose words began this essay, the Dalits today have a hero of extraordinary proportions, one who is seen as militant, as self-sacrificing, as creative, as the revealer of the truth of Dalit origins in the proud Indian past.

REFERENCES

Abrams, Tevia. 1974. *Tamasha: People's theatre of Maharashtra State, India.* Ph.D. Dissertation, Michigan State University.

Ambedkar, Bhimrao Ramji. 1917. Castes in India—Their mechanism, genesis and development. In *Indian Antiquary* XLVI: 81—95.

Id. 1948. *The untouchables.* New Delhi: Amrit Book Company.

Id. 1969. The great conversion. In *Thus spoke Ambedkar,* vol. II. Ed. by Bhagwan Das. Jullundar City: Bheem Patrika Publications.

Barnett, Marguerite Ross. 1976. *The politics of cultural nationalism in South India.* Princeton: Princeton University Press.

Blackburn, Stuart H. 1978. The folk hero and class interests in Tamil heroic ballads. In *Asian Folklore Studies* 37: 131-149.

Cadell, Sir Patrick. 1938. *History of the Bombay army.* London: Longmans, Green and Co.

Cokhamela. 1950. *Cokhāmeḷā abhaṃga gāthā.* Bombay: Balkrishna Lakshman Pathak.

Dharwadkar, Vinay. 1989. The future of the past: Tradition,

modernization, and the transforming of two Indian traditions, ch. II. Ph.D. Dissertation, University of Chicago.

Dumont, Louis. 1970. *Homo hierarchicus.* Chicago: University of Chicago Press.

Egnor, Margaret T. 1986. Internal iconicity in Paraiyar "Crying Songs." In *Another harmony: new essays on the folklore of India.* Ed. by Stuart H. Blackburn and A. K. Ramanujan. Berkeley: University of California Press.

Enthoven, R. E. 1922. *The tribes and castes of Bombay,* vol. II. Bombay: Government of Bombay. [Mahar: 401-418].

Fernandes, Braz A. 1927. *Bandra: its religious and secular history.* Bombay: author.

Gazetteer of the Bombay presidency. 1880. Vol. XII: *Khandesh.* Ed. by James M. Campbell, General Editor. Bombay: Government Central Press.

Id. 1882. Vol. XIII. *Thana.* Ed. by James M. Campbell, General Editor. Bombay: Government Central Press.

Gazeteer of the Central Provinces and Berar. 1910. Vol. A: *Akola District.* Ed. by C. Brown and A. E. Nelson. Calcutta.

Juergensmeyer, Mark. 1982. *Religion as social vision: The move-*

ment against untouchability in 20th century Punjab. Berkeley: University of California.

Kamalanathan, T. P. 1985. *Mr. K. Veeramani is refuted and the historical facts about Scheduled Caste struggle for emancipation.* Tiruppattur: Ambedkar's Self-Respect Movement.

Khairmode, C. B. 1961. *Amrutnāk*. Pradna Publishing Company. (first published 1929). [In Marathi].

Kolenda, Pauline. 1960. Changing religious practices of an untouchable caste. In *Economic development and cultural change* VIII.3: 279-287.

Id. 1964. Religious anxiety and Hindu fate. In *Journal of Asian Studies* XXIII: 71-81.

Lorenzen, David N. 1987. Traditions of non-caste Hinduism: The Kabir Panth. *Contributions to Indian Sociology* (N.S.) 21.2: 263-282.

A Marathi Sampler. 1982. *The Journal of South Asian Literature* XVII.1: 48-63, 93-101.

Mathai, M. O. 1978. *Reminiscences of the Nehru age.* New Delhi: Vikas.

Mencher, Joan P. 1974. The caste system upside down, or

the not-so-mysterious east. *Current Anthropology* 15.4: 469-493.

Moffat, Michael. 1979. Harijan religion: Consensus at the bottom of caste. *American Ethnologist* 6: 244-260.

Miller, Robert J. 1966. Button, button...great tradition, little tradition, whose tradition? *Anthropological Quarterly* 39.1: 26-42.

O'Hanlon, Rosalind. 1985. *Caste, conflict and ideology: Mahatma Jotirao Phule and low caste protest in nineteenth-century Western India.* Cambridge: Cambridge University Press.

Pandian, T. B. 1899. *Slaves of the soil in Southern India and Pandian and the Pariah.* Amsterdam.

Paranjpye, Sai. 1971. Dadu Indurikar. In *Times Weekly,* October 24: 7.

Pawar, Daya. 1974. Introduction to *Koṇḍvāḍā.* Pune: Magova Prakashan. [In Marathi].

Id. 1976. Four Poems. Tr. by Graham Smith. *Vagartha* 12: 34-35.

Rai, P. Shivaprasad (Sq. Ldr. Retd.). 1989. Bali Chakravarti, the great Dalit emperor, killed by the wily Vaman. *Dalit Voice,* January 16-21: 15-16, 18.

Redfield, Robert. 1956. *Peasant society and culture: An anthropological approach to civilization.* Chicago: University of Chicago Press.

The Reforms Committee (Franchise). 1919. *Evidence taken before the Reforms Committee,* 2 vols. Calcutta. [Lord Southborough, Chairman.]

Religion and society. 1986. Culture, counter-culture and Dalits. XXXIII: 2. [See especially A.M. Abraham Ayrookuzhiel's article, Religion and culture in Dalits' struggle for liberation.]

Robertson, Alexander. 1938. *The Mahar folk.* Calcutta: Y.M.C.A. Publishing House and Oxford University Press, 1928.

Roghair, Gene H. 1982. *The epic of Palnadu: A study and translation of Palnati Virula Katha.* New York: Oxford University Press.

Russell, R. V. assisted by Hira Lal. 1916. *The tribes and castes of the Central Provinces of India,* vol. IV. London: Macmillan.

Shulman, David Dean. 1984. The enemy within: Idealism and dissent in south Indian Hinduism. In *Orthodoxy, heterodoxy and dissent in India.* Ed. by S. N. Eisenstadt *et al.* Berlin, New York and Amsterdam: Mouton.

Id. 1985. *The king and the clown in South*

Indian myth and poetry. Princeton: Princeton University Press.

Singer, Milton B. 1959. Preface to *Traditional India: Structure and change*. Ed. by Milton B. Singer. Philadelphia: American Folklore Society.

Thorat, Major General S.P.P. 1954. *The regimental history of the Mahar MG regiment*. Dehra Dun: The Army Press.

Vincentnathan, Lynn. 1988. *Harijan subculture and self-esteem management in a South Indian community*. Ph.D. Dissertation. University of Wisconsin-Madison. [Summary given as *Harijan concept of person and ideology: cultural strategies for self-esteem*, at the 17th annual conference on South Asia, Madison, November 1988.]

Welbon, Guy R. 1982. The Candala's song. In *Religious festivals in South India and Sri Lanka*. Ed. by Guy R. Welbon and Glenn E. Yocum. New Delhi: Manohar. pp. 77-100.

Walangkar, Gopal Baba. 1894. (Petition of the) Anarya Doshparihar Mandali, Dapoli. Ms. in the Khairemode Collection of the Bombay University Library.

Wilson, John. 1857. Notes on the constituent elements,

the diffusion, and the application of the Marathi language. In *Molesworth's Marathi-English Dictionary*. Corrected Reprint. Poona: Shubhada-Saraswat, 1975.

Zelliot, Eleanor. 1976. Dalit sahitya—the historical background. *Vagartha* 12.

Id. 1977. The leadership of Babasaheb Ambedkar. In *Leadership in South Asia*. New Delhi: Vikas.

Id. 1978a. Dalit—New cultural context of an old Marathi word. *Contributions to Asian Studies* XI: 77-97.

Id. with Gail Omvedt. 1978b. Introduction to Dalit poems. *Bulletin of Concerned Asian Scholars* X.3: 2-10.

Id. 1980. Chokhamela and Eknath: Two *bhakti* modes of legitimacy for modern change. *Journal of Asian and African Studies* XV.1-2: 136-156.

M. K. Dhavalikar

THE LIVING PAST
The First Farmers of Maharashtra and Their Successors

> The past becomes something that leads up to the present, the moment of action, the future, something that flows from it, and all three are inextricably intertwined and interrelated
>
> - Jawaharlal Nehru
> (*Discovery of India*, pp. 8—9)

Tradition dies hard, and more so in India, where the antiquity of many cultural traits can be traced to a hoary past. This is very well illustrated by the study of evidence from our intensive excavations at Inamgaon, an early farming settlement dating back to the middle of the second millennium B.C. It is indeed surprising that many aspects of the prehistoric culture continue in some form or other to this day in the area around Inamgaon. This we could visualise because of the ethno-archaeological survey that we carried out in the villages around Inamgaon. Before, however, embarking upon a discussion of the archaeological evidence and the corroborative ethnographic analogies, it should be made clear at the outset that we have no evidence of what is termed the "Direct Historical Analogy" as in north America, where the present day tribals are the direct descendants of the earlier primitives, but what we have at Inamgaon is the "general comparative analogy." We need not here go into the merits and demerits of ethno-archaeology, for, as we know, there are extremes, one school totally discarding it as fallacious (Freeman 1968: 265) and the other arguing that "all archaeology is ethno-archaeology or it is nothing" (Orme 1973). Suffice it to say that Lewis R. Binford, the leader of the Processual school of archaeology, who once observed that "Fitting archaeological remains into ethnographically known patterns of life adds nothing to our knowledge of the past" (Binford 1968: 13), has now published a massive tome entitled *Nunamiut Ethnoarchaeology* and has advocated the validity of ethno-archaeology. Ethnoarchaeology is therefore gradually gaining recognition as it has proved to be quite useful in interpreting archaeological evidence, and has become an important subdiscipline of archaeology. In India, however, it has not yet received the attention it deserves at the hands of Indian archaeologists in spite of the fact that India, with its numerous tribes in different parts of the country and at different technological levels, is a veritable ethnographic museum. We carried out an ethnographic survey of the area around Inamgaon and it was observed that many of the elements of the material culture of the first farmers of Maharashtra still survive in the villages around the ancient site. Ethnographic analogies have thus proved to be of great help in explaining the evidence from our excavation not only at Inamgaon but also at Walki and Kaothe.

Before embarking upon a discussion of the excavated evidence, it is necessary to describe the culture sequence at Inamgaon. The ancient site is located 85 km. east of Poona on the right bank of the Ghod, which belongs to the Krishna system of the subcontinent. It is spread over an area of 5 ha. and is one of the most extensive early farming settlements in Maharashtra. Our twelve seasons' intensive work at the site has yielded rich evidence throwing light on the lifeways of the first farmers of Maharashtra. The occupation can be divided into three cultural periods. Period I (c. 1600-1400 B.C.) is marked by a black painted red pottery which suggests that the first settlers at the site came from Malwa in Central India. They lived in rectangular houses and also in pit-dwellings and subsisted on agriculture, stock-raising and hunting-fishing. They cultivated mainly barley *(hordeum vulgare)*, lentils, peas, horse gram etc. They buried children inside their houses in two urns, placed horizontally mouth-to-mouth in a pit specially dug for the purpose. A few pottery vessels, probably containing food and water, were also deposited inside the grave. The people worshipped a mother goddess which may be connected with fertility.

Period II (c. 1400-1000 B.C.) is characterised by the occurrence of typical Jorwe painted pottery represented by such forms as the carinated bowl and a spouted jar with flaring mouth. This was the most prosperous period in the history of the settlement. The people lived in large rectangular houses with low mud walls and thatched roofs. In addition to the crops cultivated by their predecessors, they also grew wheat, which they could do because of the facility of artificial irrigation. Wheat is a winter crop, but Maharashtra does not get winter rains, and hence even today wheat can be grown only in irrigated areas. What these early farmers did was to divert the flood water of the river through a stream, into a deep channel (70 m. long, 7 m. wide, 3 m. deep) and used the same for irrigating their fields. They could thus raise two crops, by practicing crop rotation. This constitutes the earliest and the clearest evidence of artificial irrigation in India.

The Early Jorwe people buried the dead inside the houses. They worshipped mother goddesses, one of which was without a head, and a male divinity too. Perhaps fire worship was also in vogue. The people had trading contacts with coastal Maharashtra, Gujarat and Karnataka, as is evident from such trade goods as marine fish and conch shell bangles. Some evidence of socio-political organization is available in the form of a public granary and a multi-roomed house, probably of the ruling chief, by its side. It was a chiefdom society, the chief being responsible for the distribution of water to irrigate the fields. There are also traces of fortification around the settlement which was constructed during this period.

The prosperity of the Early Jorwe period did not continue for long and the decline sets in around 1000 B.C. This was the time when the settlements in the Tapi and Godavari valleys were deserted by the early farmers, possibly because of successive droughts. But the people continued to live in the southern Deccan, as is evident from Inamgaon and other Late Jorwe settlements discovered in the Bhima valley. The Late Jorwe period III (c. 1000-700 B.C.) is characterised by deterioration in every field of human activity. The houses were small round huts with thatched walls and roofs, the pottery became coarse and crude, the dwindling agriculture forced people to subsist more on animal foods. The irrigation channel stopped functioning, probably because of decrease in rainfall, and as a result the cultivation of wheat was not possible. There is a further deterioration around 800 B.C., when people probably resorted to sheep/goat pastoralism, as is clear from the sudden increase in sheep/goat bones. In the closing phase of Late Jorwe the luxury of sedentary life was no more possible; the houses do not conform to any plan; they are irregular, circular or oval or rectangular, with flimsy floors suggesting a seasonal occupation. Slightly later, towards the close of 8th cent. B.C., the settlement was deserted by the Late Jorwe people. The inroads of the megalith builders from the southern Deccan may also be partly responsible for uprooting the pastoral nomads of Inamgaon. The site has remained unoccupied ever since.

Our excavation can be said to be intensive rather than extensive for the simple reason that we concentrated our work mostly in an area admeasuring 100 x 50 m., exposing each structural level carefully. The approach was conjunctive, with each artifact being recorded in its context, and we could therefore associate the artifacts to different structures, and identify a number of houses of craftsmen such as the potter, the goldsmith, the lime-maker, the lapidary and so on. We could also recover vast quantities of charred seeds of cultivated grains which have enabled us to reconstruct the early history of agriculture in Maharashtra.

A fairly good number of houses were laid bare by us in the course of excavations at the site and we could therefore study the micro-settlement pattern. It was observed that the houses of craftsmen such as the potter, the goldsmith, the lime-maker etc., were situated in the western part of the principal area of habitation (INM-I), whereas the houses of well-to-do people were located in its central part. This is precisely the same as today, for in the villages around Inamgaon we find the same residence pattern. In sharp contrast to this, the occupation in other localities, viz., INM-II, III, IV and V, was flimsy, for no house plans could be recovered in these areas. It is highly likely that the men of means occupied the main area (INM-I) whereas others, who may have worked as labourers, might have inhabited other areas. It must be stated here that INM-I is a very extensive area, about 200 x 100 m., whereas the other localities are much smaller.

Although a number of houses of each structural phase have been laid bare, it was not possible to reconstruct them completely. We had discovered in the course of excavations only patches of house floors, which nevertheless were carefully made, and dilapidated walls standing to a height of only a few centimeters. Sometimes we no doubt came across mud lumps bearing impressions of the thatched roof and wattle-and-daub walls. But these were not adequate for the reconstruction of dwellings and many problems in respect of mud architecture remained unsolved. From the quantity of mud lumps on house floors we could infer that the walls must not have been high, about 30 to 50 cm., and we were then wondering what ultimately would have been the total height of the house. They appeared more like the raised edges of the floor than walls (Pl. I).* The same was the case with the roof because from mere impressions on mud lumps it was well nigh impossible to say anything about it. However, we can now completely visualize what the chalcolithic

* Editor's note: The illustration and plates of this article are found at the end of the book.

houses would have looked like because of ethnographic analogies.

Almost all the different house types unearthed in the course of excavation have parallels in the present day dwellings in the villages around the ancient site. There are three main house types, viz., i) pit-dwellings, ii) rectangular and iii) circular. The earlier settlers at the site lived in pit-dwellings and large rectangular houses. The pit-dwellings were quite few in number but they were all circular on plan. Most of the dwelling pits in fact were like sunken floors, about 30 cm. deep, and their average diameter was 2 m. But the instances of deep pits are also not wanting. The floor was well made and lined with lime. Along the margin of the floor on the outside were a number of post-holes and the roof in all likelihood was gabled. The courtyard too was well made and the hearth for cooking was located outside in the courtyard. We could identify these structures as pit-dwellings only because of modern parallels. It is only very poor people who presently live in pit-dwellings for they cannot afford to buy wooden posts of adequate lengths. In order therefore to obtain height for the roof, a pit is dug. Perhaps for the same reason some of the first settlers at Inamgaon built pit-dwellings.

The earliest settlers of Maharashtra lived in pit-dwellings. The people of the Savalda culture, whose settlement at Kaothe (Tal. Sakri, Dist. Dhulia) we excavated, lived in pit-dwellings some four thousand years ago. The dwelling pits were both large and small, either round or oval on plan, but were quite shallow, not more than 30 cm. deep. They were found in clusters, and if the hearth is any indication, each cluster can be said to constitute one household. Large pits were obviously used for human occupation whereas smaller ones may have served as storage. The smallest ones, with a diameter of 1 m. or less, which are round on plan, were probably used for keeping poultry at night under a basket as is done today.

A vast majority of the Malwa houses are rectangular on plan (about 7 m. x 5 m.), having low mud walls and smooth floors composed of sand, black clay and yellow silt rammed hard and repaired periodically after every alternate year as is the case today. The roof, probably gabled, was supported by wooden posts. But the disposition of wooden posts in many cases was rather enigmatic, for some of them were found inside and some outside the walls. This made the relationship of walls with wooden posts problematic. The ethnographic parallels provided a clue to the nature of mud walls from our dig. There are quite a number of huts in Wangdari, the village opposite the ancient site across the river, which have extremely low mud walls not over 30 cm. in height. They have nothing to do with the roof and their only function is to prevent the rain water from entering the hut. This then obviously must have been the function of mud walls in chalcolithic houses. Similarly the roof is supported on wooden posts in huts at present and in between are fixed reed screens which may or may not be daubed with mud. For roofing, people presently use the Typha grass *(typha latifolia)* which grows along the banks of streams around Inamgaon and is known for its waterproofing quality. There is evidence to show that the first farmers of Inamgaon also used the same material for roofing.

There seems to be same modicum of planning in the Malwa and Early Jorwe settlements at Inàmgaon. The rectangular houses were usually built with their longer axis in a roughly southeast - northwest direction aligned in parallel rows. The average distance in between them was about a meter or so, which space would have served as a road or lane; it was sometimes rammed with pebbles and potsherds as at Daimabad (Sali 1986: 159). We know from archaeological record that in India the people of the Indus civilisation were the first to plan their settlements on a chess-board pattern, and that after the decline of the Harappans the same type of planning was introduced into India by the Greeks who ruled in the northwestern part of the sub-continent from c. 250 B.C. to 40 B.C. But for these two instances, planned settlement was not a characteristic feature of early Indian cities, at least in ancient times. There is literary evidence to show that in the beginning of the early historical period in the 6th cent. B.C., a legendary architect, Mahagovinda by name, is said to have planned and built a number of cities in the Ganga valley. But this is not corroborated by archaeological evidence from such early city sites as Rajgir and Kausambi. In the light of this evidence it is remarkable that the first farmers of Maharashtra should have planned their settlements with due care (Dhavalikar 1975). But what is important from the standpoint of the present study is that there exists even today a tribe in Maharashtra which is technologically not above the level of incipient agriculture and which plans its settlements with due care. This tribe is the Kolams, who presently live in parts of Vidarbha and Marathwada bordering on Andhra Pradesh (Mandavkar 1966: 77-79). They practice shifting cultivation and their settlements are not permanent. For cultivation they select hill slopes and then build their huts on the periphery. Their settlements are known as *poḍa,* a word derived from the Dravidian *poḍu,* which means shifting cultivation. The *poḍas* are characterised by rectangular huts which are all of almost equal size. Their chieftain *(naik),* along with a few elders, visits the spot and selects the area for locating the settlement. It is surprising that their planned settlements should resemble that at Inamgaon, which, though not far removed in terms of space, is at least three thousand years older.

As already stated, the Late Jorwe settlement is characterised by round huts in sharp contrast to the spacious rectangular houses of the earlier periods. We have so far exposed a good number of such huts and the method of their construction can be properly understood by studying similar huts which are built even today in nearby villages. Those from our excavations have rather low mud walls and well made floors. They had thatched walls and roofs, as the impressions on mud lumps suggest. The roof, probably gabled, was supported by wooden posts. The ethnographic parallels indicate that for a conical roof over a round hut, there must be a post in the centre. Most of the houses from the excavation had a central post.

The shift in the plan of the dwelling from rectangular in the Early Jorwe period (c. 1400-1000 B.C.) to round in the Late Jorwe (c. 1000-700 B.C.) is indeed noteworthy. If we go by modern parallels, it will be clear that, although it suggests general economic decline, it also has something to do with the environment. In this connection it must be noted that the scientists of the Andhra Pradesh Government who are carrying out experiments on houses which can survive a cyclone in the coastal region—which is a recurrent feature—have come to the conclusion that it is only a round hut which can withstand a strong wind. It has been observed that there was a drastic change in the climate in Central and Western India at the close of the second millennium (Kale and Rajguru 1987), as a result of which it became more and more arid, forcing the people gradually to resort to a semi-nomadic existence. Aridity is usually marked by stong winds and perhaps that may be one reason why the Late Jorwe people preferred a round plan for their dwellings.

A few of the Late Jorwe huts are oval on plan. However, these were extremely flimsy structures which had no mud wall around them but instead the edge of the floor was raised, obviously with a view to preventing the rain water from entering the hut, serving the same function as that of a low mud wall (Pl. II). But these huts do not have post holes around the margin; instead there is a single post hole in the centre or two post holes, one on either side. This was rather puzzling, for we could not visualise a hut without posts. But the ethnographic analogy clarified the whole situation. Such small oval huts are even at present built in fields, during the harvesting season. First, the area of the huts is cleared and the framework of split bamboo or wooden sticks is erected around it. The thatched walls are sloping and join in a conical top. Thus there is no need to fix the posts in holes because the walls do not have to support the roof; they rather rest on the beam. Such huts in fact do not need the central post. Similarly, for building round huts a bundle of sticks tied in a bunch at one end are spread on the ground obliquely and are covered with thatch. Such huts were found in the excavations at Walki, near Poona, where similar ones are built frequently by the casual labour working in sugarcane fields.

All these houses, both rectangular and round, had well made courtyards where usually a hearth was located. This is the practice in villages today, where, except during the rainy season, the cooking is done outside in the open. This also bespeaks the importance of the courtyard in Indian architecture, for in fact much of life is lived in the courtyard. In the courtyard there were also pit silos cut into the ground. They are perfectly cylindrical, about a meter deep and of equal diameter. Their bases and sides were usually plastered with lime. Sometimes the pit silos were also located inside the house. They were quite identical with their modern counterparts. But a most curious feature inside the rectangular houses recovered from our excavation was a round mud platform, having a diameter of one meter or more and about 15 cm high (Pl. I). It was made of rammed clay and contained sand. We could comprehend its function properly when we noticed to our surprise that such platforms still exist in the houses around Inamgaon. They are meant for supporting storage bins made of wicker work and plastered with cow-dung and mud. Inside the platform the people deposit sand and thorny bushes to prevent rodents from destroying the grain in the bin.

There were hearths inside the house and outside in the courtyard also. The one inside the house was a small roundish fire pit, but very rarely have we come across what looks exactly like our two-armed *chulah*. They were found in the houses of well-to-do people and one came from the house of the ruling chief. But far more interesting are large oval fire pits which sometimes had a baking pan fixed to them in the centre over a stem of clay. This baking pan is identical with the *khāpar-tavā* we find in Maharashtrian villages today.

The excavations have yielded vast quantities of charred grains from all levels. It may appear rather enigmatic that there should have been charred seeds when the houses were not burnt. What is more, they mostly come from outside the courtyard, where there was no trace of burning. This is obviously due to roasting the grain for dehydrating it as much as possible because the people had no flour mills or even rotary querns and had to crush it on stone querns with rubber stones. This is what some of the tribals in Bihar do even at present.

The huts unearthed in the course of excavations at Walki (Tal. Daund, Dist. Poona) are of great interest. These were found in clusters and each cluster contained five huts, built in a circular fashion (Fig. 1). They were either round or oval or irregular on plan, and being extremely flimsy were extremely difficult to trace. The floor was neither well made nor did the huts have walls; the only feature which distinguished them from the surrounding area was the slightly different colour of the floor, which was a little whitish and a bit hard. Some of them had post-holes along the margin. Each cluster had a hearth in the centre in the courtyard. The larger huts were obviously used for human occupation and the smaller ones for animals. The bin platform in each cluster was of mud and round on plan (average diameter 1 m. and height 10 cm.); it was rammed hard as at Inamgaon. Similarly a large round floor (diameter 2 m. or more) was equally rammed hard; it was in all likelihood used as a threshing platform.

The flimsy nature of structures at Walki has led us to identify the settlement as a chalcolithic farmstead of the Jorwe period (c. 1400-1000 B.C.) which was a satellite settlement of the chalcolithic Inamgaon, about 30 km. to the west whence people came there only during winter for cultivating barley. What is interesting is that even today similar huts are built by people who come to Walki and the nearby villages to work as casual labour on the sugarcane fields from October to March every year (Pl. III). These huts, which are round on plan, are built in clusters of five or six, in a round fashion; they too have a hearth in the centre of the courtyard. One or two huts are for living and others for sheep and goats. The huts have no well-made floor and no post-holes because the walls, which form a cone, consist of a bundle of sticks tied at the top end and spread on the ground; they are covered by mats. The chalcolithic huts, when standing, may not have looked much different.

An important part of cultural life is social organization. No attempt has so far been made to reconstruct the social organization of prehistoric India, solely for want of adequate evidence. But this aspect can also be studied with the help of ethnographic evidence. It is generally taken for granted that the rectangular house type is a token of a fully settled life whereas the round hut suggests a seasonally settled life (Flannery 1972). The evidence from our excavation shows that the Malwa and Early Jorwe people lived in large rectangular houses, some of which were even multi-roomed. Their prosperity is reflected in the variety of grains they cultivated as also in other artifactual remains, such as brightly painted pottery, beads of semi-precious stones, tools and ornaments of copper and even gold. But in utter contrast to the spacious houses of the Malwa and Early Jorwe those of Late Jorwe are small round huts. This house type is said to be a distinguishing feature of seasonally settled life (Flannery 1972). This is corroborated by the Inamgaon evidence for the Late Jorwe period, which is marked by a sharp decline in agricultural production and an increase in the number of animal bones, indicating a shift in subsistence pattern. In the upper levels of Late Jorwe, there is a sudden increase in the number of sheep/goat bones, suggesting that people may have resorted to sheep/goat pastoralism around 900 B.C.

A noteworthy feature of the Late Jorwe huts is that they are found in clusters of three or four or five, each cluster having a common courtyard. One is likely to be misled into identifying each hut as an independent household unit. But a careful examination of artifactual remains shows that not all the huts in a cluster had a hearth and storage facilities but only one hut or sometime two had cooking facilities. The only obvious conclusion that we could draw was that each cluster was an independent household unit and as such occupied by a single family. But the question that then necessarily arises is: Where was then the need to have several huts for one family? The possiblity in this case appears to be that the Late Jorwe society was probably polygamous and hence, whenever the head of the family acquired a new wife, he built a hut for her. We are told that this is precisely what the Kohalis of Vidarbha, a polygamous tribe, do today (Karve 1951: 112-13), and the number of huts in a cluster in their settlement represents the number of wives. It has rightly been observed that "the separate living houses, functionally not self contained, are merely the residences of cowives in a polygamous family" (David 1971: 120).

The problem of the plough in farming communities has attracted the attention of the scholarly world in recent years. In western Europe actual wooden specimens have been found (Steensburg 1986: 138-39, fig. 52) and experiments have also been made, but in India the problem still exists so far as Central and Western India are concerned. Clay models of Early Harappan ploughs have recently turned up at Banavali (Bhisht 1987: pl. 26) but it is doubtful if such wooden ploughs would have been effective in ploughing the hard, compact black cotton soil in Maharashtra. The adage goes that the black cotton soil ploughs itself because it develops large wide fissures in summer; nature thus completes the job of circulation of nitrogen. Even at present, the land where *jowar (sorghum vulgare)* is grown is ploughed only once in three years. All the same a British agricultural expert has reported that in Western India the people used a hand plough (Wallace 1888: 168). In form it resembled an antler and it is, therefore, highly likely that the first farmers of Maharashtra may have used antlers as hand ploughs. Such antlers have been found in the excavations at Inamgaon. As a matter of fact antlers were used for mining flint in Europe. Although no specimen of a hand plough has survived, the ethnographic evidence no doubt throws welcome light on a very important aspect of early farming.

Another important artifact which comes from our excavations at Walki is very intriguing. It is an antler which is hollow from within, as its core has been scooped out. Its exact function could not be determined. But if an antler was used as a hoe or a hand plough, then it is highly likely that a hollow antler could have been used as a seed drill. This is a conjecture but no other function could possibly have been served by a hollow antler.

We need not go into all the aspects of the chalcolithic lifeways in the short span of this paper. But one aspect, their religious beliefs, deserves special mention. The first and foremost are the mother goddesses. They were of two types, one with a head, and the other without (Pl. IV). Small female figurines of ill fired or unbaked clay have been found in good numbers. One of them was associated with pit silos and can therefore be said to be connected with the fertility cult. The other was found in a clay box over which was placed yet another goddess without a head along with a clay bull. All these objects of unbaked clay were found carefully deposited in a small hole in the corner of an Early Jorwe house. The fact that the figurines and the box are unbaked shows that they were meant for use on a particular occasion, after which they were deposited carefully in the hole. This reminds us of the custom in villages in Maharashtra where even the water from the room of a parturient woman is not allowed to drain out of the room, but is collected into a pit specially dug for the purpose. Secondly, the female figurine, without head, recalls the goddess Vishirā, one of the divinities who nurtured the newly born Kārtikeya. The neck of the newborn child is not strong enough and perhaps for this the goddess Vishirā may have been worshipped. All this would lead us to infer that these clay figurines may have been connected with childbirth.

It is interesting that a headless goddess is even presently worshipped by the Warlis, a tribe near Bombay on the west coast in Thane District (Pl. V). She is called Pālghat, which in the Warli language means the position of a woman at the time of giving birth to a child. The Warlis draw pictures of Pālghat on the walls of their houses in rice paste at the time of a wedding in the family. She is without head and her legs are stretched sideways. She is the goddess of fertility. Equally interesting is the occurrence of stone sculptures of a headless female divinity who is represented nude with legs stretched sideways. She has been variously identified as Lajjā-Gaurī or Śākambharī (Dhavalikar 1987). The images are generally dated from c. 2nd cent. B.C. to 6th cent. A.D. and are mostly found in the Deccan. The chalcolithic headless goddess thus can be said to be associated with childbirth and fertility.

These first farmers also worshipped a male divinity. Two such figurines were noticed in the courtyard of a Late Jorwe house where they were found deposited near a hearth. They are unbaked and hence may be said to have been used only on a particular occasion. Even today people at Inamgaon make such figurines of wheat flour and worship them when a community meal is cooked. The god, now known as Gaṇesha, is placed by the side of the hearth and is immersed in the river after the community feast is over.

There is yet one more curious divinity. We do not know whether this god is as ancient as the prehistoric settlement at Inamgaon. To the west of the ancient habitation, about 100 m. away, is the shrine of what is now locally known as Mhasobā. It is the aniconic representation of the god in the form of a huge, amorphous rock which is presently worshipped, surprisingly enough, not by the people from the surrounding areas, but by Bhils who come in large numbers from distant places like Nagar, Nasik and Dhulia districts. They come any time of the year according to their convenience, worship the god and offer live chickens and wooden bulls. Year after year we have been observing this with great curiosity and talking to them, but the antiquity of the god could not be established. Here the ethnographic analogy throws a welcome light. The Kolams of northeast Maharashtra are said to instal an image of their god Aiyyāk' whenever they select an area for locating their settlement. It is installed to the west of the habitation, slightly away from it. He is their principal god, identified as Bhimadeva, who is the same as Bhivsena of the Gonds. Could it be that the pioneering colonisers of Inamgaon installed this aniconic representation of their god when they arrived here to locate their settlement?

The ancient inhabitants of Inamgaon believed in life after death. They buried the dead inside the house; probably they wanted the departed soul to be with them. The adult was buried in a supine position in a pit dug into the house floor and pottery vessels, probably containing food and water, were also deposited in it. One of the vessels invariably was a spouted jar which was painted with the design of a boat with oars. This recalls the Hindu belief that the soul of the dead has to cross a river in a ferry. But more interesting is the custom of chopping off the portion of the legs below the ankles. Except in very rare instances, such as that of the ruling chief, this was the rule of the community. This may have been done with a view to preventing the dead from running away and turning into a ghost. This is precisely the reason for chopping off the legs of a woman who dies immediately after childbirth in Goa today.

The foregoing discussion of the evidence from the excavations at Inamgaon and other sites and the ethnographic parallels which still survive in some form or other amply shows how we can explain many of the customs and traditions of the prehistoric period. We can do no better than quote a great anthropologist who observes: "It is a phenomenon peculiar to India that throughout the great civilisations have risen without obliterating or absorbing all that has gone before; the older, more static cultures gave way not by disintegrating, but by seeking refuge in remote areas uncongenial to civilisation based on an advanced agricultural economy. There can be no

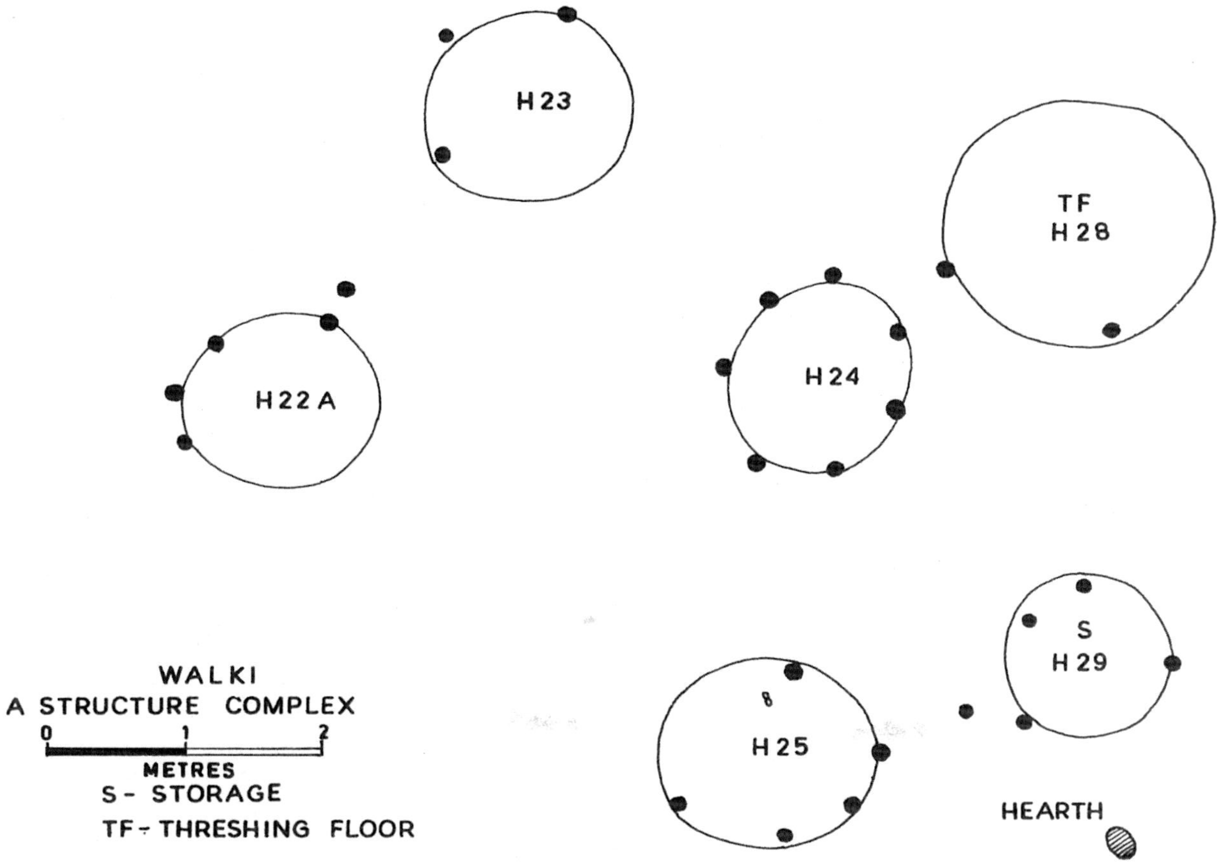

Fig. I Walki, house complex, c. 1200 B.C.

Pl.I Inamgaon, house with low walls, Period I, ca. 1600-1400 B.C.

Pl.II Inamgaon, a flimsy hut, Period III, ca. 1000-700 B.C.

Pl.III Walki, modern flimsy huts for seasonal occupation.

Pl.IV Inamgaon, a headless female figurine of clay, Period I, ca. 1400-1400 B.C.

Pl.V Palghat, the headless goddess of the Warlis in Western India.

Pl.VI Inamgaon, god Mhasoba at an ancient site which is worshipped by Bhils.

doubt that the so-called aboriginals inhabiting such refuge areas represent comparatively old and primitive culture types" (Fürer-Haimendorf 1948).

REFERENCES

Bhisht, R. S. 1987. Further excavations at Banavali 1983-84. In *Archaeology and history—essays in memory of A. Ghosh*. Ed. by B. M. Pande and B. D. Chattopadhyay. Delhi: Agam Kala Prakashan. pp. 135-156.

Binford, Lewis R. 1968. Archaeological perspectives. In *New perspectives in archaeology*. Ed. by L. R. and S. R. Binford. Chicago: Aldine. pp. 5-32.

Id. 1978 *Nunamiut ethnoarchaeology*. New York: Academic Press.

David, Nicolas. 1971. The Fulani compound and the archaeologist. *World Archaeology* 3: 111-131.

Dhavalikar, M. K. 1975. Settlement archaeology of Inamgaon. *Puratattva* 8: 44-54.

Id. 1987. Śākambharī—The headless goddess. *Annals of the Bhandarkar Oriental Research Institute* 68: 281-293.

Flannery, Kent V. 1972. The origin of the village as a settlement type in Meso-america and the Near East. In *Man, settlement and urbanism*. Ed. by Peter Ucko, Ruth Tringham and G. W. Dimbley. London: Duckworth. pp. 25-54.

Freeman, L. G., Jr. 1968. A theoretical framework for interpreting archaeological materials. In *Man the hunter*. Ed. by Richard B. Lee and Irvin De Vore. Aldine. pp. 268-273.

Fürer-Haimendorf, Christoph, von. 1948. Culture strata in the Deccan. *Man* 48: Art 99, 87—90.

Kale, V. S. and S. N. Rajguru. 1987. Late quaternary alluvial history of the north-western Deccan upland. *Nature* 325: 612-14.

Karve, Irawati. 1951. *Marathi lokanchi samskriti*. Poona: Deshmukh & Co. [In Marathi].

Mandavkar, Bhau. 1966. *Kolam*. Amaravati: Seva Prakashan. [In Marathi].

Orme, Bryoni. 1973. Archaeology and ethnography. In *The explanation of culture change—Models in prehistory*. Ed. by Colin Renfrew. London: Duckworth. pp. 481-492.

Sali, S. A. 1986. *Daimabad 1976-79*. New Delhi: Archaeological Survey of India. [Memoirs of Arch. Survey of India, No. 83.]

Steensberg, Axel. 1986. *Man the manipulator—An ethno-archaeological basis for reconstructing the past.* Copenhagen: The National Museum of Denmark.

Wallace, Robert. 1988. *India in 1887.* Edinburgh: Oliver and Boyd Tweedle Court.

Erik Reenberg Sand

GOPĀLPŪR-*KĀLĀ*
Some Aspects of the History of the Sacred Places South of Pandharpur

This paper deals with the brahmin and the Vārakarī traditions as reflected in the history of two sacred places in Pandharpur. It is my hypothesis that the so-called *kālā* ritual has played an important part in this history as a popular ritual mainly connected with the Vārakarīs. As will be seen, this paper combines several years of studies of the hitherto hardly known Sanskrit material about Pandharpur[1] with different Marāṭhī sources, a method which I believe to be very fruitful.[2]

---

[1] This is not the place to go into detail about the dating problems of the Sanskrit *māhātmyas*. I will just mention that there are good reasons to believe that both the *Pāṇḍuraṅgamāhātmya* attributed to the *Skandapurāṇa* (hereafter abbreviated *Sk.Pdm.)* and the *Pāṇḍuraṅgamāhātmya* attributed to the *Padmapurāṇa* (hereafter abbreviated *Pd.Pdm.)* are pre-Ekanātha, and that of these the *Skandapurāṇa* version, of which I am presently preparing an *editio princeps*, is the oldest, the oldest layer probably going back to the period between 1189 A.D. and 1270 A.D. For a more detailed discussion of these problems see Dhere 1981 and Sand 1990.

[2] Considering the way of transmission of the *abhaṅgas*, it is, of course, not without problems to use them as sources of historical data. However, in this case I consider their evidence sufficient to use them as supplementary sources to the *māhātmya* literature.

The Present Situation in Brief

One way of getting an idea about which places and rites are important to the present-day visitor to Pandharpur is to consult the local Marāṭhī guide-books sold to pilgrims. After consulting five such booklets (viz. Jośī *et al.* 1960, Kulkarṇī 1981, Sunṭhaṇkar 1980, Bhiṅgārkar 1981, and Cendavaṇkar 1965), one gets the impression that only two localities to the south of Pandharpur are important today, namely, Gopālpūr and Viṣṇupada. In fact, these are the only sacred localities of this part of Pandharpur dealt with in these booklets.

This impression is corroborated by an informal investigation carried out by myself and an assistant during the Pandharpur *yātrā* in 1984. When pilgrims were asked whether they knew of other *tīrthas* in Pandharpur than the Viṭṭhala *mandira*, Gopālpūr and Viṣṇupada were the only localities of the southern part of the town they mentioned.

Furthermore, it is interesting to note that both these places figure in our investigation as respectively number one and two among all the places mentioned by the pilgrims, which seems to indicate that Gopālpūr and Viṣṇupada are not only the only places known to be important on the southern outskirts of Pandharpur, but also, apart from the Viṭṭhala *mandira*, the two localities in the whole of Pandharpur best known to the pilgrims.[3]

[3] Thus, of a total of 111 interviewed, out of whom 31 did not mention any places at all, 50 persons named Gopālpūr and 25 Viṣṇupada, whereas celebrated places in the centre of town like the Puṇḍalīka *samādhī*, Diṇḍīravana, and Lohadaṇḍatīrtha were mentioned by only 11, 7, and 6 pilgrims respectively.

Present-day Gopālpūr and Viṣṇupada

Before proceeding with a historical analysis of the two localities Gopālpūr and Viṣṇupada and their mutual relationship, I would like to present a brief survey of the most important data about them. I will begin with Gopālpūr, which, to judge from my investigation, seems to be the most popular one at present.

Gopālpūr is a small hamlet about a mile south of Pandharpur on the southern bank of the Puṣpāvatī stream.[4] What is more interesting in this connection, however, is a temple built on a small hill just in front of the hamlet, which also contains the temples of Gopālakṛṣṇa, Mahādeo, Bhīmakarāja, Lakṣmīnārāyaṇa, Nārada, and the so-called cell of the saint Janābaī. The Gopālakṛṣṇa temple is the most important of these temples, and it contains an image of Gopālakṛṣṇa playing the flute and standing on the left foot, the right foot crossed and resting on its toes.

As mentioned in the *Maharashtra State Gazetteer* (1977: 937), there is an inscription in this temple which tells that construction was begun in *śaka* 1666 or A.D. 1744 by a person called Śāmajīpanta Nāndīvakara. The other temples were built later.

According to the same work, the myth connected with the Gopālakṛṣṇa temple runs like this:

> Gopalkrishna or Krishna had 16,000 milk-maids and eight wives, who, out of respect to Rukmini the chief favourite, used to stand whenever she appeared. One day while he was living in Dwarka, Krishna sat amusing himself with Radha one of the eight

[4] The most comprehensive surveys of sacred localities in and around Pandharpur are to be found in Khare 1963, *Maharashtra State Gazetteers* 1977, Deleury 1960, and Mate 1962.

> favourites, who was sitting on his thigh. Rukmini suddenly came in, but remained standing unheeded; and Radha elated with Krishna's attention offended Rukmini by not rising. Taking this to heart, Rukmini left Dwarka and came to Dindirvan now known as Pandharpur, and sat near the site of the present temple. When Krishna found that Rukmini had left him, he started in search of her with his cattle and cowherds. The mountain of Govardhan in Dwarka learning that Krishna was leaving, not caring to remain without the god, followed and forms the knoll on which the temple is built. The river goddesses Ganga and Yamuna also followed the party and settled in Dindirvan, Ganga as the Bhima now called Chandrabhaga or Bhagirathi, and Yamuna as the Pushpavati. When Rukmini and Gopalkrishna made friends they held a feast on the hillock along with their companions each bringing his own food. This gathering or feasting called kala or the mixture is said to have happened twice in Pandharpur: first on the full-moon of Ashadha (June-July) the day on which they arrived and again on the full-moon of Kartika (October-November) on which Krishna is believed to have died.
>
> (ibid., 940f.)

With the small, but, as it will become clear in the following, not unimportant difference that their common meal took place near the Viṣṇupada-shrine, the various Marāṭhī guide-books also refer to the same myth when, almost unanimously, they tell that the Gopālpūr temple is the site where Kṛṣṇa and his companions came to rest themselves, and where Kṛṣṇa played the flute *(muraḷī)* (see Sunṭhaṇkar 1980: 87, Kulkarṇī 1981: 22, Jośī *et al.* 1960: 56, and, more specifically about the image of Kṛṣṇa in the Gopālakṛṣṇamandir, Bhiṅgārkar 1981: 37). Furthermore, in their descriptions of the Bhīmakarāja temple within the Gopālpūr temple precincts they tell that this is the place where Rukmiṇī's father came to see her after she had left Dvārakā in anger, and where her anger against Kṛṣṇa ended (see Sunṭhaṇkar 1980: 87, Bhiṅgārkar 1981: 37, Jośī *et al.* 1961: 56, Kulkarṇī 1981: 22, and Cendavaṇkar 1965: 78).

Ritually, the most important ceremony connected with the Gopālpūr temple, and undoubtedly the phenomenon to which Gopālpūr owes its great fame and reception among the pilgrims, is the so-called *kālā* ceremony, also sometimes called *gopāla-kālā* or Gopālpūr-*kālā*. This ceremony is performed on the full moon days of the months Āṣāḍha and Kārttika, and marks the end of the Pandharpur *yātrā* for most Vārakarīs. Taking into consideration the very few rituals performed by the Vārakarīs in Pandharpur, this *kālā* is an important, though not compulsory, element in their *yātrā*.

Although it has already been described more than a century ago (see Mitchell 1882: 153f., and, for a very brief survey, *Census of India* 1969: 158), I shall give a brief description of the *kālā* ceremony as I witnessed it on the morning of the full moon day of Āṣāḍha in 1984.

During the morning thousands and thousands of pilgrims proceeded from Pandharpur to Gopālpūr, where they surrounded the temple *diṇḍī*-wise. Each *diṇḍī* gathered around a *kīrtanakāra* who performed a *kīrtana*. The main component of the ceremony was, however, the breaking of an earthen pot filled with a mixture of curds *(dahī)* and parched grains *(lāhyā)* which was hung up in a tree, and the contents of which were poured on the pilgrims when it was broken. It is from the contents of this pot, the mixture *(kālā)* of grain and curds, that the whole ceremony has taken its name. Presumably, since it is not possible for everyone to take part in the *kālā* itself, provisions had been made to supply all pilgrims with popped grains from a stand near the western wall of the temple where pilgrims flock in order to take *prasāda* home from the *kālā*. After this was over, many pilgrims gathered inside the temple precincts, where they spent some time playing various games, the so-called *phugaḍī*-dance, which is really a women's dance, seemingly the most popular one.[5] And, finally, they hurried back to Pandharpur again, and most of them left during the afternoon.

Although space does not permit me to go into detail with the history and interpretation of the *kālā* ritual here, I find it necessary to say a few words about it. First of all, the performance of *kālā* rituals is not a phenomenon restricted to the Gopālpūr-*kālā*, but is a more general practice in rural Maharashtra and, according to Ghurye (1962: 172), in some parts of Tamilnadu and Andhra Pradesh too. It seems, however, that the *kālā* ritual is generally associated with the Janmāṣṭamī or birthday of Kṛṣṇa, where it is performed as part of the festivities on the 9th of the dark half of Śrāvaṇa (see Molesworth under *"gopālakālā," Dharmasindhu:* 54, Ghurye 1960: 55f., Ghurye 1962: 171f., Kane 1974: 139, and Dingre 1968: 148). Whether the practice of breaking an earthen pot *(dahīhaṇḍī)* is an integral part of the *kālā* or whether it is a later addition is difficult to say, but none of the older sources seem to mention it. As is obvious from the *abhaṅga*-literature, the *kālā* commemorates Kṛṣṇa's boyhood among the cowherds in Vṛndāvan. In the case of the Gopālpūr-*kālā*, these activities have then been relocated and moved from Vṛndāvan to Gopālpūr by the help of the tradition of Kṛṣṇa's arrival in Pandharpur, as we saw it in the above quoted myth. Apart from the partaking in a common symbolic meal, the main elements of the *kālā* ritual seem to be the practice of sprinkling each other with curds, milk and ghee *(secana)*, and the playing of different popular games *(kheḷa)*. This is evident from many *abhaṅgas* of the Vārakarī saints as well as from the *Dhar-*

---

[5] For the *phugaḍī* dance in Gopalpur, see the very vivid, but somewhat unsympathetic account in Mokashi 1987: 243-46. This is an account by an educated Indian of a popular custom.

masindhu of Kāśīnāthopadhyāya (quoted by Kane 1974: 139), who quotes the *Bhāgavatapurāṇa* 10,5,14 as evidence of these practices.[6] To conclude, it seems that the *kālā* ritual as it is performed in Gopālpūr is only a special instance of an old, popular, pastoral cult of Gopālakṛṣṇa, the main representation of which is found in the more overall, regional festival of the Janmāṣṭamī.[7]

The temple called Viṣṇupada is situated about three quarters of a mile south of Pandharpur on a small island which is reached by a low bridge. The main attraction of this temple is a square piece of rock showing the footprints of Kṛṣṇa and a cow. The footprints are shown in two positions: one in which they are even (called *samacaraṇa)*, and one in which he is supposed to have stood on his left foot with the right crossed and resting on the toes (called *dehuḍācaraṇa)*. In front of these lies a cup-shaped hollow in the rock, said to be the cup out of which the god ate, and at each corner of the square is the footprint of a cow. In front of the second pair of footprints is a mark said to be caused by Kṛṣṇa's stick.

According to myth, the Viṣṇupada temple, just like the Gopālpūr temple, is presently connected with the story of the the wrath of Rukmiṇī and her escape to the Diṇḍīravana, followed by Kṛṣṇa's arrival at Pandharpur in search of her. Thus, the *Maharashtra State Gazetteer* (1977: 909) says that the Viṣṇupada rocks and the footprints "are supposed to be the spot where Krishna and his companions held a festive party in honour of the peace-making between Krishna and his queen Rukmini," and all the Marāṭhī guide-books agree that this is the place where Kṛṣṇa arrived together with the

---

[6] It has, however, to be noted that the context from which Kāśīnāthopadhyāya here quotes is not the context of Kṛṣṇa's youth, but a passage which describes the joyous behaviour of the other cowherds on the message of his birth. This fits, of course, well with the fact that these practices are normally connected with the Janmāṣṭamī, but it does not fit as well with the more popular interpretation of the Vārakarīs that they commemorate the deeds of Kṛṣṇa.

[7] Cf. also Deleury 1960: 183.

cows, the cowherds and the muni Nārada, and where they took part in a joyous meal together (see Sunṭhaṇkar 1980: 84, Cendavaṇkar 1965: 77, Jośī *et al.*, 1961: 55, Kulkarṇī 1981: 22, and Bhiṅgārkar 1981: 38). Two of these versions of the myth, namely the versions of Sunṭhaṇkar and Bhiṅgārkar, are still more explicit since they suggest that Viṣṇupada is the very spot where the meeting of Kṛṣṇa and Rukmiṇī took place, and that the meal was arranged in honour of their reconciliation. Finally, the version of Sunṭhaṇkar also has Kṛṣṇa rest and play his flute here, just as in the case of Gopālpūr.

The main purpose of this myth is, of course, to explain the footprints of Kṛṣṇa and his cows which are shown on the rock in the Viṣṇupada temple, and of which the so-called "*dehuḍācaraṇa*" footprints are taken to be the marks of Kṛṣṇa's feet while playing the flute. The tradition that Kṛṣṇa was accompanied by Nārada should be seen in relation to the fact that there is a small temple called Nārada in the river-bed just in front of the Viṣṇupada temple. It contains a *liṅga* and is probably an early example of the "Vaiṣṇavization" of Pandharpur, as it can be traced back to the earliest *māhātmya* source of this town, the *Sk.Pdm.*[8] However, this in itself could be taken to indicate that a tradition of the arrival of Kṛṣṇa was connected with this place at a very early date. Such a tradition is, in fact, without mention of Nārada, already attested in an *abhaṅga* of Nāmadeva, where it is connected with Kṛṣṇa's visit

---

[8] Cf. the following passages of the *Sk.Pdm.*: *siddhānām īśvaro devi dakṣiṇadvāram āśritaḥ // viṣṇunā sthāpitaḥ prītyā nārado liṅgamūrtimān* / *Sk.Pdm.* 2,28cd-29ab.
tasmāt sarvaprayatnena sevyaṃ suramunīśvaraiḥ / dvāraṃ dakṣiṇabhāge tu mahatkautūhalānvitam // puṇyaṃ pāpakṣayakaraṃ yatra tiṣṭhati vai bhavān / siddhair vidyādharair yakṣair munibhiś ca samanvitaḥ // sthāpito hariṇā pūrvaṃ kṛpayā brahmanandana / dṛṣṭvā liṅgākṛtiṃ tvāṃ tu ūcus te kṛtabuddhayaḥ // siddhānām īśvaraḥ tvaṃ ca siddheśvara itīritaḥ / *Sk.Pdm.* 10,16-19ab.
dakṣiṇadvāram āśritya yatra tiṣṭhasi nārada // tatsannidhau japan mantraṃ mantrāt siddhim avāpsyasi / *Sk.Pdm.* 11,78cd-79ab.
anujñāto nāradas tu yayau kṣetraṃ mahāmuniḥ / snātvā tīrthe mahāpuṇye dṛṣṭvā viṣṇuṃ sanātanam // dakṣiṇadvāraṁ āsādya tiṣṭhaty adyāpi nāradaḥ / *Sk.Pdm.* 12,38-39ab.

to Puṇḍalīka.[9]

Ritually, Viṣṇupada is the place where pilgrims, observing the more orthodox way of performing a *tīrtha-yātrā*, must offer *śrāddhas* to their deceased ancestors. Furthermore, Viṭhobā is supposed to stay in the Viṣṇupada temple during the whole of the month Mārgaśīrṣa, when his *pādukās* are carried to and fro in procession. At that time, he is supposed to be feasting out there with the cowherds, and it is the custom of the local people to take their meals in the precincts of the Viṣṇupada temple at least once during this month (see Dingre 1968: 153f., *Maharashtra State Gazetteer* 1977: 909, and Vaudeville 1976: 148).

Historical Analysis

Having now presented the major facts about the current situation concerning Gopālpūr and Viṣṇupada, I shall continue with a historical survey of these two places.

From the above description, and from the results of my own investigation of the reception of sub-*tīrthas* among pilgrims, one might get the impression that to-day Gopālpūr is the more important of the two places, at least in the tradition of the Vārakarīs. However, already the fact that in some versions of the Gopālpūr myth it is mentioned that Kṛṣṇa and his comrades first came to Viṣṇupada and took their common meal there, seems to indicate that formerly the Viṣṇupada temple was the most important and that it was here, and not at Gopālpūr, that the *kālā* took place. As I shall now show, this hypothesis is in fact confirmed by a historical analysis.

---

[9] *gokuḷīṃhūni deva paṇḍharapurā pātalā / tvarita pāvalā veṇunādīṃ // 4 // tethūni paratalā vāḷuvaṇṭhīṃ ālā / taṃva deva dekhilā puṇḍalīkeṃ // 5 // Sakalasantagāthā*, vol. 2, No. 974.

As in the preceding survey, we may begin with Gopālpūr. As already mentioned, the present Gopālakṛṣṇa temple is of recent origin, its construction having been initiated in A.D. 1744. After this date, Gopālpūr is referred to in Mahīpati's *Bhaktavijaya* (from A.D. 1762),[10] as the place where Kṛṣṇa left his companions before looking alone for Rukmiṇī, thus showing that, already at this time, Gopālpūr was connected with the myth about Rukmiṇī's wrath. Before this date, Gopālpūr is, however, mentioned several times in the *abhaṅgas* of Ekanātha,[11] once as the place where Kṛṣṇa engaged himself in the *melā* of cows and cowherds,[12] and once in the *abhaṅgas* of Bhānudāsa.[13]

Thus, knowledge about the importance of Gopālpūr might be said to go back to the time of Ekanātha at the end of the 16th century, if not to his great-grandfather Bhānudāsa about the end of the 15th or the beginning of the 16th century. Since we have no knowledge of a temple of Gopālakṛṣṇa at this time, these references are perhaps only to the village Gopālpūr. If these references are genuine, the spread of the popularity of Gopālpūr among the Vārakarīs at this time, however, is questionable, since, according to my information, it is not mentioned at all in any of Tukārāma's *abhaṅgas* or in the writings of his disciple Bahiṇābāī. Neither is it mentioned by Pralhāda Mahārāja in his Marāṭhī *Pāṇḍuraṅgamāhātmya* from around the beginning of the 18th century.

Gopālpūr is not mentioned in any of the Sanskrit *māhātmyas*. It seems probable, however, that the Gopālaparvata or Gopāla mountain, mentioned in the *Pd.Pdm.*[14] in connection with *śrāddhas* to be

---

[10] This work has only been available to me in the translation of Kincaid 1927: 1ff.

[11] *Sakalasantagāthā*, vol. 3, Nos. 319, 389, 412, and 459.

[12] Ibid., No. 319,7: *"gāī gopāḷāṃcā meḷā gopāḷapurīṃ to ṭhevilā."*

[13] Ibid., No. 21,3.

[14] *Pd.Pdm.* 31,14. The published edition of this text is rather poor and seems to be based on only one MS.

performed south of Pandharpur, is identical with the hill where the present Gopālpūr temple stands. Thus, it seems that we have evidence about Gopālpūr at least since the days of Ekanātha, even though we cannot say anything for sure about its popularity among the Vārakarīs until after the building of the present Gopālakṛṣṇa temple on the hill in front of the Gopālpūr village.

In the case of Viṣṇupada, we are informed by the *Maharashtra State Gazetteer* (1977: 909) that the rocks described earlier were formerly found to the east of the present temple, where now there is a temple to Māruti. They were originally open-air, but were set in masonry in the centre of a square platform in about 1640. About 1785, they were removed by a *Baḍava* named Cinto Nāgeśa, who built the structure as it now stands.

In Marāṭhī literary sources, the name Viṣṇupada is found in an *abhaṅga* of Ekanātha where he gives it as a synonym of the so-called *samapada* or *samacaraṇa* mentioned earlier.[15] Apart from this, we find the name in the *māhātmyas* of both Śrīdhara and Pralhāda Mahārāja from around the beginning of the 18th century.[16] In the case of Pralhāda Mahārāja, it also seems to be a name for the *samapada* as distinguished from the other, or *dehuḍācaraṇa* footprints, which are here called Veṇunāda, and to which I shall return below.[17]

In the Sanskrit *māhātmyas*, the name Viṣṇupada is found in only one chapter of the *Pd.Pdm.*, which deals with the *śrāddhas* or ances-

---

[15] *Sakalasantagāthā*, vol. 3, No. 320,2: "*joḍaleṃ jetheṃ samapada tayā mhaṇatī viṣṇupada.*"

[16] *Pāṇḍuraṅgamāhātmya* of Śrīdhara 31,15 and *Pāṇḍuraṅgamāhātmya* of Pralhāda Mahārāja, verse 84.

[17] *parisoni nāradavacaneṃ / dehuḍā pāvalīṃ yadunandaneṃ / ubheṃ rāhūni veṇūvādaneṃ / karunī godhaneṃ vaḷiyelīṃ// veṇunādī bhakti karūna / viṣṇupadīṃ piṇḍapradāna / karitī tyāṃce pitṛgaṇa / vaikuṃṭhabhuvana pāvatī //* Ibid., verses 68 and 84.

tor rituals to be performed south of Pandharpur.[18] And the fact that it appears here in connection with the performance of *śrāddhas*, as well as the fact that the whole area to the south is called Gayā,[19] clearly indicates which associations were involved, if not in the coining of this name then at least in the use of it: it is the Pandharpur replica of the famous Viṣṇupada shrine in Gayā where from time immemorial *śrāddhas* have been praised as most efficient. This is also confirmed by the fact that some of the verses mentioning the Viṣṇupada are, in fact, quotations from the *Gayāmāhātmya* of the *Vāyupurāṇa*.[20] Although it is not possible to say anything specific about when and under what circumstances this place was connected with Gayā and given the name Viṣṇupada, it seems to be comparatively recent, since the name is found neither in the older *abhaṅga* literature, nor in the older *Sk.Pdm.*

The *samapada* footprints themselves seem to have been worshipped already at the time of the composition of *Sk.Pdm.*, not under the name Viṣṇupada, but under the name Śrīpada, and from the fragmentary references in our text it seems that at that time they were connected with the story of a *daitya*, called Saṃgama, who was crushed by the feet of Visnu.[21] Although the story of the demon Saṃgama could of course be inspired by the story about Gayāsura, there are no indications in the text of *śrāddhas* being offered here, still less of the place being identified with Gayā, as is the case in the *Pd.Pdm.*

---

[18] *Pd.Pdm.* 31,11ff.; 31,24; 31,43f. and 31,48.

[19] *śṛṇu devi pravakṣyāmi gayāyātrāṃ vicakṣaṇām / niṣkṛtiḥ pitṛkartṝṇāṃ brahmaṇā gīyate tu yā // Pd.Pdm.* 31,1. Furthermore *adhyāya* 30 and 31 are called *gayāsuravarmakathanam* and *gayāśrāddhakathanam* respectively.

[20] Thus *Pd.Pdm.* 31,8-11ab = *Gayāmāhātmya* 1,19-21.

[21] *saṃgamākhyaṃ mahādaityaṃ nipātya ca surārihā / tasyopari ca śrīpādau kṛtvā viṣṇur atiṣṭhata // adyāpi tatra saṃlagne dṛśyete śrīpade vibhoḥ / mahotsāhaṃ tatra kurvan bhojanāny api suvrate // anantaphalam āpnoti sāyujyaṃ ca na saṃśayaḥ / tasya nāmnā ca tat tīrthaṃ snānāt sāyujyadaṃ nṛṇām // Sk.Pdm.* 4,36-38.

As can be seen from the above survey, the term Viṣṇupada probably originated as a new name for the *samapada* or even footprints now found in the Viṣṇupada-shrine, and which earlier seems to have been called Śrīpada. This is also supported by the fact that the first text to use the name Viṣṇupada, the *Pd.Pdm.*, in one place also uses the slightly differing name Śrīṣapada.[22] However, as I shall now show, it seems that the worship of the so-called *dehuḍācaraṇa* footprints is at least as old, and its tradition was originally more popular.

As pointed out above, the so-called *dehuḍācaraṇa* are interpreted as the position taken by Kṛṣṇa Gopāla as he was playing the flute. And due to this, there is an almost unanimous tradition among the Vārakarī saints and the Sanskrit and Marāṭhī *māhātmyas* of calling the place Veṇunāda or "the sound of the flute."

That it was a place of great popularity among the Vārakarī saints is beyond doubt, as it is mentioned in the *abhaṅgas* of almost all the saints from Nivṛttinātha to Tukārāma's disciple Bahiṇābāī as the place of Govinda's sport or the place where Govinda sported or used to dwell.[23]

In the Marāṭhī *Pāṇḍuraṅgamāhātmya* of Pralhāda Mahārāja, Veṇunāda is the place on the bank of the Puṣpāvatī where Kṛṣṇa landed, along with Nārada and the cowherds, on their way to visit Puṇḍalīka.[24] The identification of Veṇunāda and the *dehuḍācaraṇa*

---

[22] *Pd.Pdm.* 31,42.

[23] Nivṛttinātha: *Sakalasantagāthā*, vol. 1, No. 220; Jñānadeva: ibid., vol. 1, No. 57,6 *("veṇunādīṃ śrīdhara kheḷatātī")*; Bhānudāsa: ibid., vol. 3, 31 *("dhanya dhanya veṇunāda / krīḍā karito govinda")*; Ekanātha: ibid., vol. 3, Nos. 320, 389, 395, 436 *("krīḍā kārī govinda sarvakāḷa)*, 444 and 459; Tukārāma: 332 *("krīḍāsthaḷa veṇunādīṃ")*; Bahiṇābāī: 464,4 *("puṇya puṣpāvatī tīreṃ veṇunāda / sapremā govinda krīḍā karī")* and 465,4 *("dhanya dhanya veṇunāda")* (see Abbott 1929: 291).

[24] *Pāṇḍuraṅgamāhātmya*, verses 64ff.

footprints is confirmed here, as the text describes Kṛṣṇa as standing in the *dehuḍācaraṇa* position while resting after the journey.[25]

In the Sanskrit *māhātmya* literature, it is mentioned in the *Bhīmāmāhātmya* under the name Veṇunādaka in connection with the confluence of the Bhīmā and Puṣpāvatī,[26] and in the *Sk.Pdm.* it is referred to both in the earlier and the later portions.[27] Thus, in the second chapter we are told that Nārada was caused to stand at the southern gate in the form of a *liṅga,* and to the south of him is the flute mark *(veṇumudrāṅka)*, which, when worshipped with the six-syllabled *mantra,*[28] is said to provide all kinds of powers. Even though the term *veṇumudrāṅka* might be somewhat ambiguous, this location is most probably identical with the Veṇunāda of the saints. This is also confirmed by the fact that the place is called the sporting-ground of Visnu,[29] just as Veṇunāda in the *abhaṅgas* is the sporting-ground of Govinda, or the place were Govinda sported. Speaking again about the places near the confluence of Bhīmā and Puṣpāvatī in the 10th chapter, the text clearly describes the *dehuḍācaraṇa* in saying that at that place is found the foot position of the one engaged in the *veṇunāda* (?), one mark showing only the fore part and the other showing the full foot.[30]

---

[25] Cf. note 13, above.

[26] The chapter dealing with Pandharpur has been edited by the present author and will be published soon; the mention of *veṇunādaka* is found in 35,51:
bhīmāyāś ca taṭe ramye bhaved vai veṇunādakaḥ /
tasya darśanamātreṇa sarvān kāmān avāpnuyāt //

[27] *dakṣiṇe veṇumudrāṅko namaskāryaḥ prayatnataḥ // ṣaḍakṣareṇa mantreṇa pūjitaḥ sarvasiddhidaḥ /* Sk.Pdm. 2,29cd-28ab.
veṇunādena devānāṃ manaḥśravaṇamaṅgalaḥ // adyāpi tatra devarṣe dṛśyete caraṇāv ubhau / veṇunādasthitākāro dṛśyate tatra pādayoḥ // prapādākramaṇenaiva sampūrṇakramaṇena ca / Sk.Pdm. 10,41cd-43ab.

[28] I.e., the Kṛṣṇa *mantra: oṃ kṛṣṇāya namaḥ.*

[29] *"viṣṇoḥ krīḍanakaṃ sthānam." Sk.Pdm.* 2,32.

[30] Cf. *Sk.Pdm.* 10,42f. in note 27.

The only *māhātmya* sources which, to my knowledge, do not mention the name Veṇunāda are the *Pd.Pdm.* and its two Marāṭhī versions by Śrīdhara. Considering the fact that the *Pd.Pdm.* is probably also the first source to mention the name Viṣṇupada, one cannot help seeing herein a possible legitimation of an attempt to redefine this sacred place, perhaps to make it correspond better to the needs of local brahmanic tradition.

The *Kālā*

Let us now return to the *kālā* ritual. As already mentioned above, the Gopālpūr myth, quoted from the *Maharashtra State Gazetteer,* is closely connected with the *kālā* ritual. Thus, it explains the meaning of the ritual by explaining its origin in the feast held at Gopālpūr by Kṛṣṇa and his comrades to celebrate the reconciliation between Kṛṣṇa and Rukmiṇī. The performance of the Vārakarīs is then a reenactment in commemoration of this mythical event.

However, we already noticed that the fact that some versions of the Gopālpūr myth mention that Kṛṣṇa and his comrades first came to Viṣṇupada and took their common meal there might indicate that formerly the *kālā* took place there and not at Gopālpūr.

Let us therefore inquire whether any of the sources corroborate this hypothesis. In a general sense, the fact that both the *Sk.Pdm.* and many *abhaṅgas* characterize Veṇunāda as the sporting-ground of Visnu or Govinda, or as the place where Govinda sported, might point to an early tradition about Kṛṣṇa's arrival in Pandharpur in connection with the Veṇunāda. This arrival was probably not originally connected with Dvārakā and Rukmiṇī's wrath, but rather with Gokula and Puṇḍalīka, as is the case in the earlier mentioned *abhaṅga* of Nāmadeva.[31]

---

[31] Cf. note 9.

Furthermore, the *Sk.Pdm.* seems to indicate the performance of rituals similar to the *kālā* ritual near the Veṇunāda, when it says that sprinkling sports *(siñcanakrīḍanāni)* and picnics out in the green with rice prepared with curds *(dadhyanna)* and dishes cooked in oil *(tailapakva)* are recommended there.[32]

However, there are more specific references to the *kālā* ritual in Marāṭhī sources. Unfortunately, space does not allow us to go into detail about the best and most exhaustive description of how Kṛṣṇa celebrated the *kālā* along with his comrades. This is found in Pralhāda Mahārāja's *Pāṇḍuraṅgamāhātmya*, and here the *kālā* takes place without doubt near the Veṇunāda.[33] The same holds true in the *abhaṅgas* of Nivṛttinātha, where at least two *abhaṅgas* point to the *kālā* being celebrated at Veṇunāda,[34] and with the *abhaṅgas* of Bhānudāsa, where there is one reference[35] to the *kālā* being held at Veṇunāda. Perhaps this is also indirectly corroborated by one of Sopānadeva's *abhaṅgas*, where he says: "We performed the *kālā* on the sandy beach."[36]

As in the case of the references to Gopālpūr, where the *abhaṅgas* of Ekanātha seem to mark a change, the same seems to be the case with regard to the references to the *kālā*. Thus, whereas all earlier references seem to point to the fact that the *kālā* was originally performed at Veṇunāda, in the case of the *abhaṅgas* of Ekanātha, we find only one reference to the *kālā* being held at Veṇunāda,[37] and at

---

[32] Cf. *Sk.Pdm.* 2,35: *siñcanakrīḍanādīni tatra śastāni bhāmini / dadhyannais taila-pakvaiś ca śāḍvalakrīḍanāni ca //* The sprinkling with water and buttermilk fits well with the *kālā* ritual, although there is also a slight possibility that the text is referring to the practice of eating out there during the month of Mārgaśīrṣa.

[33] *Pāṇḍuraṅgamāhātmya*, verses 69ff.

[34] *Sakalasantagāthā*, vol. 1, Nos. 228 and 240.

[35] Ibid., vol. 3, No. 14 *("veṇunādīṃ kālā gopāḷa karitī")*.

[36] Ibid., vol. 1, No. 2,6 *("amhīṃ vāluvantīṃ kelā kālā")*.

[37] Ibid., vol. 3, No. 436 *("paurṇimecā kālā veṇunādīṃ jāhalā")*.

least four references to the *kālā* being held at Gopālpūr.[38]

Conclusion

In this paper, we have dealt with two different sacred localities south of Pandharpur, namely, the places that are today called Gopālpūr and Viṣṇupada. The first references to both names are relatively recent and seem to come from the period around, or sometime before, Ekanātha, maybe from the end of the 15th and beginning of the 16th century. Whereas in the case of Gopālpūr, we have no evidence of any religious activity before the reference to the Gopālaparvata in the *Pd.Pdm.*, in the case of Viṣṇupada, we know both from the Vārakarī and from the *māhātmya* traditions that religious activities took place in the vicinity, which is quite natural considering the fact that it lies just near the confluence of the Bhīmā and the Puṣpāvatī.

Furthermore, we saw that in the present Viṣṇupada temple there are two pairs of footprints of Kṛṣṇa, one which is even, called *samapada*, and one which is interpreted as Kṛṣṇa Gopāla playing the flute, called *dehuḍācaraṇa*, and we saw that both these pairs of footprints are mentioned and described in what is probably the oldest Sanskrit *māhātmya* about Pandharpur, namely, the *Sk.Pdm.*, the first being called the Śrīpada and the second Veṇumudrāṅka or, in the vocabulary of the Vārakarīs, Veṇunāda. To judge from the high frequency of references to the Veṇunāda in Vārakarī sources and the nearly total lack of references to the Śrī- or later Viṣṇupada, there is no doubt that the Veṇunāda was more popular among the Vārakarīs, connected as it is, at least since the time of Nāmadeva, with the myth of the arrival of Gopālakṛṣṇa in Pandharpur. However, it seems that the introduction of the name Viṣṇupada and its association with the orthodox practice of *śrāddhas*, started a devel-

---

[38] Ibid., vol. 3, Nos. 400, 406, 411, 444.

opment which has strengthened the more brahmanic traditions in connection with Viṣṇupada, culminating in the building of a temple about A.D. 1785.[39]

Parallel with this development, there seems to have been a decrease in the originally more popular cult of Gopālakṛṣṇa and the *dehuḍācaraṇa,* culminating in its moving to Gopālpūr and the building of the Gopālakṛṣṇa temple around A.D. 1744. This process is indicated by at least four factors: firstly, by the fact that the *mūrti* found in the Gopālakṛṣṇa temple is precisely a *mūrti* of Veṇugopāla, thus clearly replacing the *dehuḍācaraṇa;* secondly, by the fact that just as there is a Nārada *liṅga* in the river bed to the north of the Viṣṇupada temple, which has its mythical counterpart in the fact that Nārada is said to have accompanied Kṛṣṇa on his arrival in Pandharpur, we also find that a small temple of Nārada has been built within the precincts of the Gopālpūr temple; thirdly, by the fact that the myth of Gopālpūr seems to be more or less identical with the myth connected with the Viṣṇupada temple and still contains reminiscences of this relationship; and fourthly, by the fact that the so-called *kālā* ritual, which is now one of the most important ritual events connected with Gopālpūr, originally and at least to the time of Ekanātha, and possibly also after his time, was performed near the Veṇunāda or Viṣṇupada, as it later came to be called.

Of course, nothing can be said with certainty with regard to the circumstances of this development. It seems, however, as if it might to some extent have represented a conflict of interests between local brahmins and the Vārakarī *saṃpradāya.* Thus, it is certain that the cult of Gopālakṛṣṇa and the performance of the *kālā* at Veṇunāda

---

[39] Another aspect of this development is probably the connection between the Viṣṇupada temple and the Viṭṭhala *mandira* which is expressed by the simultaneous worship of Viṭṭhala at both these places during the month of Mārgaśīrṣa (see Dingre 1968: 153f.).

was early on very popular among the Vārakarīs. On the other hand, the *kālā* with its obvious "folk" features and its commensality must have seemed repulsive to the caste ideology of the brahmins, and perhaps one might attempt the hypothesis that the caste opposition inherent in the *kālā* might be the reason why this cult from the start took place so far from the centre of Pandharpur, thus allowing all Vārakarīs to take part, including the outcastes; and that the Veṇunāda was originally a place outside of the management of the brahmins.

When this Vārakarī monopoly might have started changing is difficult to say. However, as we have seen, it was probably sometime before Ekanātha and the composition of the *Pd.Pdm.*, maybe sometime in the late 14th or the 15th century. Since the Viṣṇupada temple is run today by the *Baḍavas*, this suggests its intimate connection with the main temple in Pandharpur. A qualified guess on this point would perhaps be that the brahmin interest in Veṇunāda might have been caused by the advent of the *Baḍavas* some time before A.D. 1519, when we first hear of them in Pandharpur (see Dingre 1968: 60ff.).

REFERENCES

Abbott, Justin E. (trans.) 1929. *Bahiṇā Bāī: A translation of her autobiography and verses*. The Poet-Saints of Maharashtra, No. 5. Poona.

Bhiṅgārkar, K. Jñ. 1981. *Śrī Viṭhṭhala māhātmya*. Puṇe.

Cendavaṇkar, S. 1965. *Paṇḍharapūracā Viṭhobā*. Mumbaī.

Deleury, G. A. 1960. *The cult of Viṭhobā*. Poona.

Dharmasindhu of Kāśīnāthopadhyāya. Ed. by K. R. Shāstri Navare. 1888. Bombay.

Ḍhere, R. C. 1981. "Pāṇḍuraṅgamāhātmya" āṇi tyācī prācīnatā. In *Mahārāṣṭrācī Sattvadhārā* (Dā. Rā. Cin. Ḍhere Abhinandana-grantha). Puṇe.

Dingre, G. V. 1968. *A study of a temple town and its priesthood*. Poona. [Unpublished doctoral dissertation, submitted to the Deccan College Post Graduate & Research Institute].

Gayā Māhātmya. Edition critique, traduction française et introduction par Claude Jacques. 1962. Pondichery. [Publications de l'Institut Français d'Indologie, No. 20].

Ghurye, G. S. 1960. *After a century and a quarter*. Bombay.

Id. 1962. *Gods and men*. Bombay.

Government of India. 1969. *Census of India. 1961. Volume X. Maharashtra., Part VII-B. Fairs and festivals in Maharashtra*. Bombay.

Jośī, G. V. B., Karakambakar, R. Jñ. and Gurujī, P. Jñ. Bh. 1960. *Śrīkṣetra Paṇḍharapūra darśana*. Puṇe.

Kane, P. V. 1974. *History of dharmaśāstra*, vol. V, part I, second edition. Poona.

Khare, G. H. 1963. *Śrīviṭhṭhala āṇi Paṇḍharapūra*. 3rd. ed. Puṇe.

Kincaid, C. A. 1927. *Tales of the saints of Pandharpur*, 2nd. ed. London etc.

Kulkarṇī, S. C. 1981. *Śrīkṣetra Paṇḍharapūra māhātmya*. Beḷgāṃv.

Maharashtra State Gazetteers. Sholapur District (revised edition). Bombay, 1977.

Mate, M. S. 1962. *Temples and legends of Maharashtra*. Bombay.

Mitchell, J. Murray. 1882. Pandharpur. In *Indian Antiquary* 11: 149-156.

Mokashi, D. B. 1987. *Palkhi. An Indian pilgrimage.* Trans. by Philip C. Engblom. Albany.

Molesworth, J. T. 1857. *A dictionary, Marāṭhī and English,* second edition. Bombay.

Pāṇḍuraṅgamāhātmya. (Attributed to the *Vārāhasaṃhitā* of the *Padmapurāṇa*). 1869. Bombay.

Pralhāda Mahārāja. 1929. *Pāṇḍuraṅgamāhātmya.* Paṇḍharpūr.

Sakalasantagāthā. Ed. by Rā. Ci. Ḍhere, 5 vols. 1983. Puṇe.

Sand, Erik Reenberg. 1990. The legend of Puṇḍarīka: the founder of Pandharpur. In: *The history of sacred places in India as reflected in traditional literature.* Ed. by Hans Bakker. Leiden etc., 33-61.

Śrīdhara. 1981. *Pāṇḍuraṅgamāhātmya.* Ed. by R. C. Ḍhere. Puṇe.

Sunṭhaṇkar, S. 1980. *Asā Āhe Śrīviṭhṭhala.* Beḷgāṃv.

Śrī Tukārāmabāvāṃcyā abhaṅgāṃcī gāthā. 2nd edition. 1973. Mumbaī.

Vaudeville, Ch. 1976. Pandharpur, the city of saints. In: *Structural approaches to South Indian studies.* Ed. by Harry M. Buck and Glenn E. Yocum. Chambersburg, Pennsylvania, 137-161.

Günther-Dietz Sontheimer

THE FOLK FESTIVAL *(JATRĀ)* IN THE RELIGIOUS TRADITIONS OF MAHARASHTRA: The Case of Khaṇḍobā

I

Unlike other religious traditions—as, e.g., the bhakti of the saints; the brahmanical approach to deities who, according to the *purāṇas,* mostly reside in heaven; or such ascetic-yogic Śaivite movements as that of the Nāths—folk religion does not describe or explain itself. Modern Hindus who take the position of an external viewer of folk religion would not assign it the status of a category in Hinduism and might at the most call it some kind of an aberration from "standard" religion. I would argue that folk religion indeed is a category of its own which has constantly interacted with other currents for thousands of years and yet maintained its identity. It is part of the composite culture of Maharashtra and, as with folklore in general, one should first strive to see it as "a realm for analysis and to avoid the tendency to use it as supplementary data for other concerns." (Blackburn and Ramanujan 1986: 26). The second step would be to see *how* folk religion interacts and forms a part of the composite Maharashtrian religion and culture. Folk religion may not describe or explain itself, yet as a structure of religious consciousness it can be empirically identified. Folk religion is something which is *done* by those who are involved in it, and especially *jatrās* provide an occasion for different communities and individuals to affirm or dramatize the self-perceptions and reciprocities of their social milieux by actively participating in the rituals. Folk religion does not explain itself to outsiders and thus empirical observation is one of the most important means to identify it. Another source is oral literature, but here we may find a degree of self-awareness which causes folk religion to view itself as an object. This may be in response to the subtle influence of other religious currents and their literary genres, like the *Purāṇas, Māhātmyas* and bhakti poetry. The literature of these other currents would be another, though indirect source of identifying folk religion. We must keep in mind that we mostly get facts of folk religion in these texts as a reflection which may assume many forms, e.g., criticism. The very emphasis with which authors of *māhātmyas* or bhakti poets treat certain topics and try to interpret or improve them shows that these topics formed an important part of religious life.

II

I have chosen the *jatrā* for discussion because it is one of the central topics of folk religion for consideration in this context. A cursory glance at the part of the Census Report which deals with *Fairs and festivals of Maharashtra* will indicate the importance of the *jatrā* in Maharashtra: there are 11,425 *jatrās* every year. I am concerned with the local village *jatrā* for a village deity or the *jatrā* for a family deity, which is in most cases also of regional importance. I am not concerned with the sectarian or the all-Indian *jatrā*. The terms *jatrā* and *yātrā* are differentiated depending on the social background of the speaker and/or the context. *Jatrā* is in many ways synonymous with the original meaning of the word *utsav*, that is, the "periodical renewal of the cosmos."

The *jatrā* emphasizes seasons and agricultural cycles rather than brahmanic chronology, e.g., the astrological calculation of *auspi-*

cious time. Thus the date may be fixed by the ritual of *kaul*—which, in this context, means asking the deity's permission to hold a *jatrā*. Festivals are celebrated as a sign that life and fertility have been bountiful and will continue, that processes of human growth and agriculture are proceeding in an anticipated way. Many *jatrās* end with possession by a deity who, with the help of the medium, declares the prospects for rain and harvests and the possibility of wars. Wars often meant the destruction of harvests, e.g., after Dasarā, by robber bands or conquering would-be kings. The prediction is sometimes called *vhaīk* or, in the Mhaskobā cult, *bhākaṇūk*. One of the basic aims is the winning of life out of death. The *jatrā* may take place on dates which may be astrologically inauspicious, as Stanley has shown in the case of the Somvatī Amāvāsyā festival of the Khaṇḍobā cult. But danger and death are turned into the auspicious by the god and his devotees. (There are many rituals which suggest the challenge and defeat of danger and death, e.g., the ritual of *halāvar cālṇe* may point to such a motif. The ritual of fire-walking seems to have been widespread in the Khaṇḍobā cult; I have seen it still being performed in the similar Mallanna cults of Andhra.)

The element of danger, death and disease, which has to be overcome, is perceptible in *jatrās*. For instance, the "dead" ancestors participate in the Somvatī Amāvāsyā festival and celebrate together with their descendants, and self-mortifications are frequent, however stylized they may have become. At the source of a cult there may be violent death and sacrifice. For instance, at the beginning of the Mhaskobā cult at Vīr there was a termite mound, the "Gate to the Underworld" (D. König) and to the world of the dead. When the termite mound was ploughed over by the Māḷīs with a twelve oxen plough despite the warning of the Dhangar, the devotee of the god, the ploughman disappeared along with the oxen into the abyss, though all of them, including the twelve oxen, were restored to life by the deity. The Gadkoṭ of Jejuri, the hill temple of Khaṇḍobā, owes the permanent presence of the god to the self-sacrifice of a

Māng known as Yeśvant Rao. His death not only caused him to win immortality as the guardian deity, the *havildār*, of the god's fortress, but guarantees the presence of the god as a source of life for his devotees. Non-vegetarian *nived*—involving the sacrificing, e.g., of sheep—is basic to *jatrās* of folk deities. It sustains the deities and is eaten by the devotees. The author of the prose *Mhaskobā Caritra* in 1880 explains the term *jatrā* by means of a folk etymology. The author was a devotee of Mhaskobā, though his description is informed by other currents. He writes: "*Jatrā* means *yātrā*. The reason it is called a *jatrā* is that on the day of the *jatrā* hundreds of kids are killed, so it's called a *jatrā*."

Folk deities and their festivals are replete with rituals that aim at winning power and renewal of life, or physical immortality through children, or well-being for oneself and the family, increase of cattle and prosperity, crops etc. Music, dance, drumming, *khel̤*, and shouting in various forms are elements of *jatrās*. They all have an essentially religious meaning and aim at winning life out of death. The more we go into tribal areas we find that the *jatrā* can be an occasion of love-making. And the Khaṇḍobā cult is well known for all sorts of "licentious" customs. Another feature is that there are many ritual competitions, or survivals of competitions, often stick-fighting and bullock cart races. Behind these are the attempts to conquer the "goods of life." Most of these rituals are meant to cause fertility, like the cart races at Nimgav. But such ritual competition, often expressed in violent acts, is not directed to the deity and performed to provoke him or please him; rather, it takes place between parties. The price that the folk deity has to pay is his active involvement in the world, and this may result in Khaṇḍobā, for example, becoming an object of humour or even banalisation. Eroticism is attributed to him and some songs of the Vāghyās leave it in abeyance whether physical love is involved or bhakti. The tale of Khaṇḍobā's courtship of Bāṇāī shows him behaving in a deluded and irresponsible manner, active but imbalanced. He is affectionately called *veḍā*, "mad," because of his being engrossed with the beautiful Bāṇubāī.

Gods like Khaṇḍobā reflect the divine king, and it is the folk king as a god rather than the secularised king who is controlled by *dharma* and *varṇa* and is left with only a residue of divinity. He tends to be rather a rising robber king than a king subordinated to *brahman*. He is a king who does not insist on *varṇa* or *jātī*, and privileges—the *mān* of the *mānkarīs*—are based on extraordinary feats of devotion. He is the agent of the powers of nature and provides fertility, e.g., through rain. His involvement in human life makes him a mirror of the life and occupation of his devotees. For the merchant he is a merchant, for the robber a robber; for the king he is a king; for the hero he is the divine hero; for the Dhangars, because of his involvement with Bāṇāī, he is a Dhangar, too. The human king as god or the folk god as king resembles Indra and Rudra, including all their human weaknesses and mortifications. The modes of devotion are not those of classical bhakti, but are expressed, e.g., by mortification by *vīras* leading even to suicide. The folk god-king is also a trickster *(cāravḍā)* who knows how to work miracles and magic: *māv*—derived from *māyā*—does not mean "illusion" in this context, but the power of the god to work miracles *(camatkār)* and assume different forms. Especially at a *jatrā* devotees may not only experience miracles but may be empowered by the god to enact miracles themselves.

III

The uneasiness about the constant involvement of man and gods in the world is as old as the Vedic period. The compulsion to win life out of death, the agonistic rites in which the loser had to accept the loss of the goods of life and had to accept Death, e.g., in the ritual game of dice, the impurity and violence connected with such rituals, was the target in the classical *śrauta* ritual of the *Brāhmaṇas* and *Śrautasūtras*. As Heesterman has shown, death was eliminated in the sacrificial ritual and the ritual was made transcendent, aloof from any involvement in the world or any contact with mundane reality. The ritual was not directed to any god who could respond with some mystical or magical faculty, but the ritual itself caused some invisible force called *apūrva*. It is interesting to note that all the elements which are found in the unreformed, so-called pre-classical ritual, occur *mutatis mutandis* in the *jatrā*. There is a famous passage in the *Jaiminīya Brāhmaṇa* which refers to the ancient *mahāvrata* festival. This festival contained all sorts of contests which are a part of *jatrās:* a chariot race, an arrow shooting contest, a tug of war, or a wrestling match between an Ārya and a Śūdra for a hide representing the sun. The latter reminds us of the "tug of war" (Stanley) between the Rāmośīs and the Marāṭhās while carrying the *pālkhī* of Khaṇḍobā, who is also the Sun, at the Somvatī Amāvāsyā festival in Jejuri. Besides we learn that the *mahāvrata* festival involved dancing, singing, drumming, ritual reviling and copulation. The *JB* relates that these were the weapons of Death, who competed with Prajāpati. After a long time the contest remained undecided, but finally Prajāpati overcame his rival through the discovery of certain liturgical means which eliminated Death as a participant in the ritual. By the means of liturgical equivalences Death was made ritually subservient and ritual rivalry was excluded. Thus the classical *śrauta* "sacrifice" was eventually a ritual with a single *yajamāna* who performed the sacrifice in himself and by himself without outside intervention. This was only one step short of the interiorisation of ritual which becomes especially explicit in the *Upaniṣads*, where it is called *ātmayajña*, the sacrifice in the self, a mental sacrifice which, according to Manu 2.85, was a thousand times more efficacious than the normal ritual.

But we find a similar trend in the *jatrā* to replace agonistic rites by symbolical actions. For instance, after the real wrestling bouts between different groups of Kaikāḍīs at the Pūrṇimā *jatrā* at Jejuri in the month of Pauṣ, the opponents started again wrestling, but only to symbolically clasp each other. Thus the conflict was neutralised. Or: the cart races in Nimgāv during the Māgh and Caitra *jatrā* are not competitions for prize money, but each individual cart races up the hill with breathtaking speed without competing with others. This reminds us of the development of the sacrifice in the *śrauta* ritual, which became, as we have said, an individualistic affair of a single *yajamāna.*

IV

The tension between the mundane world and supramundane transcendence is also found in the Sanskrit *Mallāri Māhātmya.* The author, like the author of any *sthala-māhātmya,* must have been in a more difficult position than the authors of the *purāṇas,* who located their gods in heaven and thus made them nearly inaccessible. The *MM* had to make a compromise between ultimately unrelated abstraction and too much involvement in particular details of folk religion, which would deprive the work of its supramundane sanction.

In the *MM* Śiva the distant, sublime ruler becomes involved in the world out of compassion. Śiva as Mārtāṇḍa Bhairava kills the two demons, restores the order of the world and returns the Ṛṣis or Brāhmaṇas to their place. The demons—rather, the demon Maṇimalla—resemble the divine folk king; one of Maṇimalla's most aggravating features is that he allows himself to be worshipped as a god. What actually happens in the process is that the folk deity is separated into two parts and god and demon are distinguished, though not entirely delinked. The god in the same process is identified with Śiva who is the Cosmos, who is the creator of the world, pervading the universe. The wide range of human desires expressed by different kinds of worship are hierarchised; they spread from mundane enjoyment *(bhukti)* to superior powers *(siddhis)* up to salvation *(mukti)*. *Bhukti* and *mukti* are not separated, but rather represent a continous encompassing set of values. This reaches from the goods of life, physical well-being and immortality (through progeny) up to spiritual immortality through salvation. Violence and Death, however, are, as far as possible, deprecated. There is, for instance, no mention of the religious suicides of the *vīras*. The royal cult, so important in folk religion, is deemphasized, though the *Māhātmya* makes Śiva take over elements of the royal warriors Maṇi and Malla, e.g., the horse. Śiva becomes king Mārtaṇḍa. Other elements of the folk cult are conspicuous by their absence, e.g., the *jatrā* on Somvatī Amāvāsyā which has or had strong resemblances to a royal hunt and shows vestiges of the ancient *aśvamedha* ritual. The notorious rivalry and asymmetrical relationship between the two wives of Khaṇḍobā, which constitutes a great source of oral folk literature, is replaced by the suggestion that the two wives are one.

The rather unclassical, folk-religious forms of bhakti are hierarchised: e.g., hook-swinging is *rākṣasī bhakti*, the possession by the god and making a living on it is styled *piśācī bhakti*, and feeding a Brahman, who has to be imagined to be a form of Mārtaṇḍa Bhairava, is called *sāttvikī bhakti* and is the highest form of bhakti.

The *jatrā* according to the *MM* is not just a seasonally determined *jatrā* to fertility and life, but it remembers a unique, mythological event in the life of the god *illo tempore* when Śiva appeared as *svayambhū liṅga* for those who are afflicted by mistakes in the Kali time. The date is fixed astrologically. It is on Sunday, the sixth day in the Amalapakṣa, in the month of Mārgaśīrṣa, when the moon is in the Śakatāra *nakṣatra* (18.6). On this day the gods with their wives and sons, the munis with their families, the *nāgas* with their *nāginīs*, the serpents, the *siddhas* with their beautiful women, *gandharvas, kinnaras, yakṣas*, and celestial harlots beginning with Menakā—all come for the *jatrā*. It was on this day that the demons were defeated. Thus whoever performs the *jatrā* on this day will have the fruit of one *yajña* for each step. One gains heaven in good shape (21.61-63). Though in some places *jatrās* are held on this day, it seems to me that the festival is *mainly* observed by the Deśastha Brahmans and is confined to celebrations within the family. A *ghaṭasthāpana* takes place and a *jāgraṇ* is performed. A Brahman would never participate in a *jatrā* where the differences between social groups are at least temporarily abolished and where the "impure" is a source of auspiciousness and a higher value than purity. As the *Arthaśāstra* stated earlier:

> *pravaṇeṣu caiṣāṃ brāhmaṇā nākāmāḥ kuryuḥ /*
> *aṃśaṃ ca labheran*
>
> (3.10.44)

> The Brahman should watch the village festivals
> at the most from the outside.

V

The bhakti of the saints has many roots in folk religion. The saints do not ignore or discard it and each of them has a slightly different approach worthy of separate study. Much of their imagery can be understood better if one sees it as a reflection of folk religion on the bhakti level. For Tukārām the rituals and implements in the Khaṇḍobā cult became metaphors for the "inner religion." One of Tukārām's *abhaṅgas* reflects the typical situation of a *jatrā* after the harvest season on a bhakti level. People are clad in their finest clothes and are in a joyous mood. The better the crop the bigger the crowd. All become one with god in a seemingly chaotic festival of ritual processions around the temple marked by dancing and resounding drums. It is appropriately called *mārāmārī* in the Mhaskobā cult, which literally means "mutual fighting or beating." This reminds us again of the objection to the violent and antagonistic aspects of folk rituals. But the term has also the connotation of "exceeding plentifulness." The festival nearly visually enacts a kind of rebirth or renewal of life of the devotees and also the god out of an orgy of red colour. In the case of Tukārām the god is Viṭhobā and the *jatrā* would reverberate as follows according to the somewhat free translation of Arun Kolatkar:

Tuka 9

Harvest done
Good times ahead.
Now's time our own
To lose in love.

From everything
Is freedom.
Fatigue is not
Anymore.

How singularly Pandurang
Are all things!
The world belongs
To no one in particular.

We are all about
Bejeweled, bespangled
Each one of us sparkles
Like a jewel on the other.

We serve, says Tuka,
The great all-timer
And none else if any
There be besides.

Rāmdās has sympathy with folk deities like Khaṇḍobā and does not reject their worship by the people. He identifed Khaṇḍobā with Rām. At the same he has his reservations about *jatrās* and, according to oral traditions, he discouraged the violent sacrifices at Jejuri. About the Rāmnavamī *utsava* he says:

Dāsa doṅgarī rāhato
yātrā devācī pāhato

Deva bhaktāṃsaveṃ jāto
miḷoniyā.

Rāmdās stays on the hill.
He watches the God's yātrā.
God goes and joins in
with the bhaktas.

His description of the *jatrā* at Jejuri is famous, but it could also have been Pāli in Satara District. He shows the many splendours of the *jatrā,* as well as mankind and even animals joining in the celebration with Khaṇḍobā.

> I saw the God Khaṇḍerāv / All the pilgrims gathered / How can I tell of the manifold splendour? / Crowds of people, the mass of horsemen / Throngs of pilgrims, bands of musical instruments //1//
>
> Huge drums, kettle-drums, cymbals, tabors / The *burugas* [and] the tabors merging into a tumultous noise / The horns and the cymbals join the symphony //2//
>
> Elephants trumpet, camels grunt / Horses neigh, bullocks bellow loudly / The name [of God] //3//
>
> One does not know who is where / in the *jatrā* / One gets lost in surprise //4//
>
> In front there is a dense crowd, behind there is a dense crowd / On both sides are the shops huddled together / Up in the sky are clusters of parasols //5//
>
> Standards bearing the sign of the Bull, all kinds of flags / The huge banner poles / Parasols and fly-whisks, ornamented standards //6//

I saw the God diffusing a fragrance / Shining with glory / I saw those holy grounds, soft and pure //7//

All kinds of flowers, garlands of flowers / All kinds of jewels, garlands of jewels / The Three are the very substance of beauty //8//

Fierce and horrid [are] Vetāḷ and Khaṅkāḷ, / the watchmen on both sides [of the gate] / Both are seated on horses [and] watch motionless //9//

Who has counted the dancing girls owning the glory of the art [of dancing], who came / Glittering and started dancing under the various festive canopies? //10//

The glories [of the God] are sung to the accompaniment of tambourines / There was stickfighting of different kinds / When a group was formed / The competition started //11//

If one went to the bazaar there was wonder / what to buy and not to buy / There is no limit to the blessed glory of the God //12//

On one side there was the silent heath / Where the simple and innocent should go / One should go to the God['s temple] at a quiet time //13//

In the night the time was quiet / In many a place music sounded / One felt as if Kokilās were singing //14//

Rāmdās says: with the strength of discrimination / One should be in the midst of all and yet remain aloof / That is the highest happiness //15//

But from where should the true bhakta watch the *jatrā?*

> Yekekaḍe nivāṃta māḷī
> tetheṃ jāveṃ teṃ balīṃ bholīṃ
> Dāsa mhaṇe vivekabaḷā
> sakalāṃmadhye parī nirāleṃ
> teṃcī sukha sarvāṃ-āpaḷeṃ
>
> On one side there was the silent heath
> Where the simple and innocent should go.
> Rāmdās says: with the strength of
> discrimination
> One should be in the midst of all
> and yet remain aloof.
> That is the highest happiness.

VI

In the *Jñānoday* there are many typical examples of Christian disapproval of folk religion and of the *jatrā* and its elements. Naturally the criticism singles out the more obvious and extreme examples. I have to confine myself to two. The journal notes on the 15th March 1845:

> A Christian writes in a letter that near Ghodnadī in the village of Nimuṇe a certain person gets possessed by Khaṇḍobā's wind *(vāreṃ)* and then pulls twelve to thirteen bullock carts. In front of the god he kills sheep. He jumps like an animal. Near the *pādukās* of Khaṇḍobā he pierces his back with a hook and to the hook he fixes the rope and ties it to the car. The surrounding people help him pull the car. Moreover there is a steep slope so that one can pull the cars with little strength. If the car stops then the mother

> of the *bhakta* curses the gods: "Khaṇḍyā, you have become one who has no child!" In sum there is a lot of clever scheming in it. It is necessary to put an end to the ignorance of people.

The *jatrā* is always a spectacle and it would not be complete without a number of wonders and miracles to be talked about. The fact that the miracle looks sometimes rather stylized would not bother the participants, for whom the *jatrā* means participation in a play which is inspired by the deity. The fact that the bhakta's mother reviles the god not only shows the intimacy with god but is nothing unexpected for the historian of religion who knows the meaning of ritual reviling. The humanization and banalization of the god is a phenomenon which devotees in folk religion would prefer to the distant, supramundane, but aloof and otiose god. Humanization means that there is also humour involved in the worship of the god. But let us first cite the *Jñānoday* of 9th December 1850:

> If Khaṇḍobā becomes angry, he affects people with cough, fever, stomach ache and similar troubles. If there is some mistake in the worship, in the fulfilment of the *kuladharma* or in the gondhaḷ, then all kinds of distress start. If someone has not fulfilled his *navas*, then he is angry. In sum, this god troubles even an intimate *bhakta!*
> One person made the *navas* to present god a golden vest: *sonyāce aṅgaḍa*. Later, when god fufilled his wish for a child, he gave the boy the name Sonyā and presented the god with the boy's vest. Such clever *bhaktas* are there, too!

The involvement of the god in the life of the humans makes him human himself. The intimate relationship is reflected in a version of the story of Sonyā told by a Dhangar:

> A woman did not have a child. "What to do now?" she said. "To which god should I go and make a *navas* so that I can have a child?" She remembered: "There is Khaṇḍobā, who is so close to many people. Even to thieves he is close. I shall go to Khaṇḍobā." She went to the god and made the following *navas:* "If I get a child, I shall give you a *sonyācā ghoncā* (a golden cap). When she mentioned a golden cap, the interest of the god was aroused. After all a golden cap meant a lot of gold. And thus he accepted *(pāvlā)* the request and she got the child.
> One year passed, another year passed—and what did she do finally? She called her son "Golden" and went to Khaṇḍobā to pay off the debt. She put Golden's cap on his head. Khaṇḍobā enquired: "Didn't you want to give a golden cap?" "I have given you a golden cap haven't I?" "But it is not golden." "But it is the cap of Golden, of my son." The woman had tricked him. She had called her son Golden and put the cap of "Golden" on Khaṇḍobā's head. Now can we say that the woman has really tricked the god or hasn't she? End of the story.

VII

Thus, I wanted to suggest that the *jatrā* is an important topic of folk religion and a part of Maharashtrian religious traditions. The *jatrā* for a god "here and now" who is *"jāgṛt"* fulfils an important function in satisfying basic religious needs. The worship of the folk deity is not just practical but an instinctive realignment with the powers of nature. It expresses the desire to humanize god. Once we have identified the *jatrā* and folk religion as a separate topic it is worthwhile to study its interaction with other religious currents of Maharashtra. These express the constant tension between, on the one hand, the god and worshippers being involved in the ways of the world by collective worship, and, on the other hand, the abstraction of the individual from the world to another, other-worldly sphere of individual worship and salvation.

REFERENCES

Blackburn, Stuart H. and Ramanujan, A. K. 1986.	*Another harmony. New essays on the folklore of India.* Berkeley and Los Angeles: University of California Press.
Government of India. 1969.	*Census of India. 1961. Volume X. Maharashtra. Part VII-B. Fairs and festivals in Maharashtra.* Bombay.
Jñānodaya. 1845.	Puṇeṃ (journal).
König, Ditte. 1984.	*Das Tor zur Unterwelt: Mythologie und Kult des Termitenhügels in der schriftlichen und mündlichen Tradition Indiens.* Stuttgart: Franz Steiner Verlag.

P. B. Mande

FOLK CULTURE, FOLK RELIGION AND ORAL TRADITION IN MAHARASHTRIAN CULTURE

This paper makes an attempt to show that the oral tradition of Maharashtra is not just the remnant of the past but is a continuous process of creation, acceptance and rejection of many genres. Thriving in a living society, Maharashtrian culture has been enriched through centuries by the rich diversity of folk elements permeating it. Oral tradition has added strength and vitality to it. Maharashtrian culture reveals a commingling of vital folk elements, which are not only alive today but are still becoming stronger. Oral tradition breathes the intense life of the people.

The social, religious, and cultural life of Maharashtra lies embedded in its folksongs. These are varied and colourful. They are simple, charming and full of sincerity of emotion and purity of feeling.[1] Folksongs are connected with the current customary practices, ways of behaviour, rites and beliefs among the people. The main object of this paper is not to study various forms of oral literature prevalent in the area but to underline its significance in folk culture. The author has made an analysis of the features of folk culture in his book entitled *Some aspects of folk-culture.* The following is a summary of the conclusions arrived at in that book.

---

[1] The "Maharashtra Lokasahitya Samiti" has published a number of collections of folksongs in Marathi edited by Dr. Sarojini Babar, the Chairman of the Samiti.

While studying the beliefs, customs and practices, I have observed that, by and large, people in Maharashtra believe in the existence of some supernatural and invisible power. This concept of a supernatural cosmic power dominates popular practices in the area. It is believed that this power is manifested in various forms. It can be acquired, used and also transferred. It is a power which acts both for good and for evil. If one studies minutely it can be noticed that underneath all the magical practices and religious rituals prevalent in the area there is an attempt to get control of this power. People want to use it for their own benefit and try to accumulate a fund of it as a potential source of all forms of blessings.

In the villages of Maharashtra, if a family member falls sick, instead of consulting a physician immediately, it is customary to make the diagnosis of the disease at home. The method used to make such a diagnosis is the oracular method *(śakun pāhaṇeṃ)*. With the help of the divine prophecy, the category of the disease is ascertained. The order of these categories is as follows:

1. The displeasure and wrath of some deity.
2. Possession by some evil spirit.
3. Some bodily disease.

If the oracular method gives a verdict that the disease is caused by the anger of some deity, a family member, in order to appease the deity, utters a vow *(navas)*. Such a kind of cure-treatment is still popular in the villages of Maharashtra. It is difficult to find a family in Maharashtra which has never engaged in the practice of binding itself by a vow in order to appease some deity, and of fulfilling that vow by giving necessary offerings to the deity. This tendency to appease a deity instead of giving proper treatment to a patient is very dominant in rural areas in Maharashtra.

It is believed that some deities are closely related to some particular diseases. The deity Bhairava is associated with the cure-treatment of snake-bites. If a person is bitten by a snake, he is immediately carried to a temple of the deity Bhairava or Bhairobā. This custom is prevalent in the area of Marathwada and Vidarbha. To cure snake-bites, *nāg-mantriks* are invited. They sing *baryācī bhajane* and also utter certain mantras. A person bitten by a snake gets possessed by the snake. In course of time he gets free from the poison.

Various methods of ascertaining prophecies *(śakun)* prevail in Maharashtra; people have faith in magico-religious treatments. Prophetic methods are used not only for curing diseases but also for fulfilling personal desires. There are numerous examples of uttering a vow *(navas)*, such as offering the first son to the deity or binding oneself to pay regular visits to the temple of the deity. It is observed that deities like Hanumān, Vetāḷ, Śani, Muñja, Mhasobā etc. are associated with cure-treatments using chants and spells.

Possession by evil spirits is considered one of the prominent causes of disease. There are many expiatory methods to cure the diseases caused by possession by evil spirits, such as tying sacred threads and amulets *(gaṇḍā-dorā)*, chanting sacred words *(mantras)* etc.

If we take into account the nature of folk medicine in Maharashtra, it becomes apparent that the cure-treatments employed are a mixture of superstitions, magico-religious rituals and the use of medicinal herbs. These three types of cure-treatments have intermingled with each other to such an extent that it is almost impossible to draw a line of demarcation between them.

In Maharashtra various customary practices for getting rain and stopping it are in vogue. Some mystical rites are also performed to increase the production of grain and pulses and to ward off attacks on the vegetative kingdom. Many of the details regarding these occult and mystical practices bear testimony to the continuity of the tradition revolving around fertility myths.

Religious and social rites found in Maharashtra can be classified under three categories. The first category includes rites in which people of all castes in the town or village can take part collectively. In the second category the performance of the rite is restricted to the people of a particular caste. The third category is restricted to rites which are to be performed by individuals only.

In its origin, if all these varied rites signify the struggle of human beings to make human life comfortable and happy, the main object of these rites is to weed out all evil influences and to gain a divine power that will ward off all evils and enable human beings to lead a life free of obstacles. The idea is to get a kind of protection for human life and for the whole region. For this the help of an unseen power is sought through the performance of these rites. Since in course of time the help of this unknown power weakens, these rites are performed at regular intervals. They are performed on some particular days every year. There is a belief that the non-performance of the rites brings some calamity on the village community. The rites which are to be performed by the people in the village collectively include such rites as can be performed when a calamity is felt to threaten the whole village. These calamities that befall the people are divine or human in their origin. It is presumed that the *kṣetra devatās* take care of the village and protect it.

There are certain ceremonies to propitiate the village deities. The village is supposed to be a complete unit in itself. This living, organic unit consists of two parts, *i.e., kāḷī* and *pāṇḍhrī* (the land and the people who are dependent on it.) The village is protected from external evil influences. For securing protection of the village a continuous stream of some mixed substance is poured around it. The procession of the cart of Marī-Āī is held in the month of Āṣāḍh. *Potrāj,* a devotee of Lakṣmī-Āī, pulls the cart up to the outskirts of the village. After the devotee returns from the outskirts a scapegoat is sacrificed and the devotee dips his palm in the blood of the scapegoat.

In some villages a fair of twelve carts is observed every year. The days fixed for these fairs differ from village to village. The devotees of different deities hold the fair. These fairs of twelve carts are held in the name of Lakṣmī-Āī, Khaṇḍobā and Mārutī. The devotee has to observe a complete fast for seven or three days before going to draw the twelve carts full of children. He has to abide by certain rules like observing celibacy, not mixing with other people etc. The devotee is worshipped. The devotee, charged with divine power, makes his body throb. The devotee ties the row of carts around his waist and amidst cries of victory to the goddess Lakṣmī-Āī he pulls all the carts over a distance of nearly a kilometer. In some villages on the very day of this ceremony the ritual drama of *pañcamī*, in which the village folk experience the visit of the deity, is performed. In Nasik District this folk drama is named *bohāḍā*.

After studying some ceremonies and rituals prevalent in some areas of Maharashtra such as the fair of Marī-Āī, the cart of Marī-Āī, the fair of twelve carts, the battle of stones, and purification practices in the Konkan, we find that among all these ceremonies the following four traits are discerned:

1. All these religious performances are carried out to seek protection for the village.
2. The custom of offering a victim is observed in actuality or in a symbolic fashion.
3. The village is supposed to be an organic unit.
4. People of different strata take part in the ceremony.

If we study a variety of customary practices we find one common idea behind these performances. All these practices have power to remove all dangers and evils from the village. It is believed that this divine power weakens in the course of time because of the sins and trivial wrongdoings *(pāp)* of the people in their everyday life. So the object of customary practices is to bring about purification of all the people by cleansing them of their sins. To purify the entire village from the sins, the blame of incurring sins is attributed to some person or to some animal at some kind of religious ceremony. The animal is sacrificed and thereby all sins are washed away. Such rites are still in vogue in almost every part of Maharashtra.

There are some rites in which people of only one particular caste take part while others offer their cooperation and watch merely as spectators. Sometimes people of more than one caste take part in such rites but the participation is limited to that particular group of people. The celebration of *huīk* among the shepherds, or *baḍhaṇ* among the depressed classes and the rite of *bhaḍvā* are the chief examples of such rites. These rites have great importance in the life of the people in the village and it is generally believed that the life of the people will not go on smoothly if these rites are not performed. These rites are essential to the protection and growth of the society and it is generally believed that if they are observed rightly, some kind of power is generated which keeps people happy during the rest of the year.

In Maharashtra a ritual called *huīk* is observed by people every year in many places. During the celebration of *huīk* the whole future is foretold to the people through a devotee. In the villages Savkhed, Kharadi, Valuj, and Chincholi of Aurangabad District *huīks* are held on the day after *Vijayādaśamī;* in the villages Chakalamba, Nandur, and Devi-Paithan in Beed District, *huīks* are held in the month of Caitra.

Performances of the *huīk* rite have the following features:

1. The rite is performed every year on a particular day.
2. During the *huīk* performance the god pulsates with abnormal force in the body of the devotee and also in the bodies of other votaries.
3. The god predicts future events.

4. At last thc gods are immersed, i.e., set at rest.
5. At the very commencement of the function, the devotee has to put on a wreath of knowledge *(genmāḷ)* and only then does the god pulsate in his body.
6. The devotee has to observe certain rules; if they are not observed rightly, his special power weakens.
7. Some songs are sung to invoke the god.

In the villages of Aurangabad District there are some more rites which have the traits of the *huīk*. Among the Mang community there is an important rite called *baḍhaṇ*. Before their conversion to Buddhism, Mahars also used to perform this ritual. The rite of *baḍhaṇ* is performed in almost all parts of Maharashtra, but in some places the details differ. The devotees of Lakṣmī-Āī and Marī-Āī from among the Scheduled Caste communities are called *potrāj*, or in some places *bhutyās*. Some people dedicate their first son to the goddess, by way of return of their fulfilled wish. A son who has been dedicated in this way becomes a *potrāj*. Every *potrāj* has to receive certain mantras from his preceptor before becoming a real devotee. Then the goddess Lakṣmī-Āī or Bhavānī begins to pulsate with abnormal force in his body. Then the same person performs some abnormal feats like eating bitter *nimb* leaves, placing a burning piece of camphor on his palm and then eating it, swallowing vermilion powder, bearing onslaughts of uncovered swords, twisting his body with a bee-like humming noise with closed lips, making circular movements of his bent head with his hands on his waist, or making strange movements of his body and peculiar screams. All these are supposed to be signs of the supernatural force in the body of the devotee. This is true of the devotees of other gods also. These devotees are dedicated to gods. The boy dedicated to the god is in a way a symbolic victim given to the god. Such a victim is supposed to be reborn with divine power in the form of a devotee. Special rites like *baḍhaṇ* are celebrated on such an occasion.

At the origin of these varied rites is the struggle of human beings to make human life comfortable and happy. The idea is to get a kind of protection for human life and for the whole region. For this the help of supernatural power is sought through the performance of these rites. By examining the corpus of beliefs, customs and rituals prevalent in Maharashtra, one may arrive at a theoretical formulation that underlies all these rites: the struggles of human beings to make life comfortable by creating the direct accessibility of live *(jāgṛt)* deities.

Though the conservatism of Maharashtra still tries to preserve these traditions, it has its own limitations. Class consciousness and the force of communal sentiment are fast disappearing in the face of the disruptive forces of modernity. Because of social change, the impact of technological development and improved agricultural practices, the rituals pertaining to agriculture in particular are changing fast. Of all the areas of culture, folklore has been tremendously affected by technogical factors. In the present century, it has undergone a remarkable transformation since independence. Changes were, at first, slow, imperceptible and less pervasive, but during the last three to four decades they have been rapid. Traditional norms and beliefs remain strong obstacles in the way of adopting innovations.

Maharashtra is a repository of folk arts. Such arts have thrived for ages among the rural people. During festive occasions folk arts are performed with gaiety in most of the villages. The arts serve to give expression to people's talents in different artistic forms. But seldom is there the feeling of an auditorium in them.

All three of the forms of dancing—i.e., *nāṭya, nṛtya,* and *nṛtta*—are blended in folk dance in Maharashtra. It is not just aimless whirling, but each folk dance has a definite motive behind it. It may be for the propitiation of gods or for warding off evils. This can very well be identified in the traditional performing arts. Performing arts in Maharashtra have a long tradition and a rich heritage. The variety of these art forms is greater in Maharashtra than in other regions of India.

In the present paper we propose to discuss only certain aspects of dramatic performances.[2] Traditional performances which have dramatic elements can be classified as follows:

1. Performance by an entire village, e.g., *pañcamī, ākhāḍī, bohāḍā* etc. It is supposed that the deity visits the village in the form of *suaṅge* or *svārī*. Adivasis of Maharashtra also experience the visit of their deity every year. They celebrate it by performing *dandar*, a ritual drama.
2. Performances of ritual dramas, namely, *gondhaḷ, jāgaraṇ, bharāḍ* etc., by devotees of different deities. They sing songs to invoke the deities and also perform *līlās*.
3. Performances like *kīrtan, soṅgī bhajan, bhārūḍ, lalit* etc.
4. Performances of '*māgtes*', *i.e., rāyrāṇḍ, dakkalvār, citrakathīs, vāsudev, jogatīs, potrāj* etc.

Every form has its own traditional characteristics which distinguish it from others. It is worth noting that performances by devotees or *bhagats* have their own identifying features. These common patterns are typical of Maharashtra. The ritual is of theatrical performance even when the theme may not be religious. Certain assumptions are also present in folk theatre. For instance, notions of possession are never far from the mind of the audience. The performance is accepted as a true experience. Rituals akin to ritual dra-

---

[2] This part of the present paper is based on an analysis of the performances prevalent in Aurangabad District of Maharashtra State as observed by the author. However, all over Maharashtra such performances appear to be essentially similar.

mas are performed in many places in Maharashtra. Such rituals are called *ākhāḍī* or *pañcamī*. At certain places, they are also called *caitī* or *bohāḍā*. It is presumed that the deity visits the village at a particular moment. When the village folk experience the descent of the deity amidst them, they go into a trance.

It may also be noted that people presume that, during the festival related to a deity, the deity visits the home and offers blessings to the family members. The period of such a visit is celebrated. *Ghatasthāpanās* of Khaṇḍobā, Devī, Narasimha and other such deities are examples of such celebrations.

The *pañcamī* festival of Marathwada is similar in many respects to the festival *bohāḍā* celebrated in the Konkan. In Marathwada the day on which the presiding deity is supposed to visit the village is called *bohāḍā*. It is also called the *jatrā* of the deity. People gather from distant places to see the performance and to take *darśan*. They are thrilled with joy when they see the actors who have assumed the role of the deities on the stage. Though it is just a *suaṅg* the people feel that the deities have themselves appeared before them.

This festival is never celebrated just for the sake of entertainment. It is treated as a religious rite and is an annual feature of the social life of a village. The people believe that the village would face many difficulties, such as scanty rains, if they failed to celebrate this festival. After the celebration of the festival, village life seems to be spurred with joy and enthusiasm.

As regards the celebration of *pañcamī* there is one more aspect to be noted: the actors who present the deities on the stage behave as though they are possessed by the deities. The spectators, too, believe that they are not seeing the assumed roles but the deities personified. This naturally results in the utterance of vows *(navas)* in the name of the deities.

No stage is built especially for the performance of this ritual drama. An open enclosure about twenty feet in breadth is enough for this purpose. The corridor, which becomes a part of the performing area, is necessary for the entrance and exit of the artists. The dances are started and continued with the entrance of the artists at the farthest end of the corridor. The corridor should be twenty to seventy-five feet in length and five feet in breadth. The *yavanikā* is used at the time of the actor's entrance into the corridor.

The audience sits on the bare ground which encircles the enclosure. The performance continues for the whole night. The last item is the visit of the presiding deity.

At the beginning of the performance, the musicians appear and display their talent for a considerable time. After this preliminary is over, three or four vocalists appear on the enclosure with folded palms and sing a brief invocation to Gaṇeśa, who is traditionally offered worship before any auspicious work is undertaken. Immediately the character of Gaṇeśa appears at the farthest end of the corridor. He comes dancing with an attractive mask of Gaṇeśa and, with two additional hands made of wood and adjusted from his back, he offers his blessings. Sarasvatī follows Gaṇeśa. A *vidūsaka* plays mischief in various ways while the *sūtradhāra* and other vocalists try to invoke Gaṇeśa and Sarasvatī and ask for blessings to ensure success in performing the ritual drama.

These ritual dramas are a pleasant confluence of religious rites and entertainment programmes. Apart from the *suaṅg* of the presiding deity, many other *suaṅgs* are also presented. The nature and number of these *suaṅgs* vary from place to place. Who should perform which *suaṅg* is generally decided by tradition. The dialogues and songs are unwritten and are orally transmitted. Though an element of improvisation is present, the traditional form is kept intact.

There are many superstitions prevalent regarding the actors who play the roles of the deities. Miracles are also attributed to them. The following are some of the beliefs and practices that prevail amongst the village folk:

1. The person who performs the role of the deity is possessed by the deity.
2. Such roles are performed exclusively by male actors. Women who are menstruating must not even cast their shadows upon the actors. If this happens, the deity gets enraged and does not move further.
3. Such a deity fulfills a vow taken in its name.
4. The actor playing the role of a deity experiences tremendous physical power. Not even ten or fifteen persons can control him.
5. Any obstacles in the way of the procession automatically get removed.
6. At the time of the procession, there is a huge crowd. No one gets hurt and no fatal accident takes place.
7. The actors wear genuine ornaments. If by chance, any ornament falls down, the deity stops and does not move further. These ornaments are never stolen.
8. Only bachelors can present the role of Devī. The bachelor-actor gets married within a year.
9. The actor falls unconscious immediately after the performance is over. It takes him three to four hours to regain consciousness.
10. All the people in the village are involved. They do not remain mere spectators but also participate in the ritual drama.

In every village the masks are kept in onc particular temple. When the *pañcamī* festival approaches, these masks of Gaṇapati, Devī, Mārutī, Narasiṃha and other deities are repaired and repainted with coloured powder and red lead. Similarly, the vehicles of the deities, such as the peacock of Sarasvatī, the bull of Śaṅkar, the horse of Khaṇḍerāyā, and the eagle of Viṣṇu are also repaired and decorated with coloured papers. For the necessary make-up, materials such as turmeric powder, *kuṅkūṃ*, red lead, coal, *gulāl* and *hiṅgūḷ* are used. *Rākṣasas* are decorated with coal, white powder etc. Black strips are painted on the faces of bufoons to make them appear ferocious. They are generally asked to wear black trousers, and leaves of the *nimb* tree are fixed around their waists. Little jingling bells are also tied to their ankles and waist. These bufoons jump awkwardly all the time here and there to create laughter. The decoration of the *vāghe, muraḷī, kañjāriṇ, pardeśī, brāhmaṇ* etc. is done in a manner suitable to the character. When the decoration of a character is over, a lemon is sacrificed in the name of that deity. There are tribes called Goṇḍ, Kolam and Andha in Maharashtra who also perform some such ritual drama. They experience the visit of the god Persapen to their *pod* or village. Every year in the month of Āśvin they perform a ritual drama called *dandar*. Bhils and Bañjāras also have such a ritual.

Our present age is a time of rapid cultural change. The whole way of life of the village folk and the tribals is in constant flux. This change is influenced by many forces, both internal and external. The world-view is changing, and as a result, traditional folk religion and culture are being influenced. But still the pattern of the ritual drama is retained. Yearly recurrent descent of the deities *(devatā-avataraṇ)* is experienced by the people. This ritual still has functional importance in Maharashtra.

Because of the rigid structure of village society and the traditional concept of caste-occupation, those who do not have any traditional caste profession could not be accomodated in the *gāvgāḍā* (village life).[3] The communities of the devotees of different deities prevalent in Maharashtra could not live a settled life. The descendants of such people formed separate castes which were kept outside the *gāvgāḍā*. They could not become one with the mainstream society. These devotees or *bhagats* earn their livelihood by performing rituals for and on behalf of patrons *(yajmāns)*. The performance of these rituals is of a dramatic nature. So it can be called ritual drama. There are many castes of such devotees. We can call these communities *māgate*. There are many castes of *māgate* in Maharashtra. All the *māgates* perform their respective traditional art forms. These performing art forms have their own functional importance in the society. Ritualistic in nature, they play a significant role in the cultural and religious life of the society. They form an important component of the life style through which the people's worldview is expressed.

gondhaḷīs, vāghes and *bharāḍīs* perform the ritual dramas of *gondhaḷ, jāgaraṇ* and *bharāḍ* respectively. The folk songs of the *gondhaḷīs, vāghes* and *bharāḍīs,* which they sing to invoke the deities, are repetitive, insistent, flattering and persuasive. The range of tone is often narrow and restricted to intervals. The voice production is high in the head, plangent and penetrating. Sometimes it is low, rumbling or growling, but it is seldom meek or gentle. The deity is addressed in an impressive manner. There are specific modes of singing with rhythm and specific instruments. *Jāgaraṇ* denotes the awakening of the supernatural powers in order to get blessings or protection and prosperity. The performers of traditional ritual dramas are the custodians of *jāgaraṇ*.

All of these ritual performers have developed the ritual drama in their own way and have a separate identity regarding their costumes, symbols, instruments, ways of singing, dancing and enacting

---

[3] For a detailed discussion refer to the author's book *Gāvgāḍyābāher* (Mande 1982).

the episodes etc. But the basic pattern of these ritual dramas is the same.

These *bhagat-māgtes* who lead the life of nomadic castes and have no productive traditional occupation fulfill priestly duties toward their respective deities. They have become professional singers and performers and earn their livelihood by way of charity they get from the people. Being outsiders to the rural folk, they perform the ritual dramas for them and before them. Hence they have the sense of auditorium. Because the devotees get their livelihood out of these rituals they try to make them entertaining. Ritualistic features diminish as and when a performer tries to make the performance more interesting.

$$\text{Ritual in performance} = \frac{1}{\text{Entertainment in performance.}}$$

The purposeful utilization of the performing folk arts is not new to Maharashtra. In the medieval period, the saints of the Bhāgvat sect adapted the traditional ritualistic and other folk performances and evolved a new form, namely, *bhārūḍ*. Sant Eknāth is known as an exponent of this new form. Traditional performances like *kīrtan*, *bhārūḍ* and *tamāśā* have proved to be successful means of conveying messages effectively. In this context it is interesting to trace the story of the performing art form *tamāśā*, which has evolved from traditional dramatic performances like *gondhaḷ*, *jāgaraṇ* and *bhārūḍ*. These traditional dramatic performances are ritualistic in nature. In the later Peshwa period Śāhīrs successfully amalgamated the characteristics of these forms and evolved *tamāśā*, of which the sole purpose is entertainment. It was delinked from the rituals but the basic pattern was retained. *Gaṇa*, *gavaḷaṇ*, *batāvaṇī*, *vaga* and *mujarā* are the important components of *tamāśā* which have been incorporated from traditional ritualistic art forms. The pattern of *pūrva-raṅg* and *uttar-raṅg* which we come across in the *kīrtan* has also been brought into *tamāśā*, but the basic concepts of *bhakti* and of performing rituals to the deities have been eliminated.

The process of detaching *tamāśā* from ritual is more interesting. The *gaṇa and gavaḷaṇ* of *gondhaḷ* and *jāgaraṇ* are retained. The *muraḷī* is replaced by a dancing girl *(nācī)*. The pattern of dances has also been changed, with the addition of humour and satire. In musical instruments, *ḍaph* and *ḍholakī* are added to the *tuṇtuṇe* and *kadi*. The songs in *tamāśās* are usually full only of romance. In the process of detachment from ritual the *tamāśā* became full of entertainment. Although *tamāśā* owes a lot to the traditional ritualistic performing art forms, some new features have been added with a view to make it more entertaining. Śāhīr Anant Phandi, Paraśurām, Rām Jośī, Honājī, Prabhākar, Sagan Bhāu, Paṭṭhe Bāpurāv etc. have made substantial contributions to the structure and form of *tamāśā*.

In the opening days of English rule, social reformers including Mahātmā Jyotibā Phule and his followers fruitfully utilized the popularity of *tamāśā* and developed the *satyaśodhakī tamāśā* to convey their messages to the masses. It is here that the applied form of *tamāśā* begins. Later on the followers of Dr. B. R. Ambedkar evolved what is known as *"ambeḍkarī jalsā,"* the main purpose of which is to convey the message of reform.

Traditional folk performing art is an excellent medium to communicate ideas because of its *interpretability*, its *reportability* and its *repeatability*.[4]

In Maharashtra written works as well as modern mass media are surrounded by and embedded in oral traditions—not *vice versa* as in the developed countries. Contrasts like elite-folk and great-little are not identical with written - oral. The two traditions may come into play, whether in composition or in transmission or in both. The pattern can be stated schematically as follows:

---

[4] Ben-Amos/Goldstein 1975: 14.

O -------- W -------- O
W -------- O -------- W

There may be various cycles like the above.

There has always been a give and take between folk traditions and the classical tradition. Folk forms are influenced by the art created by individual artists. The classical tradition accepts folk elements to revitalize itself. Exponents of the classical tradition are attracted towards the simplicity and vitality which they see in traditional folk arts. Out of this give and take popular religion, popular song, and popular art forms are born.

People in Maharashtra represent different levels of cultural attainments, follow different habits in economy, possess different types of social organisation and also play vital roles with separate cultural identities. These groups in the society differ from one another in their socio-cultural make-up, thus forming a cultural complex. But if we examine the cultural contents minutely, the similarities surpass the dissimilarities in both structure and contents. The ritual patterns are similar. Nowadays this cultural complex is subject to many forces and changes. Many changes have been introduced by governmental as well as non-governmental agencies. At first the people would not relish the changes being brought about in the social structure and the economic system, as there are many hazards and loads which one has to bear. Traditions play an important role in relation to economic systems. Understanding the impact of traditions is extremely important for a changing society.

REFERENCES

Ben-Amos, Dan and Goldstein, Kenneth S. (eds.). 1975. *Folklore: Performance and communication*. The Hague-Paris: Mouton.

Mande, P. B. 1982. *Gāvgāḍyābāher*. Aurangabad: Parimal Prakashan.

M. N. Deshpande

SOME ASPECTS OF FOLK RELIGION IN THE KONKAN AND DESH REGIONS OF MAHARASHTRA

The formidable mountain ranges of the Sahyādris running from north to south divide Maharashtra into two main parts: The Desh, forming the table-land of the Deccan Plateau; and the Konkan, the verdant narrow coastal strip with streams rushing down at breakneck speed to meet the Arabian Sea amidst green rice fields, coconut and areca-nut groves. These two areas, inter-connected by many mountain passes, have facilitated, throughout their long history, the absorption and assimilation of varied socio-religious influences emanating either from the north and south or from distant lands through sea-borne or overland commercial and cultural contacts with traders and migrating communities.

The earliest perceptible remnants of folk religion in Maharashtra have necessarily to be observed in the early chalcolithic settlements and in the age-old mountain passes and caravan routes criss-crossing the length and breadth of Maharashtra.

Recent excavations at Daimabad, a chalcolithic site on the river Pravara in Ahmadnagar District, by the Archaeological Survey of India and at Inamgaon on the Bhima in Pune District, by the Deccan College Postgraduate and Research Institute, Pune, have provided important clues about the religious beliefs of the early farming communities which settled in the river valleys of Maharashtra in the second and first millennium B.C.

In fact, it will not be an exaggeration to say that the new evidence provided by the finds from numerous chalcolithic sites discovered (and in a few cases excavated) in the last three decades have extended the horizon of our knowledge in understanding the foundation of the cultural profile of Maharashtra. The worship of the mother goddess, of which specimens in terracotta and copper have been discovered at Daimabad, was widely prevalent. Two ithyphalluses of agate were discovered side by side at this place in Phase I, in circular pits of fire-altars. Dr. S. A. Sali (1976-1979) in his report on the Daimabad excavations, explains the importance of the discovery as follows:

> "It should be mentioned that nowhere else in the Indian sub-continent so naturalistic a representation of ithyphallus has been hitherto recorded in so early a period. Besides representing the earliest evidence of sculptural art in the Deccan, it also suggested that the 'Savaldans' were phallus worshippers." (p. 464)

These objects quite obviously symbolise the generative power in nature or the fecundating principle and throw light on the religious ideas of the users.

A sculptured head in basalt in the Malwa Phase of Daimabad, identified as Śiva by the excavator, is another interesting object. It was found hardly fifteen metres to the east of the religious complex, which was of the nature of an apsidal sacrificial temple with mud-walls enclosing a mud platform with offerings of pots and beads, charred animal bones and grains of wheat, barley, horse gram, beans etc. Besides this stone image were found at Daimabad, by the side of the potters' kiln I, potsherds of a thick, coarse variety bearing human figures in appliqué. In fact there are three such specimens, one each belonging to the Daimabad, the Malwa and the Jorwe cultures. The appliqué decorations are of a mother goddess (Jorwe culture) and of Śiva (?) holding an arrow in the right hand and a bow in the left.

It is not proposed to deal with this early evidence in greater detail, for my colleague Dr. M. K. Dhavalikar has already presented a paper on this subject. I, therefore, pass on to later evidence, starting with the early historical period.

The earliest historical monuments in the Deccan are the Buddhist caves excavated from c. 2nd century B.C. They contain representations of deities like *yakṣas, nāgas,* and mother goddesses whose worship was not only accepted but placed on a high pedestal so as to win over the local population, who were traditional worshippers of these old deities. The Buddhist text *Mahāmāyūrī* (c. 4th century A.D.) mentions three *yakṣas* from Maharashtra.

...Pratiṣṭāne ca khaṇḍakaḥ
Pītaṅgalyeṣu Saṅkārī
Tarangavatyām Sukhāvahaḥ
Nāsikye Sundaro Yakṣa
Asaṅgo Bharukacchake

"Khaṇḍaka (lives) at Pratiṣṭhāna,
Saṅkārī at Pītaṅgalya,
Sukhāvaha at Tarangavatī,
Sundara at Nāsikya,
Asaṅga at Bharukaccha."

Pratiṣṭhāna, with the *yakṣa* Khaṇḍaka, was the capital of the Sātavāhana dynasty. Pītaṅgalya is the ancient cave site of Pitalkhora near Ambaghat in Aurangabad District, where there were unearthed from the debris in front of the principal *caitya* cave two *yakṣa* images of which one bears an inscription (c. 2nd century

B.C.) and was provisionally identified as the *yakṣa* Saṅkārī (see Deshpande 1950: 67-69). This identification has been borne out by the discovery of Sātavāhana period pottery from Hankari, a place close to the Pitalkhora Cave site. Evidently this place is no other than the one named after Saṅkārī, the *yakṣa* mentioned in the *Mahāmāyūrī* text. It is also not unlikely that the door-keeper *yakṣa* at the *caitya* cave at Pandulena near Nasik may be the *yakṣa* Sundara, for it is in graceful human form, not conforming to the usual heavy, pot-bellied *yakṣa* type. The fact that it represents a *yakṣa* is borne out by the inscribed record above the entrance door specifically referring to it as a *yakṣa*. The other type of heavy-bodied *yakṣa* is also portrayed here as *bhāravāhaka yakṣa* in cave 3, in the act of supporting the *caitya-gṛha*. There is yet another *yakṣa* figure at the Kondane cave (District Kolaba) situated at the head of Borghat and of the same type as the Pitalkhora *yakṣa*. The inscription near it clearly states that it was the handiwork of the pupil of Kaṇha, who perhaps fashioned the Pitalkhora image of the *yakṣa* Saṅkārī. Sopara, the ancient port-town of Surparaka, has also an enormous image of a *yakṣa*. Though mutilated, it is a magnificent piece from c. 1st century A.D. It is now preserved in the National Museum, New Delhi. The Buddhist cave site near Karad (ancient Karahāṭaka) is Jakhinvadi, the place-name being derived from *yakṣa-vāṭikā*. The purpose of narrating all this is to emphasize that among the various *grāma-devatās* of the Desh and the Konkan there is a clear mention of *yakṣa* or *yakṣiṇī* as the *grāma-deva* or *grāma-devatā*. In the list compiled by the late N. G. Capekar in his Marathi work *Citpāvana*, the following *grāma-devatās* from south Ratnagiri District clearly relate to the worship of *yakṣiṇī* as the village deity: Jākhāī, Jākhamātā, Jākhādevī, Jākhubāī, Jāgedārī (p. 134)

Jākhamātā and other deities are also mentioned by the saint Rāmadās in *Dāsabodha (Daśaka* 4, *Samāsa* 5*)*, together with other gods and goddesses of the same class:

Jākhamātā Māyarāṇī bāḷā baguḷā mānaviṇī |
Pūjā māṅgiṇī jogiṇī kuḷadharme karāvī ||
4.5.16

In the same strain he mentions:

Dhātu paṣāṇa mṛttikāpūjana citralepa satpātrapūjana |
Āpale gṛhīce devatārcana yā nāva pāṃcavī bhaktī ||
4.5.5

Sīḷa saptāṅkita navāṅkita śāligrāma śakale cakrāṅkita
Liṅge Sūryakānta Somakānta bāṇa tāndaḷe narbade ||
4.5.6

Bhairava Bhagvatī Mallārī Muñjyā
Nṛsiṃha Banaśaṅkarī |
Nāga nāṇi nānāparī pañcāyetna pūjā ||
4.5.7

In *Daśaka* 3, *Samāsa* 2 of *Dāsabodha,* entitled *Saguṇa parīkṣā,* while describing the reaction of people when a child gets ill, Rāmadās enumerates the various evil spirits which may have possessed the child.

Lāgalī bhūte jālī jhaḍapaṇī |
jaḷīcyā Mesako Māyerāṇī |
Muñjyā Jhoṭiṅga karaṇī | Mhaisobācī ||
3.2.27

Vetāḷa Khaṅkāḷa lāgalā | Brahmagiro sancāralā |
neṇo Ceḍā volāṇḍilā | kāhī kaḷenā ||
3.2.28

Yeka mhaṇatī Bīradeva | Yeka mhaṇatī Khaṇḍerāva |
yeka mhaṇatī sakaḷa vāva | hā brāhmaṇa Samandha ||
3.2.29

yeka mhaṇatī koṇe kele | āṅgī daivata ghātale |
yeka mhaṇatī cukale | Saṭavāīce ||
3.2.30

Let us revert to the worship of the *yakṣa* once again.

It is observed that the location of the Buddhist cave sites is generally near mountain passes and on caravan routes *(sārthavāha-pathas)*. The *yakṣas* were worshipped in these caves by travellers and caravan leaders who sought their protection, a function which was later performed, during the period of Mahāyāna ascendency, by the Bodhisattva Avalokiteśvara. Before the Buddhist caves were carved out, the *yakṣa* was found in the form of a rock or stone and not in an anthropomorphic form like the *yakṣas* in Buddhist cave sites. There are many such rocks daubed with vermilion which are either nameless gods or called Devī, Śiva, Bhairava or Gaṇeśa, and are even today worshipped by travellers. Roofless shrines of such deities are usually located in mountainous *ghāt* areas. It is an everyday sight to see the driver of a modern conveyance and the travellers flinging coins as offerings to these wayside gods. The important Gaṇeśa shrines in Maharashtra are located on ancient routes and were very likely, at one time, seats of *yakṣa* worship. The Gaṇeśa at Madha (Kolaba District), for example, is at the head of Borghat and is a transformation of the *yakṣa* in the area, the anthropomorphic *yakṣa* in the Kondane cave being an intermediary stage of this protective god. The Gaṇeśa 'Dhuṇḍirāja' at Pali-Sudhagad (Kolaba District) must have been originally a *yakṣa* in the form of a huge rock. This was located on the ancient route starting from Chaul (the ancient port town of Semulya) and going to Māmala-deś through the Tel-bailyā and Savāśnicā *ghāt*. The two rock-cut tanks *(pāṇa-poḍhi)* on the outskirts of Pali, on the way to two Buddhist cave sites of Thanala and Karsamla, must have been the original *yakṣa sthāna* which in due course became an Ekvīs Gaṇapati *sthāna*.

This time honoured *yakṣa* worship predates the Buddhist *yakṣa* worship and, in fact, it was Buddhism which legitimized and elevated the tribal and pastoral gods of the neolithic pastoralists. This is best illustrated by the Khaṇḍaka *yakṣa* of Pratiṣṭhāna, the royal *kula-deva* of the Sātavāhanas, which came to be called Khaṇḍobā. The credit for this brilliant suggestion goes to Prof. D. D. Kosambi, who says in his work *Culture and civilization of ancient India in historical outline:*

> "Finally, the patron *yakṣa* of Paithan, known well before the 4th Century A.D. as Khandaka, became the local Śiva. His cult had spread all over Mahārāshtra under the original name Khandoba, with centre at Jejuri and a powerful following among all castes. The special ministrants, male and female, still manifest the frenzied primitive nature of the original worship."
>
> (Kosambi 1983: 191)

The *yakṣa* Khaṇḍaka is the new *avatāra* of a pastoral deity which later became the ubiquitous *kula-devatā* of all castes of Maharashtra as Khaṇḍobā with shrines all over, the principal ones being at Jejuri and Nimgaon (Pune District), Sheguda (Ahmadnagar District), Satara and Pali (Satara District), and at Mangsuli, Mailarling, Mailar-devaragudda, and Mailar in Karnatak; the god also has a shrine in almost every village and town in the region.

We now pass on to other goddesses worshipped at Buddhist cave centres. At Karle in the village limits of Vihāragrāma (Vehergaon, in Pune District) there is an Ekvīrā shrine right at the entrance to the principal *caitya* cave. Ekvīrā is worshipped by men and women of the Koḷī (fishermen and sailors) community living around Bombay and Thane. Curiously enough, when I visited the Buddhist caves at Chaul, I noticed within the cave complex a shrine for the worship of Hiṅgalāja-mātā. The shrine is located in one of the ancient cells, but the circumambulation path around it was specially carved out at a later date. The shrine has been renovated in the recent past by the Bhānusālī community of Bombay. I was told by a local devotee that this deity went from here to Karle and that the Ekvīrā deity of Karle is, in fact a form of Hiṅgalāja-mātā. At Karle there is a cleft in the rock near the *vihāra* cave, located a little distance away to the south; it has within it bubble-like zeolite formations which are worshipped as Śitalā-mātā. There is a water-tank *(pāṇa-poḍhi)* nearby and all the worshippers of Ekvīrā also propitiate Śitalā-mātā for protection against smallpox. At Bedsa there is a crude image of a goddess in the *vihāra* cave which is worshipped as Yamāī. Professor Kosambi records a legend which is current at Bedsa that the 'four brothers' who started the excavation of the Bedsa caves were scared away by the goddess to Bhaja and went thence to Karle, where they excavated the other retreats.

The Buddhist cave site at Thanala, on the Konkan side of the Karla-Bhaja area, was also a centre of mother goddess worship. These caves contain four representations of Gaja-Lakṣmī and were anciently known as *śrī-sthāna,* the *'siri-tana'* of the Vasathiputa Pulumavis' inscription, in cave 3 at Nasik.[1] The place-name Thānālā also indicates the place as a *thāṇa* or *sthāna* of the goddess. It appears that all such places which were once hallowed by the worship of the mother goddess or *yakṣa* were appropriated by the Buddhists for locating the caves, and the local gods were reinstalled under a new appellation and given an anthropomorphic form. The Mānmodī cave at Junnar, with standing Gaja-Lakṣmī on the *caitya* window, and the Pitalkhora cave with Gaja-Lakṣmī on the *vihāra* entrance, were also old centres of mother goddess worship. The *ghāt* nearby is known as 'Ambā', the mother. It is not unlikely that the Mānmodi cave was named after a mother goddess of that name who when propitiated cured children of tetanus. Their original character lingers in the *devī-sthāna* at Patan near Pitalkhora and Śivāī at

[1] See Mirashi 1981: part II, 49-55.

Shivneri fort.

Some of these places were also centres of *nāga* worship. The caves at Pitalkhora, Kondivate, Thanala, and Nasik bear *nāga* images near water tanks, on the façade or in the *vihāra* caves. There are numerous towns and villages in Maharashtra named after *nāgas:* Nagathane, Nagavadi etc. The *Nāgpañcamī* festival of Battis Shirale in Satara District is well known. In every village, on the *Nāgpañcamī* day, clay images made by the local potter are worshipped; curiously, the priest is the village barber. At least, such is the case in my village, Rahimatpur in Satara District. The cult of snake worship has permeated all major sects of India. Its emergence can be traced back to the Harappan period and it has persisted all through the centuries and is present in all parts of India.

Earlier there was a reference to the Hiṅgalāja-mātā shrine at Chaul and to the fact that this goddess is worshipped by men of the Bhānsālī or Bhāvasār (weaver) caste in Maharashtra. This deity is also worshipped by the Lambāḍīs, also called Lamāṇīs or Vañjāras, who are found living in *tāṇḍās* (cattle camps) in Gujarat, Maharashtra, Karnataka and Andhra Pradesh. They are also found in Madhya Pradesh and Rajasthan. It is very interesting to find how Hiṅgalāja-mātā came to be worshipped in Maharashtra and further south in Karnataka and Andhra Pradesh. The original home of Hiṅgalāja-mātā is in Baluchistan, below the peak of the same name on the bank of the Hingol river (25° 30° 0'N and 65° 31'E). A pilgrimage to this place is considered a must for the yogīs of the Nātha Saṃpradāya. The place is also sacred to the Muslims, who call her Bibi Nānī and consider her to be the same as Naina Devī of the Kulu Valley. It is believed that this mother goddess, in her original form, is Nanā or Nānaia, or Nanā-Shāo, a Sumerian mother goddess. It is very likely that the worship of this deity was introduced and popularised in Maharashtra by the Lambāḍīs (Vañjāras), among others, who worshipped her for protection in their hazardous travels, as they carried goods on pack-animals along transcontinental caravan routes. The worship of this deity may have begun in Maharashtra around the first or second century A.D. or perhaps earlier, when the Bhānsālī weavers specializing in dyeing and printing cloth possibly migrated from a distant region like Sindh-Baluchistan through Rajasthan and Gujarat and settled in the Deccan. No early images of this deity have been found and quite possibly the image was a nondescript vermilion-daubed stone which was later replaced by a crude form of a *devī*, perhaps Mahiṣāsuramardinī. The reason for the migration of these craftsmen (weavers) must have been the brisk trade in cotton textiles in the beginning of the Christian era from the Deccan to the Mediterranean world. The mallow-coloured cloth mentioned as an item of export in the 'Periplus' must have been dyed and printed by the people of this weaver caste. The Bhāvasārs mention Muṅgī-Paiṭhaṇ as their original home. It is not unlikely that the Sātavāhana royalty induced these craftsmen to settle in the neighbourhood of their capital. The Bhānsālīs trace their origin to a mythical king, Bhānusāla (Bhānu = Sun). They also claim to be Solankis of the solar race.

The chief god of the Vañjāras and the Bhānsālīs is Bālājī. Dr. Durga Bhagwat has told me that the nomadic tribe of Phāse Pāradhīs also worship this deity. Next to Bālājī the Vañjāras revere Hiṅgalāja-mātā, Tuljā Bhavānī, Ambābāī, and Mariammā. The Hiṅgalāja-mātā shrines attract both the Bhānsālīs and the Vañjāras. The brightly printed costumes of the Lambāḍīs may have been dyed by the Bhāvasār-Bhānsālīs. At traditional textile centres like Malegaon, Aurangabad, and Sholapur there are, even to this day, shrines dedicated to Hiṅgalāja-mātā. There is a place called Hiṅgalaja-wāḍī about seven kms. southeast of Ter, the ancient Sātavāhana emporium, and this may have been a suburb of Tagara where the Lambādis had a *tāṇḍā* and the Bhānsālīs had settled. Besides Hiṅgalaja-wāḍī, there are many places like Hingle (Parbhaṇī District) Hinglad (Thana District) Hingone (Jalgaon District) and Hiṅglāj-garh in Kolhapur District. There are probably other places also that are sacred to this *devī*, but a systematic search will have to be made for shrines dedicated to this deity at such places. In Madhya Pradesh, in Mandasore District, there is an early medieval temple town named Hiṅglāj-garh. From this place, hundreds of Śaiva and Śākta images have been collected. These are now housed in the Indore State Museum, and the curator in charge, Shri R. S. Garg, has published catalogues of these images. Among them there are many representations of Durgā Mahiṣāsuramardinī, which may have been the same as Hiṅgalāja-mātā. The only image bearing the *devanāgarī* inscription 'Hiṅgalaja' that has been brought to my notice is among the victory tower sculptures at Chittorgarh (Rajasthan) built by Rana Kumbha between A.D. 1442 and 1449.

At this point an explanation must be given for suggesting the identity of Hiṅgalāja-mātā with Mahiṣāsuramardinī. In her book *Yogini cult and temples* (1986: 116), Vidya Dehejia states: "Today every cell of Khajuraho's Yogini temple is empty and not one of the images has been traced. Our only data consists of photographs of three of the sixty-four Khajuraho Yoginis, taken in the year 1955. The first Yogini, labelled Hiṅglāja, is clearly Mahiṣāsuramardinī, the inscription providing us with a local name for this important, widely worshipped goddess". Dehejia describes the image, which is undoubtedly of Mahiṣāsuramardinī (see photo). The Yoginī temple at Khajuraho is dated to circa ninth century A.D. Dr B. N. Mukherjee, commenting on the association of Nanā with Durgā, states in his book *Nanā on the lion* (1969: 20): "Lion appears also in the majority of the Devī's images showing her as slaying the demon Mahisha. The association of lion with Durga in her demon slaying form may echo the concept of Ishtar (Nanā) as a war goddess". He further points out (p. 47): "It appears that in or by about the time of Kanishka III the fusion of different aspects of the concept of Nanā (and/or Anāhitā), Ambā, Tyche and perhaps also Artemis (and/or Aphrodite?) had taken place. Such intermingling of ideas pertaining to different deities worshipped by peoples geographically separated from one another could have been made possible through migration, conquests, colonisation, or trade and commerce". It will now be abundantly clear how Hiṅgalāja-mātā in the form of Mahiṣāsuramardinī travelled to the Deccan along with the nomadic Lambādis escorting caravans of traders.

The next part of this paper deals with aspects of folkreligion and worship as influenced by Tantric Vajrayāna and the Nātha Saṃpradāya at a place called Panhale Kaji, in Dapoli Taluka of Ratnagiri District, in the Konkan. Twenty-nine caves have been discovered here on the banks of the stream Kotjāī, near its confluence with another mountain stream named Dhāktī. Religious and architectural activity at this place began in the 3rd century A.D. when monks of the Hīnayāna order of Buddhism started their activities in the Konkan region. Later this place developed into a prolific centre of Tantric Vajrayāna ritual and worship, with Akṣobhya as the chief patron god. Still later, the place gained importance as a centre of the Gāṇapatya, Śaiva and Nātha Saṃpradāyas, with two caves specially devoted to the worship of Nātha teachers like Matsyendranātha, Gorakhnātha, Curaṅginātha etc. In fact, this place is unique, inasmuch as one of the caves contains sculptural representations of eighty-four Nātha *siddhas*, a feature not to be found elsewhere in India. Nāthism is intimately connected with the later Vārkarī movement in Maharashtra and, therefore, this discovery is of great significance. With such a long tradition, from the 3rd century A.D. to the 14th century, a study was undertaken by this writer of the religious traditions and rituals current among the people of the Konkan in general and Panhale in particular (see Deshpande 1986). For all the twelve *vāḍīs* into which Panhale is divided, there is a common place of worship, namely, the temple of Jholāī which is located on the top of a hill close to Durga-wadi to the south-east of the cave-group and not far away from the hill fort of Panhaledurga. In this temple the following deities are worshipped: Jholāī, Antarālā, Mānayā, Vāghjāī, Navasīrī and Koṭeśvarī. Of these, Jholāī is also called Pāndhardevī and is considered the principal one. All the other deities conform to the iconography of Mahiṣāsuramardinī except Navasīrī, who stands in the *samabhaṅga* posture and has nine heads, four on either side of the principal one. She has two hands and holds a sword in the right hand and a shield in the left. All the images, including that of Navasīrī, belong to c. A.D. 18th century. What is significant, however, is that Jholāī is placed on a large and old *adhisthāna* which can be dated to c. A.D. 10th century. The *adhisthāna* is a piece meant for the image of the Buddha in the *dharma-cakra-pravartana-mudrā,* as can be surmised from the *dharma-cakra* or 'Wheel of Law' with deer on either side that is carved on the pedestal, signifying the first sermon delivered by the Buddha at Sarnath after he attained enlightenment at Bodh Gaya. There is another image of Mahiṣāsuramardinī placed on another old *adhisthāna* but it has no figure sculpture on the pedestal.

Pāndharā Devī is the other name of Tārā or Pāndarā and it is quite likely that the old Buddhist tradition of the worship of Pāndarā is perpetuated in the worship of Jholāī. Perhaps Jholāī is a derivative of Dhavalāī, which has the same meaning as Pāndarā ("white"). Some scholars of linguistics might question the derivation of Jholāī from Dhavalāī, but we do have instances like Sanskrit *upādhyāya* changing to *uvajhjhāya, ojā* and even to *jhā,* and Upādhye into Pāndhye and Vaze. Similarly, from *dhvajadaṇḍa* we have the Marathi and Hindi word *jheṇḍā* or *jhaṇḍā.*

The other goddess, Navasīrī, is also derived from multiheaded deities in the Vajrayāna pantheon like the eleven-headed Avalokiteśvara.

The other centres of the worship of the mother goddess in the vicinity of Panhale are at Rasalgad, Gavatala, Matvan, Deganve, Anjanvel and Palgad.

At Khed in Ratnagiri District, where there are Buddhist caves, a village deity *(grāma-devatā)* called Khedujī is worshipped, whose shrine is also in one of the caves, although this cave is a little away from the main group of Buddhist caves. At Dabhol, in the same district, the goddess Candikā is worshipped. She is also located in a cave. All these instances suggest that the Buddhist centres came to be established where there was some earlier worship of a male or female deity and when the Buddhist worship ceased, the original worship was resumed, sometimes influenced by the Buddhist worship. A similar observation is possible with respect to the Lonad caves near Kalyāṇ (District Thane). Here, after the Buddhist affiliation of the cave was forgotten, the cave was turned into a shrine of Khaṇḍeśvarī, a form of Mahiṣāsuramardinī. The name Khaṇḍeśvarī derives from *khaṇḍa* (*khaḍga,* sword).

In conclusion, I would like to say that, for the study of folk religion in Maharashtra, we must take up intensive work at some centres, and among such places, Ambejogai in Marathawada and Lonad in Vidarbha would call for early attention. At both these places there is plenty of interesting material.

REFERENCES

Briggs, G. W. 1938. *Gorakhnāth and the Kānphaṭa yogīs.* Calcutta.

Cāpekar, N. G. 1966. *Citpāvana.* Badlāpūr (Thāṇe District). Second edition.

Dehejia, Vidya. 1986. *Yoginī cult and temples. A Tantric tradition.* New Delhi: National Museum.

Deshpande, M. N. 1950. The Rock-cut caves of Pitalkhora in the Deccan. *Ancient India* 15.

Id. 1983. *Ṭhāṇālā Bauddhaleṇī, Panhāle Vajrayāna kendra, Śaiva, Gānapātya va Nātha saṃpradāyavara navā prakāśa.* Nāgpur: Vidarbha Saṃśodhan Maṇḍala. [Marāṭhī].

Id. 1986. *The caves of Panhale Kaji.* Archaeological Survey of India.

Joshi, S. B. 1952. *Marāṭhī Saṃskṛti.* Puṇe: Antar Bhāratī Prakaśan.

Karve, Iravati. *Marāṭhī Lokāncī Saṃskṛti.*

Kosambi, D. D. 1983. *The culture and civilization of ancient India in historical outline.* London: Routledge and Kegan Paul.

Mirashi, V. V. 1981. *The history and inscriptions of the*

M. N. Deshpande

Satavāhanas and the Western Kshatrapas. Bombay: Maharashtra State Board for Literature and Culture.

Mukherjee, B. N. 1969. *Nanā on the lion. A study in Kushana numismatics.* Calcutta: Asiatic Society.

Prabhudesai, P. K. 1968. *Ādiśakti Viśvasvarūpa, Devīkośa,* (in four parts). Puṇe: Ṭiḷak Mahārāṣṭra Vidyāpīṭh. [Marāṭhī].

Sali, S. A. 1976-1979. *Daimabad.* Archaeological Survey of India 1986.

Satīpa Dāsabodh. Ed. by S. S. Dev. 8th ed., published by K. B. Dhavale.

N. K. Wagle

ON RELATIONS AMONGST *BHŪTS*, GODS, AND MEN: Aspects of Folk Religion and Law in Pre-British Maharashtra

SECTION I

Introduction

When a Maharashtrian belonging to the 18th and early 19th centuries (1730-1812) encountered difficulties and troubles, such as illness, the death of near ones or the loss of property, that had no apparent human explanation, he would likely attribute their cause to non-human agents. He would respond by saying that the trouble might be due to sorcery (*jāduṭoṇā*) by some living persons, it might be due to the activity of a *bhūt* (the disembodied spirit of someone who has died) or it might be due to one or more of a wide range of gods. The interactions amongst humans, *bhūts* and gods, and the role of the state in controlling the troublesome activities of the *bhūts*, is a much neglected research area in the social and legal history of 18th and early 19th century Maharashtra. The subject of *bhūts* is dismissed as the "superstitions" of Maharashtrian society, and is linked with sorcery and witchcraft.[1]

[1] For a study of the contemporary situation see Stanley 1988 and Sontheimer 1989: 142-146.

The legal disputes involving the *bhūts* (*bhūtācā kajiyā, bhūtāce bhāṇḍaṇ, bhūt taṇṭā*) and the associated folk-religious practices, as examined in this paper, indicate a prevailing anxiety over property and health. The *bhūts* became socially and legally relevant by imposing difficulties and troubles upon people. Government intervention was called for to control and arrest the activities of the *bhūts*, and of the persons who were responsible for setting the *bhūts* (*bhūt ghālṇe*) upon their victims. Some of the victims accused the person whom they suspected of being instrumental in the *bhūts'* destructive actions; others were convinced that the troubles they were experiencing were caused by the *bhūts*, but could not ascertain the identity of the person or persons responsible for setting the *bhūts* on them. The identity of the person, and sometimes that of the *bhūts*, was revealed through *paḍthal*, a process of consultation with the gods. The *bhūts* often revealed themselves or made their wishes known through the medium of another person.

The main text of this paper, with description and analysis of the subject matter, appears in section one; section two contains the translations of five cases dealing with *bhūt* disputes.

The Troubles Caused by the *Bhūts*: Property Damage by Fire, Bodily Harm, Loss of Health.

The *bhūts* were held responsible for cases of arson. Bālājī Dhoṇḍdev of Mauje (village) Nivlī complained to the *hujūr* that:[2]

[2] *Peśve Daftar Ghaḍṇī Rumāl* (*PDGR*), 374, Bālājī Dhoṇḍdev, June 6, 1786; see also *Selections from the Satara rajas' and the Peshwas' diaries* (*SSPRD*), VIII, vol III, p. 116. Vad does not give a reference to the actual *Peśve Daftar Rumāl* number. The Marathi documents referred to in the main body of the text, and in section II of this paper, are available in the Maharashtra State Archives, Pune. I would like to thank Mr. M. M. Oṃkar and Mr. Bhogam for their assistance in the archives. References to the Marathi text have been transliterated from Moḍī. The transliterations may not coincide with standard Marathi spellings, e.g. **don velā** instead of **don veḷā**. **bhut** has been transliterated according to standard written Marathi as **bhūt, bhutācā,**

> For the last two years our house has been vexed by the *bhūts* in a number of ways, and we have been ruined by them. Within a year, our house was twice caught on fire unexpectedly; it was burnt by the *bhūts*. All the goods in our house perished. Nothing remained.[3]

Āpā Bhaṭ Parānjpe also complained to the *hujūr* that his house was set on fire by the *bhūts*. Even when he moved out of his house to live with a Kulkarṇī in another village, the Kulkarṇī's house, too, suffered because of the outbreaks of fire. Therefore, the Kulkarṇī asked him to leave the house.[4] Nene complained to the government that the house he had built on Peṇḍse's property got burnt by the bhūts.[5] Malhārjī Deśmukh of Kotul was judged to be the person responsible for setting two villages, Liṅgdev and Dhamaṇgāv, on fire. It was proven in the trial that he had commissioned *bhūts* to do the job (*bhūt ciṭṭhyā bāndhalyā*).[6]

The *bhūts* and the person who sent them were held responsible for the death of a victim. It was established in a dispute between Saṃtājī Cavhāṇ and Bhikājī Govind Khot (village headman) over a field, that the latter's peasant woman (*kuṇbīṇ*) died at the hands of Saṃtājī's *bhūts*. The local administrator, Cimājī Māṇkar, was

etc.

[3] Ibid., *āj don varṣe bhutācā updrav nānā prakāre hoūn nāś jhālā yekā varṣāmadhye akasmāt gharās āg lāgon ghar don velā bhūtānī jālale tyāt vastabhāv jhāḍūn jalālī kāhī rāhile nāhī.*

[4] See Case III of section II.

[5] *Peśve Daftar Dakṣiṇ Koṇkaṇ Rumāl*, 490, Nene vs. Peṇḍse, September 4, 1771.

[6] *PDGR*, 274, Malārjī Deśmukh, March 26, 1778. Instead of paying the fine, as agreed upon previously, Malhārjī Deśmukh absconded from the place. Hence, the government sequestered his house. But the government found a lot of building materials in the house, which were sold and, after deducting the amount of fine, the remaining two hundred fourteen rupees and eight annas were given to the Deśmukh's deputy, Dādā Moreśvar.

instructed by the central government to seek compensation for the murdered woman from Cavhāṇ, and to collect the fine from him for murder. A note was added that if the settlement could not be effected on this matter locally (*tethe mansubīcā nivāḍā na hoya*), then Cavhāṇ's [Khotī] *vatan* (tenured office) should be sequestered, and he should be sent to the *hujūr* for a settlement.[7] Viṣṇu Palsule, who had given the managment of his Khotī to Viṣṇu Ghāṭe, complained to the *hujūr* that Ghāṭe, "setting the *bhūts* upon us, got the members of our household killed". In the settlement, done through the *paḍthal* procedure, it was proven that it was Ghāṭe who had set the *bhūts* upon Palsule. The local brāhmaṇs, therefore, ostracized Ghāṭe.[8]

A dispute which took place in early 17th century Maharashtra between Gopālpant Lāhādev and Jānojī and Jāujī Thiṭe over the Deśpāṇde *vatan* of Vāī, ended in a murder.[9] After a prolonged dispute, Gopālpant secured the *vatan* from the Bijāpūr rulers. While he was returning home with the new settlement papers, the signed letters, and the new orders from the government confirming his *vatan*, he was murdered along with an escort. The murder was commissioned by the Thiṭe brothers and was carried out by Konerī Mehutā (Mhetar, Mahār), a dependent of Gaṇpatī Desāī of Āṅgāpūr, who also took away all the documents which Gopāl had on him. Jāvobā (Jāujī) Thiṭe and Konerī had made a vow to the goddess (*devās*

---

[7] *SSRPD*, VII, vol II, Saṃtājī Cavhāṇ vs. Bhikājī Govind, September-October, 1763, pp. 211-212.

[8] See case Va, section II of this paper.

[9] I am indebted to Mr. M. M. Omkar for giving me a copy of the Marathi original housed in the Bhāratīya Itihās Saṃśodhan Maṇḍal, Puṇe. The document, unfortunately, has no date. And, although it is about 9 pages long, the beginning and the end are missing. But from the internal evidence of the language and the persons mentioned in the documents, it is reasonable to assume that it was a pre-Śivājī era document when the districts of Vāī and Karādh (Karāḍ) were controlled by the Bijāpūr Sultāns. Vaṅgojī Nāīk Niṃbālkar (1570-1630 A. D.) figures prominently in the document as a patron of the Thiṭe brothers. For Vaṅgojī's genealogy, see Sardesai 1957: 72.

navas kelā hotā) at Āṅgāpūr that if they succeeded in their venture, they would celebrate the victory (*digvijaya*) by underwriting a great festivity, a *gondhaḷ* (propitiating the goddess by singing and dancing), for the goddess (*āpaṇ gondhaḷ ghālīn va devācā bahut mohachav karūn*). Since they had accomplished their objectives, they began the *gondhaḷ*. As the *gondhaḷ* began, Konerī suddenly became paralysed, the spirit of Gopāl Lāhādev itself possessed his body, and he began to rant (*konerīce khoḍ valale aṇī savec tyāce aṅgī gopāl lāhīdeū prakaṭ hoūn avtāro lāglā*):

> You became the Māhār (*dhākṇyā*) of Jāūbā. You murdered me and, having brought all my *vṛtti* (*vatan*) documents, you are now celebrating the success of the venture. I shall make you, Jāū and Jāno heirless (*nisaṃtān karīn*). I am a brāhmaṇ and was returning after securing my *vṛtti*, and you had no grounds to murder me. My family is at Uṃbraj with Datto Lāhmājī. Inform them that near the Rāmlakṣumaṇ *vaḍ* tree, which is near the well belonging to Basopant, there are two skeletons (*sāgaḍe*). The skeleton with a sacred thread (*jānve*) attached to it is mine. Bringing that skeleton to the river Kṛṣṇā, get my funeral rites (*uttara kārya*) performed through my sons on its banks. You should personally go and inform them of this news. Also tell them that it was you who were responsible for the act. You will then be released from me. Otherwise, I shall haunt you day and night (*rātradivas tuj soḍīt nāhī*, lit. I shall not leave you day and night).[10]

The entire assembly (*sabhā*) gathered at the *gondhaḷ* became stunned (*taṭastha jālī*) by this event. An investigation was conducted. Konerī was sent to Dattopant at Uṃbraj with a letter from the assembly.

---

[10] Ibid.

And the men sent to investigate the matter actually found two skeletons, one with a sacred thread attached to it. That skeleton was sent to Uṃbraj, where it was cremated and the last rites were performed by Gopāl's brothers. Eventually, the whole episode was placed before the Brahmasabhā (the assembly of the learned brāhmaṇs) for settlement. It was decided in that assembly to ostracize the Thiṭes, and that decision was endorsed by the government authorities (*hākīm*) of Karhāḍ. The ostracism became effective. For two to four years, the Thiṭes were unable to perform rituals; their daughters came of age, but none was willing to accept them in marriage. Because of their implication in the murder they were utterly disgraced (*tyāṃcī toṇḍe khunā karitā kālī jālī*). Eventually, the Thiṭes absolved themselves of the liabilities of murder by giving back the *vṛtti* (*vatan*) to the rightful owners.[11]

The Ghāṭes' case mentioned above, in which their *bhūts* killed Desāī's people, was different from the Thiṭes' case fought about 180 years earlier. In the latter case, the murdered person himself had become the *bhūt* and had exposed the murder plot. In the Ghāṭes' case, the revelation that the *bhūts* had been set upon Palsule by the Ghāṭes came through the *paḍthal* procedure, involving the gods giving the evidence. The goddess was, evidently, aware of the *bhūts'* doings in the Thiṭes' case. It was during the *gondhaḷ* of the goddess at Āṅgāpūr that the *bhūt* of Gopāl entered the body of Konerī. However, the guilty parties in both the cases were ostracized by the local brāhmaṇs with the backing of the government authorities. The absolution of the Ghāṭes had to be sanctioned by the government. An attempt on the part of one of them to coerce the brāhmaṇs into receiving him back would not do. However, they were all to be readmitted with a purificatory ritual.[12] The Thiṭes were received into the brāhmaṇ fold by giving back the *vatan*, the original source of the dispute and the murder. The two cases indicate the dynamics

---

[11] Ibid.

[12] See Case Vb in this paper.

of how the gods, the government authority, and the community, acting in consort with each other, tried to resolve the property and moral issues of individuals which resulted in murders, the *bhūts* in both cases acting as the catalyst. We find cases in which the causes of death were linked directly or indirectly with the *bhūts*. Kāḷojī Bhoī (Bhoī, the caste of palanquin bearers) was killed by Morājī Tikonā Bhoī of Puṇe, by having *bhūts* set upon him. The caste-brothers (*got bhāī*), fifty of them meeting together, established that Morājī was responsible for that action. In order to neutralize Morājī's occult powers (*jādugirīcī vidyā*), the *got* decided to remove his two front teeth, to feed him with water from the tanner's vat and then to ostracize him from the caste. Morājī rebuffed this move by threatening the caste members that he would, in consort with the Beraḍs and Māṅgs, perpetrate more killings if he were to be ostracized. The orders went from the government that Morājī should be put in jail after his powers had been nullified by the methods recommended by his caste-fellows.[13] As in the previous two cases discussed, the connection with death through the *bhūts* was an act punishable by the community by the effective method of ostracism. The government became involved because Morājī refused to listen to the biddings of his caste.

In an extreme case, the Pāṭīls of Jānorī village, suspecting the mother of Rāmjī Pāṭīl to be a Bhūtālī, killed her. The Pāṭīls were summoned to Puṇe for investigation by the government. They were made to pay a fine and had to come to a negotiated settlement with Rāmjī Pāṭīl, probably by paying him monetary compensation as the victim's near kin, as was customarily done. In this instance, however, the act of killing was done without the permission of the government (*sarkārce ājñekherīj mārlī*), although it was established through the evidence of the Pāṭīls of neighbouring villages that Rāmjī's mother was, indeed, a Bhūtālī.[14] Thus, without due legal

[13] *SSRPD*, VIII, vol. III, Kāḷojī Bhoī, November 24, 1775, p. 115.

[14] *Selections from the Peshwa Daftar* (*SPD*), G. S. Sardesai, ed., vol. 43, Jānorī

process, the right to take life, even a Bhūtālī's, was denied to the community; killing a member of a community was not the same as ostracism.

There are dispute cases associated with the *bhūts* that culminate in one of the parties suffering death, although the *bhūts* may not have been directly responsible for it. There was a dispute between Sajṇājī Pāṭīl Gurav and Aṃbājī Gurav of Mauje Yavteśvar about the cup which was placed on the ritual vessel during the Navrātra festival. The cup (*ghaṭācī vāṭī*) was therefore kept with Rām Bhaṭ Abhīsekī, the ritual priest of the temple. The Bhaṭ's house became vexed with *bhūts* (*bhūt bādhā jhālī*). Suryājī Pāṭīl, the brother of Sajṇājī Pāṭīl, became ill and soon died.[15] There was a *bhūt* dispute (*bhūtācā kajiyā*) between Devjī and Kevjī Pāṭīl Madhanī, the Pāṭīls of Mauje Kosiṃbe. Kevjī Madhanī's mother's brother Māvjī, in the meantime, was killed because Devjī had complained to Mādhavrāv Niṃbājī. Eventually, the initial arrest of Devjī led to his freedom after paying a fine of 800 rupees to the government.[16] Both the above references are cryptic, but the linkage between the *bhūt* dispute and death is self-evident.

Besides the cases involving death and arson attributable to the *bhūts*, which were few and far between, the nature of damage done and the troubles caused by *bhūts* are noted in some instances. Triṃbak Ballāl Gānū complained to the government that, because of conflict with the villagers, the latter set the *bhūts* upon him and thereby

> we were utterly ruined. Although we had become *khare* (true) and *nivāḍpatre* were written twice in our

---

Pāṭīl vs. Rāmjī Pāṭīl, c. 1750-61 A. D., p. 32 (7456).

[15] Śāhū Daftar Rumāl 10, 11290-294, Sajṇājī Gurav vs. Aṃbājī Gurav, April 29, 1731.

[16] *PDGR*, 372, Devjī Pāṭīl vs. Kevjī Pāṭīl, May 15, 1752.

> favour, we could not receive the government seal of ratification [on the *nivāḍpatra*]. Our settlement did not come to fruition. Our health began to deteriorate. When the cause had been determined through the *devadharma,* it was established that the villagers had set the *bhūts* upon us.[17]

Āpā Bhaṭ's plea to the government is rather desperate. He said:

> In our house and those of our lineage brothers, the women's garments get torn and burnt. Our women get assaulted. Our cattle die yelling and our houses get set on fire.[18]

However, in many *bhūt* disputes, the nature of the troubles casued by the *bhūts* is not specified. Paraśrām Jivājī Doṅgare's plea to the government is typical of the statements we generally find in our documents. He said, "There was much ruination of our household caused by the *bhūts.*"[19] Yesājī Nāīk Mudvaḍkar said: "Our lineage brother (*dāīja*) Pemjī Mudvaḍkar set the *bhūt* upon us (*bhūte ghātlī*) and he creates a disturbance (*nārā karto*)."[20] Sadāśiv Bhaṭ Devdhar complained to the *hujūr* (central government) that Bābdev Bhaṭ Parāñjpe occupied his place (*ṭhīkāṇ*) and that he was determined not to leave the place. Because he complained to the *hujūr,* Bābdev set *bhūts* on him *(bhūte ghātlī)*.[21] Harī Bābājī Mahājan of Mauje Muṭāt complained to the *hujūr* that there was a dispute between him and Parāñjpe concerning a house. The issue was settled in the temple of Vāḍeśvar, in which he became *kharā* (true). Despite this, the *bhūts* sent by Parāñjpe were causing trouble for

---

[17] See case I of this paper.

[18] See case II of this paper.

[19] *SSRPD*, VIII, vol. III, Paraśarām Jivājī Doṅgare, February 12, 1774, p. 111.

[20] *PDGR*, 45, Yesājī Mudvaḍkar vs. Pemjī Mudvaḍkar, May 17, 1779.

[21] *SSRPD*, VII, vol. II, Sadāśiv Bhaṭ vs. Bābdev Bhaṭ, April 24, 1768, p. 212.

him.[22] Devkī Rāvat told the local officer of Nāgāv that Bāpu Viṭhal Kavḷe's *bhūts* were set upon him in the house of Rāghobā Marāṭhe.[23] Viṭhal Rām Kulkarṇī of Mauje Kaḷvalī, Tarf Soṇḍal, complained to the goverment that the Khotī of the village belonged to Kṛṣṇa Prabhudesāī of the above Tarf and that the latter caused "the *bhūts* of the village to set upon us (*gāvcī bhūte āmhāvar ghātlī*)."[24] Saṃt Pāṭīl's *bhūts* were set upon the clerk of Sadāśiv Bhaṭ Nānaḷ.[25] In all the cases cited above, the main concern was to arrange for the dissipation of the *bhūts* by one means or another. Government intervention was deemed necessary for the control of activities involving the *bhūts*.

The *bhūt* disputes which reached the government for their resolution were deliberated on carefully, and if the accusations were proven to be false, then the party which had initiated the accusations was made to pay the fine. Dādājī Soyarājī Gurav of Kasbe Pāl and Kṛṣṇājī, the son of Lakṣumaṇ, were engaged in a *bhūt* quarrel (*bhūtāce bhāṇḍaṇ bhāṇḍat hote*). A settlement (*nivāḍā*) was arrived at, in which Dādājī became *khoṭā* (false) and had to pay a fine of fifty rupees to the government.[26] Kṛṣṇanāk and Lohanāk Māhār of Mauje Āsvalī, Tarf Nirthaḍī, Prānt Puṇe, had a better idea. They came squabbling to the *hujūr* (central government at Puṇe), engaged in a *bhūt* dispute. They were sent back to their village to provide surety for their conduct (*jamān*) before the trial could begin. In the meantime they came to a mutual understanding (*te āplyāt samajle*) and stopped their dispute. Nevertheless, they were not spared. A fine of forty rupees was extracted from them by the government.[27]

---

[22] *Peśve Daftar Jamāv Rumāl*, 601, Harī Bābājī vs. Parāñjpe, October 3, 1802.

[23] Avlaskar 1962: 90.

[24] V.K. Rājvāḍe (ed.), *Marāthyāṃcyā Itihāsācī Sādhane*, vol. 10, July 10, 1766, pp. 21-22.

[25] *PDGR*, 372, Saṃt Pāṭīl vs. Sadāśiv Bhaṭ, June 4, 1783.

[26] Ibid., Kṛṣṇājī vs. Dādājī, May 15, 1752.

[27] Ibid., Kṛṣṇa Nāk vs. Loha Nāk, June 26, 1741.

The party which was judged as true also had to pay a present to the government. Māhimājī and Vākojī, the sons of Saṅkarājī Śinde Deśmukh, of Tarf Kuḍāl started a dispute, stating that Mānsing, the son of Bāvājī Śinde, and Āpājī, the son of Sūryājī Śinde Deśmukh, had sent *bhūts* to Māhimājī's house. The dispute reached the *hujūr* and after a proper settlement effected by the *pañcāyat,* it was established that the *bhūts* allegedly sent by Mānsing et. al. to Māhimājī's house were not his; the *bhūts* really were those of the latter's own house. Māhimājī et. al. became *khoṭe* (false). Mānsing et. al. became *khare* (true) and they were given a government sanctioned settlement document (*sarkārce nivāḍpatra*) to that effect. Mānsiṅg paid the *harkī,* the present to the government, consisting of 500 rupees in cash and a horse worth 500 rupees.[28] It is interesting to note that in all three cases referred to above, the parties involved were apparently members of the same lineage, deducible from the fact that they came from the same village or town and shared a common title and surname.

The Maratha government is on record as taking steps to control the Bhutāles, the persons responsible for inducing *bhūts* to start troubles on behalf of their clients. The Bhutāles themselves, of course, could set *bhūts* upon their personal enemies. A government decree was issued in 1759[29] to punish deliberate acts of setting *bhūts* on people. Bāl Mahājanī Gogṭe's is a case in point. The *bhūt* problem must have reached crisis proportions in the districts of southern Koṅkaṇ in the mid-1770s, since we find the government establishing a separate constabulary, drawn from the Koṅkaṇ districts, headed by a special officer, Bājī Rām, who was assisted by six persons from the central government. Hiṣ duties were to counteract the influence of the Bhutāles over the populace by touring the areas, investigating the *bhūt* cases (*bhutācī caukaśī*), controlling the *bhūt* cases (*bhutāce bandobastāce kām*) and collecting reasonable fines (*gunhegārī*) rang-

---

[28] *PDGR*, 374, Mahīmājī Śinde vs. Mānsing Śinde, August 27, 1768.

[29] See Case IIa of this paper.

ing from 25 to 50 rupees from those involved in *bhūt* activities.[30]

We notice that the whole procedure of dealing with the *bhūts* was carefully laid out. The government officer investigating the *bhūt* disputes had to establish that the troublesome acts committed were those of the *bhūts* and, more importantly, to ascertain that the person who was accused of setting the *bhūts* upon the complainant was the right one.

Generally, when the government at Puṇe received a formal complaint about the troubles caused by *bhūts*, it sent the following orders to the district officer:

> The person whose *bhūts* are causing trouble in another person's house, should be told to dispose of the *bhūts* (*bhūte vārāvūn deṇe*). A surety (*jāmīn*) should be taken from the person that the *bhūt* should not cause trouble again. A fine should be extracted from that person.[31]

Hari Mahājan complained to the government that [he suspected that] Parāñjpe's *bhūts* were troubling him. He said that if "it were to be proved that the *bhūts* are his (*bhūte nivḍon ālī*), then he should dispose of them (*vārāvar karvāvī*).[32] In a *bhūt* dispute between Saṃt Pāṭīl and Nānal, the Pāṭīl, after the settlement of the dispute, is actually stated to have disposed of the *bhūts*. A *jāmīn* was taken from him that the *bhūts* would not cause any trouble. And he had

---

[30] See instructions to Kṛṣṇājī Viśvanāth, Bājī Māhādev, and Moro Bāpujī from the Peśvā's office sent by Nāro Āpājī, *Peśve Daftar Dakṣiṇ Koṅkaṇ Rumāl*, 421 and 495, February 25, 1775 and March 9, 1775. Cf. *SSRPD*, VIII, vol. III, pp. 112-115, where the same instructions are repeated. However, the original *rumāl* numbers are not found there. The dates given in the *SSRPD* are incomplete. There are other minor errors in the transcriptions of the Modi originals.

[31] *PDGR*, 374, Bālājī Dhonḍdev, June 6, 1786.

[32] *Peśve Daftar Jamāv Rumāl*, 601, Hari Mahājan vs. Parāñjpe, October 11, 1812.

to pay a fine of fifty rupees.[33]

The important procedure to determine the identity of the person who sent the *bhūts*, before the *bhūts'* activities could be controlled, was to initiate a *paḍthal*, i. e., to consult the gods. The central government routinely ordered the district officer to institute a *paḍthal* proceeding to settle a *bhūt* dispute. The operating instruction, in one instance, reads:

> You should appoint a *paḍthal* of four gods. Whoever is proven as the sender of the *bhūts* according to the *paḍthal* should be made to dispose of the *bhūts*. A surety (*jāmīn*) should be taken for the non-recurrence of the *bhūt* trouble. (*tumhī cau devās paḍthale nemūn paḍthalī jyāce bhūt nivḍel tyā pāsūn vārvūn. yās phirūn upadrav na lāge te karūn jāmīn gheūn*...).[34]

Yesjī Mudvaḍkar complained to the government that Pemjī refused to comply with the results of the *paḍthal* which proved that he had set the *bhūts* upon the former. The government sent the instructions to the officer at the district level:

> If it is established through the *paḍthal* of 10 villages that it was Pemjī Mudvaḍkar who sent the *bhūts* to Yesjī and that the *bhūts* were responsible for the disturbances, then the person who sent the *bhūts* should be forced to dissipate them (*vāravaṇe*). A fine should be collected from that person.[35]

---

[33] *PDGR*, 372, Saṃt Pāṭīl vs. Nānal, June 4, 1783.

[34] *SSRPD*, VIII, vol. III, Paraśrām Ḍoṅgre vs. Bābū Ḍoṅgre, February 12, 1744, fl, p. 112.

[35] *PDGR*, 45, Mudvaḍkar vs. Mudvaḍkar, May 17, 1779.

That Bāl Mahājanī Gogaṭe had set *bhūts* upon Gaṇeś Gokhale was established through the *paḍthal* of five to seven places. But Gogaṭe did not dissipate the *bhūts*. The penalty, after further investigation, was rather harsh: Gogaṭe's Khoṭī *vatan* was sequestered by the government and his house was razed to the ground.[36] Devdhar stated that *bhūts* had been set upon him by Parāñjpe: "it was established as those of Parāñjpe (*tyācyā āṅgī lāvlī*)." But he did not dispose of them. The government orders went to the Subhedār: "In the past, the *paḍthal* was done. But appoint two to three additional *thal*. Then, without caring for anyone, collect a fine from the sender of the *bhūt* and have him dispose of the *bhūt*".[37] The *paḍthal* procedure involved a process of consultation with gods about the *bhūts*. The response of or the evidence given by one god had to be compared with those of the gods of nearby localities. When the results of one round of the *paḍthal* were not acceptable, then another *paḍthal* could be appointed. As in the case of Gogaṭe vs. Gokhale, a new *paḍthal* was appointed by the government, but this time the gods had to belong to the great centres (*mahāsthān*) known to be efficacious (*jyāgrut sthale*) and situated outside the home territories (*parmahālī*) of the disputants.[38] It appears that a consensus of the gods' evidence concerning the *bhūts* was aimed at. The gods made their response known through the voice of a medium or through the ritual of *prasād* or *kaul-prasād* (the interpretation of signs, such as the falling of flowers, petals, leaves and rice stuck upon the image). What is significant in our study is that the government and the people recognized it as the "legal" procedure to settle their *bhūt* disputes. The *paḍthal* was done through the agency of the diviners known as *bhagat*, the *vaśye* and the *zāḍ*. These diviners were involved in the activities recorded in the legal documents as *devdharma* or *devaskī*, the profession of communicating with the *bhūts* and the gods. Trimbak Gānū's case illustrates the importance of

[36] See Case IVb of this paper.

[37] *SSRPD*, VII, vol. II, Devdhar vs. Parāñjpe, April 24, 1768, p. 212.

[38] See Case IVb of this paper.

devdharma, and the roles of the *bhagat* and *vaśye*. Gānū, unsuccessful in his venture, returned to the village in order to understand his series of misfortunes. It was established through the *devadharma* that the villagers had set *bhūts* on him and that they had made vows (*māṇnikā kelyā*) to the gods that he should not succeed in his task. Moreover, in order to fulfill their wish, they had presented a silk flag to the village god and had, in fact, sacrificed three goats in Puṇe before the god. When Gānū lodged an official complaint with the government, the government gave Gānū one *bhagat* and one policeman, and appointed five villages for the *paḍthal,* with official government letters authorising them to consult the gods. The *vaśye* of the village was interrogated, and he gave a deposition that villagers had set the *bhūts* upon Gānū. The villagers, who were the accused party, went, along with Gānū and the *bhagat,* to the five gods' places and performed the *paḍthal.* The gods, in the presence of the villagers, verified the statement that the *bhūts* had been set on Gānū by the villagers after they had made their vows to the gods. The documents stating the results of the *paḍthal* were submitted to the government. However, the government wanted a thorough investigation of this matter and instructed its officer to initiate, if doubts were to emerge, a new *devdharma* investigation, and to settle the matter through the *paḍthal.*[39] We may note here that the *paḍthal* procedure assumes a legal proportion, backed up by an official government letter of authorisation. The gods' evidence, too, is recorded formally in the *thalpatra,* authenticated by the parties present on the occasion. It is clearly stated in the document that the *paḍthal* was done in the presence of all the parties concerned. The deposition given by the *vaśye,* after a government interrogation, is significant, because he is also a specialist in *devdharma.* The vows made to the village gods, with appropriate goat sacrifices and a present of a silk flag, are pointed out as the causes of the ruination of Gānū. The close link between the gods and the *bhūts* cannot be denied; the gods in the above case are the de facto *bhūts.*

---

[39] See Case I of this paper.

In another case, Āpā Bhaṭ Parāñjpe alleged that the village gods, Śrī Bhūtnāth and Śrī Nātheśvar, because of the pleadings of the villagers, had set *bhūts* upon him and his family, resulting in his troubles. Āpā Bhaṭ approached the *vaśye* of the village and told him to "ask the gods the reason for the varied troubles affecting our houses." He said that he would, but did not settle the issue by asking the gods through possession or asking the gods questions through the *prasād.* Āpā Bhaṭ then complained to the government officer Gangādhar Govind, who sent a clerk to do the *paḍthal* of five villages. It was established that the village *vaśye*'s pleadings to the gods were responsible for the ruination of Āpā Bhaṭ. The gods of the five villages also concurred with the truth of that statement. The *vaśye* had the *devaskī* under control for a month or two. But the *bhūt* troubles began after that period. The government felt that, although the initial *paḍthal* had been successful (*guṇ ālā*), the settlement had been ignored by the *vaśye,* who now should be asked to put a stop to his activities. The government instructions also asked the local officer to give compensation to Parāñjpe for his losses due to the *bhūt* trouble.[40] The village diviner's role as an intermediary to the gods is borne out by this passage. But even he was exposed by the *paḍthal* procedure. One of the names of the village gods, Bhūtnāth, in translation, the "lord of the *bhūts,*" assumes significance in this context. Those gods are induced by the *vaśye* to send the *bhūts* to Āpā Bhaṭ. Although the role of the diviner is considered vital in dealing with the *bhūt* situation, his divination could be challenged. Bāl Gogṭe complained that, instead of following the *prasād* procedure at the various *paḍthale,* as recommended by the government, far too much reliance was placed on the divination of the *bhagat.* This "legal" point, when pointed out, went in favour of Gogaṭe.[41]

---

[40] See Case II of this paper.

[41] See Case IVb of this paper.

The *bhūts*, the gods, the people and the government are all linked in Case III of this paper, which is a legal document of assurance dated January 16, 1812, addressed to Peśvā Bājīrāv II (1799-1818), and signed by the brāhmaṇ dignitaries of the town of Guhāgar. The letter assured Bājīrāv that the land he had purchased for building a palace at Guhāgar should no longer be vexed by the *bhūts*, and that the brāhmaṇs of the place should be held responsible for any trouble caused by the *bhūts*. According to this letter, Bājīrāv had purchased six plots of land from the local brāhmaṇ families to build his *vāḍā* (palace). While digging for the foundation on the plot bought from Hari Parcure, the workers stumbled upon a buried pot containing the *bhūts*. The *bhūts* began causing trouble to the workers on the site. The carpenter became possessed by the *bhūts* (*bhūte āṅgī vāḍhu lāglī*). With the aid of Daulat Sāvant, the *bhagat*, the *bhūts* were disposed of next to the goddess Jholāī. A god who had possessed (*āṅgāt vāḍhlā*) one Yesu Gāvḍā was consulted to verify if the *bhūts* had really been terminated. It was established through the god that the *bhūts* who had been in the pots had been disposed of, but that the building plot was still vexed by the *bhūts* of the Rāṇe brothers, who had died a violent death four hundred years ago and had been the original owners. The god, therefore, advised against the construction of the *vāḍā* on the spot. The local village goddess, Vāghāṃbarī, sustained that advice. Bājīrāv, who was in Guhāgar at that time, gave orders to stop the work. At that juncture, the Rāṇe brothers' *bhūts* appeared in a dream of Kripālgīr Gosāvī, a courtier of Bājīrāv, who was accompanying him. The *bhūts* told Gosāvī that Bājīrāv should continue the work on the *vāḍā* and that the brothers would not create trouble on the site, since, on their own, they were giving the land to him for building the *vāḍā*. In a further development, the *bhūt* communicated with the brāhmaṇs. Saṃbhājī Rāṇe's *bhūt* told Hari Parcure that, as compensation for his place, which Hari had sold to Bājīrāv, he wanted 1200 rupees, the price Hari had received, and an area measuring 18 *hath* in his house to live in. Hari Parcure told him that he did not have the money, but was left with only his house. The *bhūt*, nonetheless, reiterated his demands. Also, he demanded and got surety (*jāmīn*) from the dignitaries of the village that Parcure would not sell his quarters to anyone. One and a quarter *sīr* of *uḍid* (black-gram) and 21 coconuts were placed on the 18 *hāth* spot at Rāṇe *bhūt*'s instructions. With his own hands, the *bhūt* broke open one coconut in each of the four corners of the area of the *vāḍā*. A coconut was given to Bājīrāv with instructions to break it open at the time of his departure for Puṇe. The villagers consulted Gāvḍā's god, to verify that what had transpired was true. The answer was in the affirmative. But the god warned them that the *bhūt* was still insisting on 1200 rupees from Parcure. The only way out for Parcure was to surrender to the villagers and ask them to intercede on his behalf with the *bhūt* to spare him the cost. Bājīrāv had left instructions with his courtier that the *bhūt* should be confronted with the argument that, as a *bhūt*, he should not be hankering after money and a house. He should instead show goodwill towards Parcure. The *bhūt* still wanted the pile of 1200 rupees to be placed before him. 1200 rupees were given to Parcure on loan and he placed them in front of the *bhūt*. The bhūt then assigned some of it to the *zāḍ* (medium), some to the *bhagat* and the rest to erect an *oṭā* (platform) for him near Rāmeśvar, where he had decided to retire. An *oṭā* was given gratis by the government from materials from the workshop of the *vāḍā*. The *bhūt* annulled the surety given to him by Hari Parcure that he would not sell his 18 *hāth* place, and gave the place to Hari as a gift. The *bhūt* was installed by the *bhagat*. The other Rāṇe brothers were disposed of in front of the goddess Vāghāmbarī. The brāhmaṇs were assured by the goddess Vāghāmbarī that the place was safe from the *bhūt*.

The Guhāgar *vāḍā* case involves the brāhmaṇ Peśvā, the head of the Maratha confederacy, or what was left of it, in 1812. And it was his intended palace which was harrassed by the *bhūt*. The supreme head of the state had to bow down to the pressure of the *bhūt*. The case, therefore, is of interest in understanding the importance of the *bhūt* phenomenon in Maharashtrian society. We shall, however, deal with observations which have relevance to what we have stated previously about the *paḍthal* and associated activities of the gods and mediums. The Guhāgar case is different from all previous ones discussed earlier in that the *bhūts* were not set upon in a deliberate manner by human agencies; they were there before. They were provoked by their removal from the pots. They were agitated enough to cause serious obstacles to the construction of the palace. Many of the *paḍthal* details concerning consultations with the gods emerge from this case. The god possessing Gāvḍā was, indeed, asked about the *bhūts'* identity, which he told. The same god advised that the *vāḍā* should not be built on the spot where it was intended to be built, and his advice was serious enough for Bājīrāv to give orders to halt the construction of the *vāḍā*. But in the true manner of a *padthal*, after Gāvḍā's god was consulted, the village god was also consulted for a second opinion. When the Rāṇe *bhūt* was demanding unreasonable consessions from Hari Parcure, the god was consulted for the steps Hari should take to pacify the *bhūt*. He was told that the community should plead with the *bhūt*. Even Bājīrāv had some input in the presentation of the arguments to convince the *bhūt* to tone down his demands. Eventually, the *bhūt* was installed in the temple of Rāmeśvar, with a special *oṭā*. It is possible that the *bhūt* may have been elevated to the status of a god, since he was given the ritual honour of a *jatrā* and other offerings (*nevedya*). The Rāṇe brothers' *bhūt* obtained an honoured position in front of the goddess's image. In the end the goddess gave her assurance of safety. It must be noted, however, that the god is not shown as stopping the activities of the *bhūts* or in any manner controlling them. The god in the above case was an agent par excellence to report on the *bhūts*. The *bhagat*, the diviner, disposed of the *bhūts* at the goddess Jholāī's compound in the initial stage of the Guhāgar case. His services were required at the end of the case to install the *bhūt* on the *oṭā*, the platform for the *bhūt*.

Some Observations: The Gods and the *Bhūts*

The relationship between the gods and the *bhūts* is well established in the legal documents. The gods are actually shown sending in the *bhūts* for those of their worshipers who perform the *māṇnukā* (vows). The services of the diviners such as the *bhagat* or *vaśye* are used by persons to plead before a god on their behalf. Sacrifices of three goats and a present of a silk flag would naturally help to expedite the process. Interestingly, the consultations with the gods for the *māṇnukā* and for the other *bhūt*-related projects are known as *devdharma* or *devaskī*. As stated earlier, the gods in the Guhāgar case act as the *paḍthal* advisors. Gāvḍā's god acts as a consultant to the brāhmaṇs and advises them on how to deal with the *bhūt*. On the advice of Gāvḍā's god, advice which was endorsed by the goddess Vāghāṃbarī, Bājīrāv decided to stop the construction of the palace. It was during the *gondhaḷ* of the goddess that Gopāl's *bhūt* manifested itself.

Law and the Gods: The *Paḍthal*

Paḍthal (the term may have come from *paḍosā thal*, the place for verification) was a formal "legal" procedure to determine the identity of the *bhūts* and the person responsible for sending them. The person identified as the *bhūt*-sender was implicated in the troubles generated by the *bhūts* and, therefore, was liable for punishment. In the cases mentioned above we find that when the "*bhūt*-sending" was established, *vatan* was sequestered, a heavy fine was imposed and, in the worst scenario, a person was forced to leave the area with his household.

In the *paḍthal* trials, a written government authorization was sent to the *paḍthal* centres. At the end of the *paḍthal*, formal letters were sent to the government informing it of the response of the gods. It was more like evidence given by the god. The final settlement (*nivāḍā*) of the *bhūt* dispute (*bhūt kajiyā*) could not take place without the *paḍthal* report. Furthermore, in the *paḍthal* procedure the god's response had to be witnessed by both the accused and the victims and in the presence of the government representatives and other witnesses present in the temples. The gods' words spoken through the medium, if required (as in the case of Bāl Gogṭe), had to tally with the gods' answers received through the ritual of *kaul-prasād*. Once the settlement was effected, the person responsible for the *bhūts* was legally bound to terminate the trouble caused by them. He had to give surety (*jāmīn*) for non-recurrence of the *bhūt* trouble and had to pay a fine to the government commensurate with the severity of the harm done by the *bhūts*. However serious the crime may have been, the punishment was generally a fine or a period of confinement in jail. The community dealt with the offender who had commited a particularly heinous crime, such as homicide, through the *bhūts*, by (social) ostracism, which was endorsed by the state authorities. Ghāṭe, Thiṭe and Bhoī had to face ostracism from the community. Ghāṭe was readmitted by purification. Thiṭe, whose ostracism was so severe that his children could not get married, had to make do without the rituals. He returned the *vatan* to the owner. Bhoī, when given a notice of ostracism, recoiled by threatening to kill the members of the community. The state then put him behind bars.

The *paḍthal* procedure was, in fact, like the *pañcāyat* court proceedings in 18th century Maharashtra.[42] In the *paḍthal* "court", the arbitrator-judges were the gods, who evidently knew the *bhūts* and their doings, and also the persons who were responsible for sending the *bhūts*. The expression "*paḍthal nemṇe*" ("institute a *paḍthal* proceeding") was the same as the phrase found frequently in 18th-century Marathi legal documents, "*pañcāyat nemṇe*". *Nivāḍā* was the

---

[42] For the structure and function of *pañcāyat* courts, see Sen 1925: 214-212; Gune 1953: 73-86. However, neither of the above authors is aware of the *paḍthal* procedure.

formal legal term for the settlement of the court used both in the *pañcāyat* and *paḍthal* trials. In the *pañcāyat* proceedings, the decision of the arbitrators emerged as a consensus of opinions; in the *paḍthal,* the responses of the various gods had to be matched. The collective wisdom of the gods was required before there could be any settlement. Lastly, the *pañcāyat,* in a dispute which reached the government, was usually convened by the government; the directives to appoint a *paḍthal* generally came from the government. Sometimes it was requested by the parties themselves.

The Guhāgar palace case was different from the trial by *paḍthal* in the *bhūt* disputes mentioned above, in that the *bhūts* were not set upon people by humans; on their own the Rāṇes harassed the people concerned with building the palace. The case was nearer to the negotiated settlement (*samjāviśī*) sanctioned and ratified by the 18th century government in Maharashtra and which had the same weight as a *pañcāyat* court settlement. The dispute in the Guhāgar case was initiated by the *bhūts* themselves. The proprietary rights of the *bhūts* constituted the issue in this dispute, and this was acknowledged by the humans. At the end of the negotiations, Saṃbhājī's *bhūt* settled for an *oṭā* in Rāmeśvar temple, as befitting a god. His brothers found a resting place in goddess Vāghāṃbarī's precincts. Hari Parcure saved his 1200 rupees and a potentially troublesome 18 *hāth* spot in his home. The initial security (*jāmīn*) he had given to the *bhūt* that he would not sell away his house was annulled at the end. But before he would be freed of the obligations, the other brāhmaṇs as a group had to negotiate the terms with Saṃbhāji's *bhūt*. The *bhagat* and the *zāḍ* got their money for services rendered. Bājīrāv got his future *vāḍā* freed of the *bhūt*.

The last point deals with the noticeable helplessness of the brāhmaṇs, the upholders of great Sanskritic tradition, in preventing the doings of the *bhūts*. The brāhmaṇs, including the powerful brāhmaṇ Peśvā, had no control over the *bhūts*. Some of the brāhmaṇ participants in the Guhāgar Palace case were temple priests and administrators, government officials and learned in the Vedas and Purāṇas. Guhāgar appears to have been a brāhmaṇ dominated town; the town's key administrative officers were brāhmaṇs. Also in the *bhūt* disputes discussed in the first half of the paper, the majority of the disputants were brāhmaṇs from Koṅkaṇ. The śāstric *mantra* and rituals, for example, the *anuṣṭhāna* to ward off the *bhūts* and *picās,* were evidently not used in the *bhūt* cases. In the *bhūt* cases, the *bhūts* were "here and now" phenomena. The concern to contain them, to keep them permanently at bay, was local and immediate. The non-brāhmaṇ diviners, the *bhagat, vaśye* and *zāḍ,* had access to the *bhūts* as well as to the local gods and goddesses. For example, in the Guhāgar case, the medium was the Sutār, and the *bhagat* was Daulat Sāvant. The god spoke through the medium of Yesu Gāvḍā. Even Kripālgīr Gosāvī, in whose dreams the *bhūt* manifested itself, was a non-brāhmaṇ person. After the installation of Saṃbhājī's *bhūt* on the *oṭā,* only the *śūdra mānkarī* (receiver of rights) remained to finalise the ritual arrangements; others were asked to leave.

SECTION II

Case I

Peśvā Daftar Ghaḍṇī Rumāl, 374, September 16, 1786.

Trimbak Ballāl Gānū, Mauje Vāsī, Tarf Saṅgameśvar, Tālukā Ratnāgirī, came to the *hujūr* [at Puṇe] and petitioned:

> We had been managing the Khotī of the above village from the beginning. But the peasants of the place (*rayat*), disputing with us that "the Gānūs were being more stern (*jājatī jalal*) in their behaviour than is required by the regulations of the place," went to the Subhā [headquarters] at Ratnāgirī, lodged a com-

plaint against us and gave the itinerary [of complaints] in writing (*kalamācī yādī lehūn dilhī*). Without enquiring into the matter, the Subhā sequestered our Khotī [*vatan*]. When we went to the *hujūr* with our complaint, the villagers (*gāvkarī*) also came to the *hujūr*. But before coming to the *hujūr*, they had petitioned the village god, presenting him with a silk flag (*gāvce devās garāṇe ghālūn yek niśāṇ tāpattyāce deū karūn*), and stating: "Something bad should happen to the Gānūs. They should emerge as *khoṭe* (false) from the settlement (*mansubī*) and the complaint lodged by us should succeed."

Having arrived there [at Puṇe], Rāmjī Gāvḍā, Rāmjī Bhekrā, Yes Vajhā, Gaṅgājī Moryā and Bahirjī Cālkā, asking the god to do their bidding (*devās jāb devūn*), sacrificed three goats (*tīn bakrī mārlī*). Because of these actions, we were utterly ruined (*nāś bahot jālā*). Although we had become *khare* (true) and twice the *nivāḍpatre* (settlement documents) were written, we could not receive the [government] seal of ratification. Our settlement in the end did not come to fruition (*mansubī śevṭās na gelī*) Our health began to deteriorate. Hence we returned home. It was established through the *devadharma* (*devadharma pāhātā*) that the villagers had set the *bhūts* upon us and had done the vows (*bhūte ghātlī va mānṇukā kelyā*). We then went to the Subhā and informed [the government] of the developments. We got one *bhagat* (the diviner), one policeman (*sipāi*) and the *thalpatra* (letters to the *thal*, place of arbitration) for the appointment of five villages for arbitration, and returned to the village. Yes Vajhā and the others were interrogated (*pursīs kelī*) and they wrote their two depositions:

> While leaving the village, because we wanted our claims to succeed, we petitioned to the god and gave him the silk flag (*tāpattyāce niśāṇ*). When we came to Puṇe we sacrificed one goat (*ek bakre mārle*) in order that the Gānūs' claims should not succeed, and that something bad should happen to them.
>
> We possess those two depositions. After that, the villagers (*gāvkarīs*), the *bhagat* and the policeman proceeded to the five villages and did the *paḍthal*. There the gods, in the presence of the villagers, verified the above statements and the other intimidating acts (*sadarhū pramāṇe va āṇkhī daṇī kelyācī purvaṇī kelī*) [of the villagers]. The *thalpatra* (the documents stating the results of the *paḍthal)* of the five villages are with us. We are submitting this letter [to the *hujūr*] so that it may take action concerning this matter.

[Instructions to the Kamāvisdār:] You should bring the peasants (*kuṇbiyās*) to the Subhā [headquarters]. You should personally investigate the matter and if, after the deliberations, doubts emerge, then initiate a new *devdharma* and resolve the matter through *paḍthal*. You should collect the fine (*gunhegārī*) from the one who emerges as *khoṭa* (false) after a proper investigation, and deposit it with the Tālukā [*district headquarters*]. You should punish the *khoṭā* (*khoṭyāce pārpatya karṇe*). Inform the *hujūr* of the actions taken. One *citṇīsī* (secretarial) letter to Mahipatrāv Kṛṣṇa [Kamāvisdār], Tāluke Ratnāgirī.

Case II

Peśvā Daftar Ghaḍṇī Rumāl, 374, October 22, 1789

Āpā Bhaṭ Parāñjpe, Mauje Muṭāṭ, Tarf Khārāpaṭaṇ, Tāluk Vijaydurga came to the *hujūr* and petitioned:

> Our house is right in the village. The village gods (*grāma devatā),* Śrī Bhūtnāth and Śrī Nātheśvar, were at the pleadings of the four (*caughāce śabde*): Ātmājī Polkar Mirāsī, the *kuṇbī* who is the officer of the *pāvṇī* (passport officer), Mahād Dhaḍī, Bāḷū Gurav and Māhār have caused trouble for the last ten months. In our house and those of our lineage brothers (*bhāūbandh*), the women's garments get torn and burnt. Our women get assaulted (*bāīkā dāḍon paḍtāt*). Our cattle die yelling (*gure vāsre ārḍon martāt*). Our houses get set on fire. We, therefore, approached the village diviner (*gāvkarī vaśye*) and said, "Ask the god the reason for the varied troubles affecting our houses." He replied that he would ask (*utar kele kī pusto*). But he did not settle the issue and stop our troubles by [asking] the god through possession or through [*kaul*-] *prasād* (*devā javlī avasarī prasādī nivāḍā karūn updrav manā hoy te karāve te na karīt*). We, then, waited for a month or two at the village, and then went over to live in the house of a Kulkarṇī of Mauje Vāghṭoṇe, Tarf Khārāpāṭaṇ. On account of the troubles caused him by fire (*agnīcā updrava*) in his house, the Kulkarṇī would not allow us to live with him. We then went into the woods where there was enough supply of water, and stayed there. We then went to the Subhā and told Gaṅgādhar Govind of what had transpired. Dispatching the clerks (*kārkūn*), through them, he did

> the *paḍthal* of five villages (*pāc gāvcī paḍthale kelī*) and the settlement was effected (*nivāḍā jāhālā*). It was established that the village diviner's pleadings [to the gods] were "responsible for the ruination of Parāñjpe (*gāvkarī vaśye yāce śabde parānjyape yācā nāś hoto*). "The gods of the village also concurred with the truth of that statement (*tyāpramāṇec gāvcyā devānīhī khare mhaṇon sāṃgitle*). There was no trouble for a month or two after the village diviner had the *devaskī* (the workings of the *bhūts* and other supernatural beings) under control (*devaskicā bandobast*). But the troubles started again as before. The [government] investigations (*caukaśī*) which should have been followed to control such events, did not take place. The village diviner should be compelled to dispose of the *bhūts*. A surety (*jāmīn*) should be extracted from him that, henceforth, the troubles would not be caused through him. Because of the troubles, our fields have been ruined. The government estimates of the revenue (*sarkār dastācā ākār*), therefore, should be recovered from him. He should be made to give that amount (*vasūl*) to the above Tāluke. We should be compensated for the loss of our clothing (*cirgu pāṃgharūṇ*). Without government efforts to settle the above matter, we would not be able to inhabit the village. The *hujūr* should give its ruling on the matter (*yevisī āñā kelī pāhīje*).

This letter is given to you [Gaṅgādhar Govind] on account of the above. Āpā Bhaṭ's and his lineage brothers' household were harassed by the village diviner's *bhūt*. You conducted the investigation by appointing the *paḍthale* from the Subhā. Although those were effective (*guṇ ālā*), the troubles have started again. The village diviner should be asked to terminate the *bhūts*; a surety (*jāmīn*) should be taken from him for the non-recurrence of the troubles.

He should be fined according to his means and circumstances (*jivan māfik gunhegārī*), and the amount should be credited to the Tālukā accounts. You should compensate reasonably the amount of loss incurred by Parāñjpe on account of the troubles generated by the *bhūts*. One *ciṭṇīsī* (secretarial) letter to Gaṅgādhar Govind.

Case III

Prānt Ajmās, Peśvā Daftar Dakṣīṇ Koṅkaṇ Rumāl, 423, January 16, 1812.

In the service of Śrīmant Māhārāj Rājaśrī Bābāsāheb Svāmī (Peśvā Bājīrāv II). The plea of his servants, the administrators and the villagers of Kasbe Guhāgar, Tarf Guhāgar, Tāluke Anjaṇvel. Salutations... (*sāṣṭāṅg namaskār vijñāpanā viśeṣa*). The Mahārājā purchased a total of six *āgar* (pieces of fertile land) in order to build a *vāḍā* (palace).

A list of the *āgars*.
Of Nāro Bābūrāv and Hari Vasudev Pālandye,
Of Satyabhāmābāī, the widow of Morār Mādhavrāv Peṭhye.
Of Raghunāth Hari and Aṃtājī Parcure.
Of Naro Bāpūjī Bhāve.
Of Bāpūjī Nārāyaṇ Parcure.
Of Sadāśiv Dikṣit Sāvarkar....

The excavation for the foundation of the *vāḍā* was started in some of the plots of land by setting up a workshop (*kārkhānā*). The pots in which the *bhūts* had long been buried were brought to the surface on the site which had belonged to Hari Parcure. The *bhūts* began causing trouble to the clerks and others in the workshop. The carpenter Bhikājī Sutār Vasaīkar was possessed by them (*aṅgī vāḍhū lāglī*). The clerk in charge of the workshop brought Daulat Sāvat, the *bhagat*, of Mauje Doṇvalī, Tarf Havelī, Tāluke Anjaṇvel to investigate. The *bhūts* of the place were disposed of with the aid of the *bhagat* (*bhagtāce gujāratine*) by Hari Parcure and Sadāśiv Keśav. It was their responsibility to do so. The *bhūts* were taken next to the goddess Śrī Jholāī of Mauje Gāvtale, Tāluke Suvarṇadurga, and were terminated there [*gatīs lāvilī*]. In order to verify (*paḍosā pahāvayāsī*) if the *bhūts* had really been terminated, we, the villagers, went to consult a god who had possessed (*aṅgāvar dev vāḍhat āhe*) Yesu Gāvḍa of Mauje Pāṭapnāle, Tarf Velaṃb, Tāluke Anjaṇvel. We asked the god's spirit (*devās avsarī pusīle*), "Have the *bhūts* inhabiting the six *āgars* really been terminated?" The god said:

> The *bhūts* who were taken to the village of Gāvtale have been terminated (*gatīs gelī*). But the original owners of this place, Suryājī, Saṃbhājī, Bāvājī, and Rāghojī Rāṇe, died a violent death four hundred years ago. Becoming *bhūts* and inhabiting their place, they have caused troubles (*upadrav karitāt*). Therefore, the *vāḍā* (palace) should not be constructed on that site.

The village goddess (*grāmdevatā*) Śrī Vāghāṃbarī of Kasbe Guhāgar, when consulted through *prasād* (*prasādī pusīle*), for verification of the response of the god, confirmed the god's statement. On hearing this news, the Svāmī [Bājīrāv] gave orders to stop building the *vāḍā*. The next day, the Rāṇe brothers appeared in a dream of Kṛpālgīr Gosāvī, who had come to Guhāgar with the Svāmī. They identified themselves and said:

> The Śrīmant [Bājīrāv] has been building the *vāḍā* in our place. He has now stopped the construction, but should not do so. On our own we have given the place to him. If this needs verification, we shall possess and communicate (*āṅgāt yeūn sāṅgū*) with any one you wish to name.

When the Māhārājā came to know of this, he ordered that the *bhūts* should enter the body of the Sutār, whom they had possessed earlier, and should tell through him whatever they wished to tell. Thereupon, we, the villagers, and the *bhagat*, got Bhikājī Sutār Gujrātī to sit with us and pleaded with (*garhāṇe ghātle*) the Rāṇes to explain the meaning of the dream. Saṃbhājī Rāṇe's spirit then said [through the medium of the Sutār]:

> We have willingly (*svasaṃtoṣe*) given our place to the Śrīmant [Bajīrāv]. He should build the *vāḍā* and live there securely. He will not be troubled a bit by us (*āmcā updrav kāḍī mātra lāgṇār nāhī*). But Rāgho Harī should give me a place to live. The 1200 rupees, the price which he received for my *āgar*, should be given to me.

Rāgho Harī then said:

> I had only one plot of land. I sold it to the government. I have only an occupied house (*nāndte ghar*).

Rāṇe then said:

> You should assign an area of 18 *hāth* in that occupied house. I shall live there. You should give surety (*jāmīn*) to me that the place I live in will not be sold to any one.

Rāgho Harī then assigned a location measuring 18 *hāth* in his occupied house and named the administrators (*kārbhārī*) among us as his surety. Following the instructions of Rāṇe, 21 coconuts and one quarter *sīr uḍīt* (black grams) were placed in that 18 *hāth* spot. The spirit (*avsar*) of Rāṇe [through the medium of the Sutār] went over to the place which was sold to the *sarkār* (government) and on which the *vāḍā* was being built. On the four corners of that place, he, with his own hands, broke open four coconuts, one at each corner. He gave one coconut for the Svāmī [Bājīrāv] to break open at his feet. When he was about to leave for Puṇe, the coconut was cracked open.

As a form of respect, the Svāmī [Bājīrāv] was presented with a flower-plume studded with emeralds (*pācū*) to wear in his *pāgoṭe* (turban). He [Bājīrāv] gave permission to build the *vāḍā* [and left for Puṇe]. We then went to the god who had possessed the Gāvḍā to verify the truth or falsehood of what had transpired (*yāpramāṇe majkur kharā jāhālā kiṃvā khoṭā yācā paḍthal pāhāvayā karitā*). The Gāvḍā's god said:

> What transpired was true. But the [*bhūt*] who was demanding the rupees will insist on taking them.

We all prayed to the god, saying, "Rāgho Hari has no money. How can he give the 1200 rupees which he received from the sale [of the plot of land]?"

The god said:

> Rāgho Hari should take refuge with the villagers (*gāvkarī yās śaraṇ yāve*). The villagers then should entreat the *bhūt* to exempt him from payment of the rupees. Heeding their entreaty, the *bhūt* may spare Rāgho Hari.

The Gāvḍā's god gave this advice. The next day, as previously arranged, the *bhūt* was induced to possess (*bhutācā avsār āṇūn*) the Sutār. All the villagers, the *bhagat* and the deputies of the government, the Rājaśrī Mor Dikṣit and the Rājaśrī Jñānobā Deśpāṇḍe and their attendants, who were assembled there, said to the *bhūt:*

> As prearranged, you have come. Now is the time to clarify the previous talk.

Rāṇe *bhūt* said:

> Rāgho Hari should give me 1200 rupees and, from his plot, he should give me a place measuring 18 *hāth* as compensation (*mobadlā*).

He began reiterating the same statement. But the Māhārājā's [Bajīrāv's] instructions to his deputies were to entreat Rāṇe, saying, becoming pleased with us, you removed the obstacle encountered by us and the villagers. Now only Rāgho Harī is in dire straits (*aḍcaṇit paḍto*). You should show your goodwill towards him and free him from difficulties. What use is it for you to crave after money and a place?

After this entreaty, Rāṇe said:

> Rāgho Hari should place the pile of 1200 rupees in front of me. Then I shall go to live in another place near Rāmeśvar.

Mor Dikṣit Marāṭhe gave Rāgho Hari 1200 rupees on loan. These were placed before the *bhūt*. The *bhūt* gave Ābā Keḷkar, in the service of Dikṣit, 10 rupees out of the pile for construction of an *oṭā* (platform) measuring one *gaj* (about two feet) at a place near Rāmeśvar. He gave 10 rupees to Ābā to give to the *zāḍ* (the medium of the *bhūt*, in this case the Sutār) as a gift (*bakṣis*). He gave three rupees to Daulat Sāvant, the *bhagat*, for the expenses of installing him on the *oṭā*. The surety deed (*jāmīn*) from the villagers given earlier by Rāgho Hari, that the latter would not sell the spot measuring 18 *hāth* in his house, was annulled. Rāgho Harī was given the place as a gift. The *bhūt* made a contract to the effect that he would keep on residing in the *oṭā* near Rāmeśvar, and that he would not cause trouble to anyone.

Next the *oṭā* was built. All the villagers assembled and the spirit of the *bhūt* was brought over for installation. The twenty rupees entrusted to Ābā Keḷkar were brought in. Dikṣit said:

> The materials for the *oṭā* were used from the workshop. We do not want recompense from you. Take this ten rupees and do what you like with it.

He [the *bhūt*] gave three rupees to Rāgho Hari and seven rupees to the *bhagat,* and the other *mānkarī* (the people entitled to dues in this connection). The *zāḍ* (medium) was given the 10 rupees as promised after the spirit left him. The *bhagat* and the *śūdra mānkarī* (non-brāhmaṇ holders of the rights) were asked to stay behind and the rest were asked to leave. As was customarily done (*gāv cālī pramāṇe*), amidst the offerings and the festivities and giving of coconuts to the people present there (*jatrā naivedya karūn nāraḷ maṇḍaḷīs deūn*) the *bhūt* occupied the *oṭā.*

The remaining three Rāṇes were installed in front of the goddess Vāghāṃbarī just outside the Devī's image (*devāpuḍhe povlī bāher*). This was done according to the wishes of Vāghāṃbarī. The instructions to conduct the festivities (*jatrā*) associated with the event were carried into effect. Under the instructions of the *bhagat,* the *grām devatā* (the village goddess, Vāghāṃbarī) was given three coconuts for forgiveness for any indiscretions committed, and one coconut for freeing the house of Rāgho Hari. The goddess gave the assurance of safety. All the *bhūts* everywhere have been kept at bay.

The Svāmī [Bājīrāv] and his descendants should live securely in that place after building the *vāḍā.* The villagers, without any uncertainty about this matter, have written this letter:

> The responsibility is ours to ensure that there shall not be any trouble from the *bhūt.* We should be considered as offenders of the government if such trouble were ever to arise.

Written on Thursday, January 16th, 1812, in his own handwriting by Govind Raghunāth Gogaṭe, representing Bābājī Āṃbeḍekar Kulkarṇī of Kasbe Guhāgar. Endorsing and testifying the above (*mānyatā va sākṣa*):
Moro Ābājī Parcure, Māhājan, Kasbe Guhāgar.
Māhādājī Hari Tāmhaṇkar, representing Govind Rāmcandra Vijhe, Māhājan of the above Kasbe.
Sadāśiv Rāmcandra Peṭhe, Mokdam of the above Kasbe.
Rāgho Hari Parcure, Māhājan of the above Kasbe.
Dād Bhaṭ Khare, Purāṇik, Dharmādhikārī, Upādhyāya of the above Kasbe.
Rāmcandra Dikṣit Paṭvardhan, Upādhye of the above Kasbe.
Gaṇeś Bhaṭ Khare, Dharmādhikārī and Upādhye.
Sadāśiv Dikṣit Khare Śāraṅgpāṇī.
Māhādev Dikṣit Paṭvardhan, Upādhye of the above Kasbe.
Mor Bhaṭ Khare Śāraṅgpāṇī (handwriting: Vāsudev Bhaṭ Khare).
Rāgho Nārāyan Āṭhavle Guhāgarkar.
Janārdan Dhoṇḍdev Gadre of the above Kasbe.
Vināyak Bhaṭ Khare Belsare of the above Kasbe.

Case IVa

The Selections from the Satara Rajas' and Peshwas' Diaries, II, vol. 2, G. C. Vad, et. al., eds., August 19, 1759, p. 70.

A letter to Nāro Triṃbak of Taluke Vijaydurga. That Bāḷ Mahājanī Khot, Mauje Gāvkhaḍī, Tarf Lāje, set *bhūts* upon Gaṇeś Viṭhal Gokhale was established through the *paḍthal* of five to seven places. But the latter did not dissipate the *[bhūts]* (*vārāvar na kelī*). Recently, both the disputants were summoned to the *hujūr*, and during the adjudication, Bāl, having confessed verbally that he did set a few *bhūts* and did some vows [to the gods] (*kāhī bhūte va mānṇukā kelyā kharyā*), admitted it in a *katbā* (a formal statement, a bond). Abiding by the recent government ordinance sent to the entire Talukā establishment [of Vijaydurga] to punish the persons found engaged in the *bhūt* activities (*bhūtāḷyāṃce pārapatyāviṣayī*), this letter is issued to you to sequester Bāḷ Mahājanī's Khotī *vatan* and to induce his household members (*kuṭuṃba*) to leave for the Ghāṭs (upland). Hence, sequester the Khotī *vatan* of the above mentioned persons. Escort his household members to the upland. Break down his house. He should [however] be allowed to take his belongings and his animals. Ten people and one clerk should be assigned for this task from the Subhā. Bāl Mahājanī is kept under detention by the *hujūr*. When his people reach the upland destination, he will be sent there.

Case IVb

Selections from the Peśvā Daftar, G. S. Sardesai, ed., vol. 43, January 31, 1761, p. 34 (7458).

Letter to Rājaśrī Nāro Trimbak, Tāluke Jañjire, Vijayadurga, from Rāmśāstrī.

Greetings. Because of the *bhūt* dispute (*bhūtācā kajiyā*) between Gaṇeś Viṭhal Gokhle and Balmānī Gogaṭe (Bāḷ Māhājanī), Balmānī Gogaṭe's children and other dependents were brought to Puṇe by the *hujūr*. Their kindred (*bandhū*) took the government orders and the list of inventory [regarding the *bhūt* dispute] to the [government] people [at the Subhā]. The [letters had ordered them] to go to the great centres (*māhāsthānī*) known to be efficacious (*jyāgrutsthale*) in ten villages outside the Mahāl (*parmahālī*), to communicate with the gods there through *kaul-prasād* (a ritual of communication with the god) concerning the list of items containing the government order and to communicate the *nivāḍā* (settlement) effected in this manner to the government in writing. These government orders were not followed by you. Without the gods being consulted through the *prasād* (*devācā prasād na ghetā*), only the *paḍthale* done through the *bhagat's* divination was taken as evidence (*bhagatāce śabde paḍthale karūn*) and the brother of Balmānī Gogaṭe was put under arrest. Balmānī is, therefore, unceasingly lodging a complaint against this [procedure] with the *hujūr*. This [procedure] should not have been followed. Abiding by the previous government order, send a clerk and a policeman from the Subhā to the ouside Mahāl (district) and ask the gods there, who are known to be potent and heedful (*jāgṛt*), questions as stated in the articles in the presence of both [disputants]. The settlement arising out of such means should be communicated quickly [to the *hujūr*]. It is not good that the *hujūr* should be encumbered with the repeated protests over this matter. Balmānī's children and his dependants have become exhausted by the past six months [of stay at Puṇe]. The brāhmaṇ is a family man (*kuṭuṃba vachala* [*vatsala*]). Hence expedite the settlement, and send it to the *hujūr* in writing.

Case IVc

Peśve Daftar Ghaḍṇī Rumāl, 374, April 21, 1768.

[The trials and tribulations of Bāl Māhājanī had a bitter-sweet ending. I have translated below only the beginning lines of the following document, which has a direct bearing on the bhūt dispute mentioned in the case IVa and IVb.]

The *nivāḍpatra* (settlement document) given to Bāl Māhājanī Gogṭā, Mulīyā Khot, Mauje Gāvkhaḍī, Tarf Lāje, Subhā Prānt Rājāpūr. In the past, Gaṇeś Viṭhal Gokhale of the above village petitioned to the *hujūr* that you set the *bhūts* upon him, on the basis of which the Gogṭes' *vatan(s)* were sequestered in 1759-1760 A. D. The *bhūt* dispute was resolved after some time. The *vatan(s)* therefore, were about to be released.

[But Kṛṣṇājī Govind Gore of Bāl's village took objection on the grounds that Bāl did not belong to the lineage of the real holder of the *vatans,* and hence, he was ineligible for the *vatans*. Bāl, however, proved that he was of the same lineage. At the conclusion of the dispute with the Gores, the *vatan(s)* were released from the government sequestration. But this time, fortunately for Bāl, the case had nothing to do with the bhūts.]

Case Va

Peśvā Daftar Dakṣiṇ Koṅkaṇ Rumāl, 594, December 28, 1774.

Viṣṇu Keśav Palsule Desāī, Tarf Rājāpūr, petitioned to the *hujūr:*

> The Khotī *vatan* of Mauje Asole Vaḍad of Tarf Rājāpur belongs to us. For the past twenty-five to thirty years, we had given Viṣṇu Anant Ghāṭe Kotāpūrkar the above village to manage. In order to appropriate the *vatan* for himself (*vatan āplyās jirāve mhaṇon*), setting the *bhūts* upon us, he got the members of our household killed. In the *nivāḍā* (settlement) concluded through the *paḍthal* in our presence, it was established that it was he who had set the *bhūts*. The brāhmaṇs [of that place], therefore, ostracized him (*vālīt ghātle*). But in the meantime the Khotī of the village has been sequestered by the government. The village has been ours from the early days (*gāv kadīm āmcā*). In this regard, we possess ancient documents dealing with division of our inheritance among brothers. The Sāheb (government) should deliberate on those letters, and on the written account kept at the Subhā, which affirmed that the *bhūts* were set upon us by him. The orders should be issued to let us manage our Khotī of the village.

[Desāī] thus submitted his petition and showed the letters as indicated above. Those were looked into, and this present letter is given to you. Judging by the [contents of the] documents dealing with the division of the property [among Desāī's brothers], you should let the Khotī of the village be temporarily managed by the Deśmukh (Desāī). Afterwards, having resolved (*nirvāha*) the issue in their presence, through a settlement (*mansubī*), the management of the village shall be given to the rightful possessor. A *ciṭṇīsī* letter to Gaṅgādhar Govind.

Case Vb

Peśvā Daftar Dakṣiṇ Koṅkaṇ Rumāl, 594, March 26, 1776.

Viṣṇu Keśav Desāī, Tarf Rājāpūr, Tālukā Vijaydurga, came to the *hujūr* and petitioned.

> Viṣṇu Anant Ghāṭe set the *bhūts* upon us and got our people killed. The Subhā appointed the *paḍthal* and an Amin (a legal officer) was assigned through whom the settlement (*nivāḍā*) was effected between the two [disputants]. He went back to the Subhā [headquarters]. Although it was established in the *pañcāyat* convened by Māhādājī Raghunāth [the Amin] that it was Ghāṭe who had set the *bhūts,* no punishment was meted out to him on that account. For that reason, he [the Amin] made a representation to the government that both [the disputants] should go to the *hujūr* [for the settlement of the *bhūt* issue]. The brāhmaṇs of the area, reading the letter given by Māhādājī Raghunāth to the government, and upon instructions from the Subhā, ostracized Ghāṭe. Afterwards both of us went to the government, and the *pañcāyat* was convened there, and Ghāṭe became

> *khoṭā* (false). Without obtaining permission from the government to undertake the purification rites [for readmittance in the brāhmaṇ fold], and not letting all the brāhmaṇs know about his intentions to do so, with the backing of Rām Ṭhākūr Desāī, Ghāṭe pressured some of the brāhmaṇs into dining with him. Ghāṭe, and the brāhmaṇs who dined with him, should be made to go to the temple of Śrī Dhūtpāpeśvar and get themselves purified.

This letter is sent to you for the above reason. If the ostracism (*bahīṣkār*) in the past was carried out [by the brāhmaṇs] at the Subhā behest (*subhāce ājñepramāṇe*), then those brāhmaṇs who dined at his house without government permission (*divāṇce ājñevinā*) should be made to pay a fine of five rupees per person, and they, along with Ghāṭe, should be administered the *paṃcagavya* (five products of the cow) and, thus, be purified. *Ciṭṇīsī* letter to Gaṅgādhar Govind.

REFERENCES

Avlaskar, S. V. 1962. *Nāgāv ārthik va sāmājīk jīvan*. Bombay: Popular Prakashan.

Gune, V. T. 1952. *Judicial system of the Marathas*. Deccan College Dissertation Series: 12. Poona: Deccan College.

Sardesai. G. S. 1957. *Maratha historical genealogies*. Bombay: Government Central Press.

Sen, S. N. 1925. *Adminstrative system of the Marathas*. Calcutta: University of Calcutta.

Sontheimer, Günther-Dietz. 1989. *Pastoral deities in western India*, translated by Anne Feldhaus. New York: Oxford University Press.

Stanley, John M. 1988. Gods, Ghosts, and Possession. In *The experience of Hinduism: Essays on religion in Maharashtra*, edited by Eleanor Zelliot and Maxine Berntsen. Albany: State University of New York Press.

Durga Bhagvat

SOME MULTI-PURPOSE ASPECTS OF INDIAN FOLKLORE

Introduction

I do not believe that Indian culture is either Aryan or Dravidian. I look upon it as indigenous. Like every other culture in the world it is not isolated. Every culture has a mysterious amorphous element in it. It is the force that gives culture its potential. You find this potential working in all the forms of culture: in living forms, decaying forms, changing and reviving forms. This amorphous element is simple, yet complex. Its durability is amazing. That is what folklore is: the amorphous element of culture. It is the mysterious force behind every cultural phenomenon.

To me the word 'folklore', with all its genres, namely, tales, songs, riddles, and beliefs, seems a misnomer. Yet, since it has a long usage, about a century and a half, it cannot and should not be discarded. We have to accept the term as it is.

Archaeology and Folklore

The archaeological discoveries of Buddhist sculptures and paintings at Ajanta pose some questions that can only be unravelled by means of folklore. One such question is that of the man-bear relationship in the Ajanta paintings.

The Ajanta paintings are the most sophisticated and marvellous cave-paintings in the world. The man-bear scene that was once extant in cave 17 at Ajanta has since been destroyed by time. Thanks to John Griffith, the scene has been preserved for posterity in his unique book, *The paintings in the Buddhist cave temples of Ajanta* (1897). In that scene a man is seen sitting on a female bear's lap. The amorous and happy expressions on the faces of both the man and the bear are too obvious to be missed. Naturally, after seeing this scene, I turned to the Buddhist sources, viz. the *jātakas* and other legends in the Buddhist canon. But I found no evidence concerning the man-bear relationship. I then turned to Indian folklore and found substantial examples relating to this curious bestial form of activity. A paper of mine on man-bear relationships has been published in the *Journal of the Asiatic Society of Bombay* (1966-1967) and a more comprehensive account of the historical, natural, cultural, and folkloristic aspects of the black bear in India are presented in my Marathi book *Asval* (1974). In the course of this study I became aware that certain popular beliefs depicted in Buddhist art are not of Buddhist origin, but are representations of common folk beliefs. These beliefs were assimilated in the sophisticated art of Buddhism and given deeper meanings.

The Almighty Bull

The bull in its representations in the art and literature of the ancient world is a symbol of power and sexual potency. Bull-sport was an integral part of the rituals of the ancient Europeans, Asians, and Africans. Bull-leaping, which originated from religious rituals, gradually became a secular sport in historical times. In bull-leaping the man leapt over the bull, rode and controlled it (Hawles 1963: 112-122).

The bull is a symbol of divine power not only in India but throughout the ancient world. In Asia and especially in India it was perceived to be the mighty creative force of the universe. The seal of the bull found in Mohenjodaro represents the majestic beauty and male vigour of the animal. God Indra was called a bull in the

Vedas. The Vedas bestowed upon him the form of the fighting bull, the fiery bull, who impregnated the female. This representation of the majestic bull is found among the paintings from Ajanta in Griffith's book.

A Story in the Mahābhārata

There is no doubt that the king of the gods, Indra, was called a bull by the Vedic sages. They associated him with rain and fertility. In many tales Indra is a protector of the bulls who help man to till the land. The first such story is in the Mahābhārata, Vanaparva, IX. A farmer maltreated an ox that tilled his field. The young ox, hardly more than a calf, cried badly when the man beat it. Surabhi, the celestial cow, grieved because her son was being tormented by the man, complained to Indra, and Indra taught the man a lesson.

Nandī

Nandī, the mighty bull of Shiva, has been a symbol of power since purāṇic times. Basavagudi, in Bangalore city, is the famous and beautiful temple of Basava, the sacred bull. The huge image of the bull is awe-inspiring and yet very attractive. Venkatesh Iyengar, in his popular book, *Popular culture of Karnataka* (1954: 141f.), narrates the following legend of the temple. In the village of the Basavagudi temple there lived a farmer who was a miser. Shiva ordered Nandī to go to earth and teach the man to live a better life. Nandī entered the field and began to graze on the groundnut plants that were in bloom. The watchman was frightened on seeing such a terrible, huge bull, and ran away. He then informed his master about the strange bull. So the farmer came out with a big stick to beat the bull. He raised his arm to strike it, but his arm would not come down. He then prayed to Nandī for mercy. Nandī took pity on him and told him to give up his miserliness and become charitable. The farmer agreed. Later on, a temple was built for Basava, the Bull-God.

Indra and Puranjaya

A man riding a leaping bull is a recurring motif in the archaeological remains of ancient Asian culture. It is found both in sport and in battle situations. In both the man is controlling the animal. A literary example of this motif is found in the story of Indra and Puranjaya in the *Devī-bhāgavata*, (7-9). The gist of the story is that Indra, in a battle against the Daityas, or demons, called Puranjaya to help him. Puranjaya made Indra assume the form of a bull and, riding him, vanquished the demons and took possession of their cities. Hence he is known as Indravahana, the rider of Indra, and Puranjaya, the conqueror of the cities.

Bull Goring Man

In a pre-historic painting from the Sahara, circa 600 B. C., a bull is depicted as having gored a man, who is lying dead on the ground. The setting is a hunting scene, probably ritualistic, but shows that bull-fighting was in vogue in distant parts of the world in such an early period (Cottell, ed. 1961: 49).

The Bhitagām Terracotta

In the Bhitagām excavation (U.P.) a terracotta was found in which a man fighting a bull is depicted. The bull is overpowering the man. This terracotta has been badly damaged, thus obliterating other details (Singh 1968).

The Bullfight

In India bullfights appear to be of two kinds, viz. two bulls fighting each other and a fight between a bull and a man. A painting of two bulls fighting each other is given by Griffith in his monumental work on Ajanta. The painting was found in cave number one at Ajanta (Griffith 1897a: 114). In Indian folk traditions both of these types of fights are considered to be forms of sport. Among the Kallan tribe in Tamil Nadu, for example, aspiring bridegrooms fight with bulls. Some are injured. But those who succeed in subduing the animals are chosen by the brides. These victors dance joyfully before preparing for their wedding (Thurston 1909, vol. 3: 76).

The Bovine Habit of Goring

Bulls and cows have a habit of goring their victims with their horns. There is a proverb in Marathi: 'The donkey hits with kicks and the bull with its horns.' To hit with the horns is an instinctive act of defence in bovines.

The evening star (Venus) is called '*halad mara taro*' in the Bhili language. The literal meaning of the epithet is 'bull-killed star'. The Bhils believe that the star is the heavenly representation of a hero who was killed in a bullfight (Thompson 1895: 1-21).

Trampling by a Bull

The earliest archaeological evidence of a bull trampling a man is found in Egypt, circa 5500 B.C. In *Arts and Crafts of Ancient Egypt*, Flinders Petrie says: "...one of the most typical of these carvings is the figure in which the king is represented as a bull trampling his enemy" (Petrie 1910: 14).

Trampling as a Form of Punishment

Being trampled by one or more bulls, or being dragged by bulls, was a traditional form of punishment in India. In many regions this form of execution of a guilty person was even predominant. In southern India, that is, in Andhra, Karnatak, and Kerala, and in Maharashtra as well, this form of punishment was customary. Sometimes the victim was tied to the yoke and dragged by the bullocks along the road or field. This form of punishment was described vividly by Saint Namdeo in the 13th century. In the collection, or *gāthā*, of his devotional poetry *(abhaṅgas)* he describes how the untouchable saint who was his contemporary and dear friend, Chokhamela, was condemned by the brahmin priests of Vithoba's temple. Chokhamela was an ardent devotee of Vithoba of Pandharpur. Once the god came to the house of his beloved Chokha at night and Chokha fed him with curds. In the morning the priests found some curds on Vithoba's clothing. They made enquiries and came to know that the untouchable had fed the god at night. This was a crime that deserved nothing less than the death sentence. This being the verdict, Chokha was tied to the yoke of the bullocks. Vithoba rushed to the scene and held the yoke so firmly that the bullocks could not move. Though to others the god was invisible, his presence was felt by his devotee. As a result of this miracle, Chokhamela was set free and the punishment was nullified.

Trampling by Cattle as a Ritual

For a human to be trampled by a bull or a herd of bulls was an ancient ritual in India. Dr. Kalipad Mitra, in his article on the Gaydana festival (1932: 1ff.), gives the following account of the festival in Bihar and Bengal. "To secure the prosperity of the cattle and crops it was customary to bury a pig with its head above the ground and pass a herd of cattle to trample on it." Dr. Mitra further says that the original victim was the human animal. The pig was a later substitution. In Madras, the custom of burying a pig and driving cattle over its head was probably borrowed from the Lambadis. As Aldec Dubois relates in his *Hindu manners and customs,* the Lambadis would carry the unfortunate victim to a lonely spot and bury him alive in a hole up to the neck. Then they would dance around him, singing and making noise, till he expired. Or they would bury a child up to its shoulders and then drive cattle over it for good luck. This was a peculiar mode of human sacrifice. The Todas drove buffalos over female children. Rai Bahadur Hira Lal (1921) tells us that the Banjaras were similarly wont to place a child in a hole and drive bullocks over it with the result that the child was trampled and the well-being of the cattle was secured.

The Avadana Story

In his monumental work *Tibetan painted scrolls* (1949, vol. II: 20f.), Dr. Giuseppe Tucci gives Avadana 7, in which the story of Muktalata is narrated: The wife of Mahanama Shakya goes with her husband to listen to a sermon of the Buddha. Ananda Thera rebukes her for wearing ornaments, so she sends her ornaments home. But later, seeing the queen bedecked with jewels, she becomes envious and sends her maidservant Rohita to bring back her ornaments. The Buddha comes to know of this. Using his mystical powers he causes the maidservant to be killed by a mad cow. She had heard half of the sermon and was reluctant to go home to fetch the jewels. She dies and is reborn as princess Muktalata, the daughter of king Simhala.

The Bull as Protector

In the *Prabandhacintāmaṇi* of Acharya Merutunga is found the story (5-6) of king Ratnakara of the town of Ratnamala. The king had no son. It was predicted by an astrologer that the son of a particular poor woman would be the future king. The woman was pregnant. The time of delivery was near. The angry king ordered that the woman be buried alive. But the woman begged for permission to retire for a short while. She went to the forest, delivered her baby, left the baby in the jungle, and returned. She was then buried alive. Meanwhile, her child was suckled by a doe and was growing. When the king came to know about this, he ordered that a herd of cows and bulls be let loose so that the child be trampled to death. But a certain bull came near the child, stood still and protected it from being trampled to death by the herd. The bull that was bringing up the rear put himself in front of the cows and, placing the boy between his feet, made the herd pass by. The king then adopted him and named him Shripuja.

King Vikram and the Bulls

In the *Prabandhacintāmaṇi,* we come across a curious tale about the great king Vikrama. While wandering in disguise, Vikrama came to a town and wanted to proclaim his generosity to the world on the following day by having a pillar of glory built there. It was dusk when Vikrama walked slowly and leisurely with these thoughts. Suddenly, two fighting bulls rushed toward him and chased him. Vikrama ran for his life, the bulls chasing him all the way. Luckily, he saw the pillar of a brahmin's cowshed and climbed up it. Night fell. The bulls disappeared. But the king still sat on the roof.

When the moon rose the brahmin came out to see the position of the constellations. He found that the moon was obscured by Venus and Jupiter. He recognised this as an astrological symbol of the king's death. In order to avoid this evil, the brahmin spoke to his wife about the danger to the king's life, and asked her to make preparations for a sacrificial rite to save it. The brahmin's wife replied that though the king was said to be generous, he had not given them any money to get their seven daughters married. Where was the need to save the life of this miserly king? Yet, the brahmin persisted and the rite was performed. Vikrama from his hiding place heard the conversation. All his pride in his own generosity vanished. His dream of a glory-pillar also died. Thereupon he gave the brahmin enough money to get his daughters married and returned home.

Krishna Kills the Bull-Demons

A. Govardhanacarya's article "A lacuna in the vamsha" (1911: 58-61) presents an episode in the life of Krishna that has so far not been included in the published text of the *Harivaṃśa.* The episode is written in Sanskrit. The gist of it is that the seven sons of the demon Kalanemi fought with Vishnu in the form of bulls and were defeated by the god. In order to avenge the defeat the seven demon-bulls attacked the child Krishna and were killed by him.

The Bull Gores

This is a tale from Gujarat. A brahmin by the name of Popaṭ used to go to bathe every day. After bathing, he used to chant the *Gāyatrī mantra* and perform the *sandhyā* ritual. On the opposite bank of the river a handsome bull came to drink water and then sat quietly. He looked as majestic as the Nandī bull. He had beautiful horns. After four months had passed, Popaṭ was struck with the idea that he could push his head through the bull's horns. And one day he did this. The bull hit him with his horns. Had people not come to his aid and rescued him, Popaṭ would have died. Hence the proverb: 'To put one's head between the bull's horns' (Shah, n.d.: 6).

Bull Gores Master

In a collection of Marathi folk tales, *Loka-kathā and lokagīte* by V. V. Joshi (1936), is found the story of a prince who lovingly reared a black calf. An astrologer predicted that the prince would be killed by the same calf when it grew up. The years rolled by and the prince became all the more fond of the bull. However, the prince remembered the predicted fatal day. He raised a high platform, put his bedstead on it, and slept on it. The bull was left on the ground. At midnight, the bull managed to reach the prince and killed him.

Bull's Goring and the River Son (Shone)

In his article "The Kaimur range", Chandra Shekhar Bannerji (1877) writes: "Mr. Wheeler gives a tradition and assigns the easterly course of the Son (Shone) to disappointment in its love for the Narmada. The story that is current here, however, is different. The Son was originally in the sacred pool of Amarkantak. On the bank of this pool stood the hermitage of Jamadagni. Nearby a rustic drove his plough to which he attached a calf and its dam. The calf resented this cruelty and drove its horns into the chest of the ploughman, who died on the spot. The taint of this sin then turned the white calf black. On going into the pool the calf was purified and became white again. Parashurama, the son of Jamadagni, observed this. In order to purify humanity by the water of this pool, he cleft the side of the spring, or pool, with his *parashu*, or axe, and made the infant Son-stream turn away."

The Cow's Quality of Smiting

Like the bull or ox, the cow and the female buffalo (as well as the male) are known for smiting people with their horns, and even killing them. The *Prabandhacintāmaṇi* (1901: 56) says this about the cow:

> "She eats filth, void of discernment.
> She loves her own son, too fondly attended.
> With hoof-points and horns she smites other creatures.
> For what good quality, O King, is the cow worshipped?

Celestial Cow Attacks

In the *Śatruñjayamāhātmya* we come across the legend that King Kandu wanted to die either by drowning in the sea or by jumping from a mountain. Surabhi, the celestial cow, attacked him. He killed her. She, however, assumed the terrible form of the goddess Ambikā and challenged him to fight. Ambikā was his family deity.

The Cow that Hits

The brahmin Sudama and Dubharam Marwari were friends. Sudama did not believe in God. Both of them died on the sacred day of *Kapilashashti.* Just before dying, Dubharam, persuaded by his wife, gave the gift of a dying cow, a dark cow of the kind known as Kapila, to a brahmin, that is, to his dying friend, Sudama. Both the friends and the cow as well died on the same auspicious day. The two men went to heaven. The cow became the *Kamadhenu,* the celestial wish-granting cow. Citragupta, the scribe of Yama, the god of death, said to the men, "You have committed sins. You shall live in heaven as long as the auspicious hours last. Then you will go to hell." Sudama heard this and said to the cow, "I am your master. You have to deal with all the dignitaries in this heavenly court. Teach them a lesson." The cow obeyed. She rushed at the gods. She lifted the god Brahma on her horns. She trampled with her hoofs the god of death, Yama. Vishnu started running. She then went to Kailasa and harassed Shiva and his bull, Nandī. By that time the auspicious period came to an end and the gods were relieved. The gods decided to send the two men and the cow to hell. Sudama heard this verdict and said, "One day I am sure to go back to the earth. I will tell men that the three great gods, Brahma, Vishnu, and Shiva, are not at all gracious. If you merely look at them the result is that you have to go to hell. Do not worship them." The gods were struck as though with lightning. They cancelled the punishment and set the three free. They returned alive to the earth (Deshpande 1963: 141ff.)

A Cow Gores a Man

In the *Majjhima nikāya,* in the *Dhātuvibhaṅga sutta* (III.40) a prince from Taxila named Pukkusati is said to have met the Master incognito in a potter's shed in Rajagaha. The commentary gives us a full account of Pukkusati's renunciation in the name of the Buddha and his travelling on foot from Taxila through Savatthi to

Rajagaha, where he sought shelter in the shed. The text says that the Master, making a round in the Magadha country, moved towards Rajagaha and arrived at the same potter's shed for one night's stay. The commentary, on the other hand, says that the Master was in Savatthi at that time. Early in the morning of the same day, the Master, scanning the world, saw Pukkusati, and knew his mission as well as his imminent destiny. So, after taking a round in Savatthi for alms, the Master started alone on foot for Rajagaha, a distance of forty-five *yojanas.* He arrived at the potter's shed towards the evening of the same day. The Master and the would-be disciple stayed in the same shed without the disciple recognizing the Master, or, as the text has it, without their recognizing each other. They both sat in meditation far into the night. The Master liked Pukkusati's behaviour and asked him about himself. Pukkusati replied that he had renounced the world in the name of the Buddha and was seeking the Teacher.

The Master asked Pukkusati a few more questions. In answer, Pukkusati said that the Buddha was in Savatthi then (as he had already missed the Buddha in Savatthi en route and learnt in the city that very day that the Master was dwelling in Savatthi). Pukksati said further that he had never seen the Buddha before and that he would be unable to recognize the Master even if he saw him. The Master asked him to listen and delivered the main principle of this Sutta. The disciple then realised that the preceptor must be the Master himself. Consequently he asked the master's pardon for having disrespectfully addressed him with the term "friend" *(avusa).* The disciple was pardoned. There and then he attained the third stage of supermundane insight. The imminent danger to the life of this unique disciple arose soon after he left the Master in search of a monk's robe and a pot for his initiation and ordination at the Master's hand. A stray cow protecting her young calf in the street rushed at him and gored him to death with her horns. The monks duly informed the Master of this tragic mishap. They asked the Master what Pukkusati's destiny or future status would be. The answer was, as stated above, the attainment of the third stage of liberation. In recognition thereof the king of Magadha, Bimbisara, then gave him a royal cremation, and ordered that a stupa be erected over his ashes (Pradhan 1968: 9-10).

A Buffalo Gores a Tiger

In some stories the buffalo is substituted for the ox or bull or a cow. An illustration is found in a Bihar folktale reported by S. C. Mitra (1910-1911: 163-166). There lived seven she-buffalos. All were pregnant. Six of them said that they would give birth to bull-calves. But the seventh buffalo said she would bring forth a female calf. But, contrary to their wishes, the six cow-buffalos gave birth to female calves. The seventh one, however, produced a male calf. The bull calf grew into a full-grown buffalo.

A tiger had cultivated a sugar cane field. He appointed the jackal, his sister's son, as a watchman. The male buffalo went there and browsed on sugar cane. The jackal said, "Don't eat the sugar cane. My uncle will kill you". The buffalo continued to eat. The tiger got the news and came there and pounced on the buffalo. There was a fight between the two. The buffalo hit the tiger with his horns. But in the fight the buffalo broke one horn. He then went to a carpenter and asked him to repair his broken horn. The carpenter refused. The buffalo said, "If you don't repair my horn I will gore you to death". The carpenter then repaired his horn.

The buffalo then went to an oilman and said, "I want to fight with the tiger, the owner of your field. So oil my horn. If you don't I will kill you". The threat worked. The Teli oiled the horn. The buffalo went back to the field and again the fight ensued. The buffalo gored the tiger to death.

Bulls and Death in Bhaja Caves

Having rambled through all possible aspects of adverse human-bovine relationship in the show of might, I now come at last to the most vital point of this rather disjointed study.

In 1935 Dr. Motichandra brought to my notice a scene in the Bhaja caves of two bulls standing facing each other and a dead man stretched on the ground. He also showed me a seal from Asia Minor on which a scene of a bull goring a man was engraved. He asked me if I could find the motif of "bull killing man" in Indian folklore. Ever since then I started collecting material on it for about a stretch of five decades. Whatever I found I have put above. The information is no doubt sketchy and inconclusive as far as the Bhaja cave scene is concerned. Yet it has, I hope, paved a way to further research that awaits a scholar more competent than myself. Dr. Anand Coomaraswamy gives no explanation or even comment on the scene, but he finds its picture significant enough to include it in his book *Art in Asia and Indonesia* (1921).

His predecessors, the pioneer archaeologists James Fergusson and Jas Burgess, do the same. No verbal description or comment do they give; but they do give the photographic impression and a sketch of the scene. Folklore reaches up to the motif of the fighting bulls and the human victim and no further. The scene is an enigma to the archaeologists and Buddhist scholars so far.

G. Yazdani has observed that "representation of the contesting bulls and the dead man lying on the ground is puzzling". He feels that the treatment is "not realistic" (1930: 3-5). The Bhaja caves are the oldest caves in western India, as old as 200 B.C. according to Fergusson (1910).

Now let us turn our attention to the scene. On the left side are the two contesting bulls facing each other; they are standing. There is a corpse of a man lying on the ground with his arms stretched up. He is lying between the bulls. The bull at the head is keeping one foot on the man's arm and the bull at the feet is keeping his foot on one of the man's legs. Both the bulls are watching the victim. On the right side of the scene is a royal horse and a royal divine male being with a band of other persons. This seems like a group of heavenly beings in a celebrating, joyful mood, dancing and playing musical instruments.

There is no legendary account at all available for this particular scene. We do not even know whether the victim was a hero who in death was glorified by the gods. Neither can we guess whether the bulls were representations of divine power and the dead man was killed by the order of the divinities. The most significant point is that this is the solitary death scene in the world of Indian Buddhist art.

The peculiarity of Buddhist art is the absence of any other depiction of death, either human or animal. Even in the Ajanta paintings, there is a battle scene but no death. The Bhaja scene is the only exception to this trend. Except for the representation of the Nirvana of the Buddha, no other dead figure is seen in any of the Buddhist caves. In Bhahut the tragic Jataka tale of the noble elephant Chaddanta is depicted. But the elephant is not dead, though he is in positively low spirits, prior to his death, when the carpenter is sawing his last tusk. In the Ganesh Ganpha Caves near Udayagiri in Orissa another scene from a Jataka tale is depicted. Three hunters are riding on an elephant with the head of a man. Even in the hunting scenes, no bird or beast is shown dead or being killed. How then do we come across a corpse here in Bhaja? I think that this represents a local legend adopted by the Buddhists as in the case of the bear-man scene in Ajanta. Another inference is that an actual incident of the glorification of the death by bulls of a hero in the locality has been made into a monument, and that too in a cemetery.

James Burgess, in the Report of the *Buddhist Cave Temples* (1883: 7), mentions that the most peculiar picture in the Bhaja Caves is a group of fourteen monolithic dagobas of several sizes. In the second edition of *The History of Indian and Eastern Architecture* (1910: 137), we come across this statement about the dagobas: "The names of the Theras or Priests still legible on several of them indicate that they served the place of monuments in a cemetery though they may have been reverenced as altars to saints. This suggests the Bhaja Caves served as a mortuary as also a sanctuary."

The mortuary aspect alone can give sanction to depict the scene with a man's corpse stamped upon by two bulls.

Iron That Does Not Rust

This is a route from folklore to chemistry and technology. In 1936, while travelling in the dense forests of the Chanda District in what was then Madhya Pradesh, now in Maharashtra, I came to a village named Jaypur on the southern border of Chanda. It was a tribal village in which the Agariyas, proficient in iron-smelting and smithery, lived for generations. They showed me their iron implements—axes, knives etc.—which had no rust on them, though they were lying in the open on the ground. For years together, said the Agariyas, weather and rain had no effect on them. Rustless iron was their pride. On being asked how they could accomplish this, they said that when the "red iron", called the female iron or "mai-loha", and the "black iron", called the "pharu-loha" or male iron, were mixed together and smelted on charcoal heat the rustless iron was formed. They used a particular charcoal to smelt it. The hatchet, axe, knife etc. I saw looked as though they were newly polished.

This bit of folklorish information I passed on to Dr. Verrier Elwin and he has used it in his book *The Agarias* (1936).

This, I feel, carries seeds of old iron technology for rustless iron. A world-famous metal monument is the iron pillar of Raja Chandra in Delhi. Acharya Prafulla Chandra Ray, in his treatise *History of Ancient Indian Chemistry* (1932: 99-100), writes about the pillar as follows:

> The famous iron pillar..., near Delhi by the side of the Kutab Minar, which, from a consideration of the script and the text of the inscription on the pillar, is believed to have been constructed sometime in the early 4th century A.D. during the reign of the King Chandravarman of Pushkarana, Rajputana, as a pillar of victory. According to the historians, the pillar was first erected on Mount Vishnupada (probably at Mathura), as given in the inscription; it was afterwards removed to its present site by the king Anangapala II in or about 1050 A.D., when he rebuilt the city of Delhi. The pillar is about 24 ft. long, 16.4 in. in diameter at the bottom and 12 in. in diameter at the top. The engraved capital at the top is 3 ft. 6 in. in length. The weight of the pillar has been estimated to exceed 6 tons. Analysis of the specimens of the material of the pillar has proved that it is made of wrought iron without any alloy. Specific gravity of the metal, as given by Hadfield, is 7.81, that of the purest wrought iron being 7.84. The results of his analysis, as given in the Journal of the Iron and Steel Industries, are: Iron, 99.720; carbon, 0.080; silicon, 0.046; sulphur, 0.006; phosphorus, 0.144; manganese, — per cent.
>
> Absence of manganese is significant. Low percentage of sulphur indicates the use of charcoal as fuel, as also the purity of the ore. The pillar has wonderfully withstood the influence of rain and air for over fifteen centuries without giving any sign of rust formation. It has been suggested that possibly high phosphorus and low sulphur and manganese content has contributed somehow to its strikingly high corrosion resistance. There might be some truth in it, for in the absence of a second

metal the possibility of the formation of galvanic couple is not realized, which constitutes one of the most fundamental conditions for rusting to occur. Or, there might be a thin protective film of magnetic oxide ($Fe_3 O_4$), produced on the surface of the pillar by treatment like heating and quenching after being painted with a mixture of different salts and organic substances. There are evidences of iron being subjected to such treatment for improvement of their quality in some of the ancient alchemical treatises. Expert observers of all classes are of opinion that this pillar presents an indisputable and permanent record of marvellous metallurgical skill and engineering ability of the ancient Indian workers, which can reasonably claim unstinted admiration even of our present time.

The Rani Mahal or the Queen's Palace

This is a rare example of huge pentangular monolithic pillars.

On the border of Betul and Hoshangabad districts are the Makrai hills. Hard by flows the Machak stream, a small tributary of the Narmada. I visited the site of this "Palace" in 1936.

Once upon a time in this forest a Gond queen planned a mighty palace. Then something happened, nobody today knows exactly what, and vast jungles crept around to hide from the world the beginnings of her project. This "Palace" is about a mile and a half from the cave of Sheikh Dalla and his disciple the dreaded robber and rebel Tantya Bhil, who is still held in respect by the denizens of this tract.

The Rani Mahal is nothing but a huge mass of stone pillars and beams carefully piled one upon another on the top of a hill. Each pillar is a monolith more than 30 feet in length and pentangular in shape—a unique feature of old architecture involving skill and knowledge of engineering. The diameter of the pillars is about two and a half feet.

About a mile or so from the Rani Mahal similar pieces of stone beams are found lying in the river-basin. It seems that the pillars and beams were manufactured here and later carried to the hill.

The Korkus say that in very ancient times, a queen—probably a Gond—wanted to build a huge palace and had the stone pillars and beams hewn out of the rocks. But before the building was even started a catastrophe came and the unfortunate lady was not able to carry out her project. Some said it was the invasion of an enemy which put an end to the life of the queen. Hoping to re-start the work when the calamity was over, she ordered the pillars to be piled on the hilltop in order to preserve them. Though the palace structure never came into being, the huge pile of pentangular monolithic pillars on the hilltop surrounded by inaccessible forest is no doubt an architectural marvel.

Fossilized Fruit?

In a portion of the Narmada valley in Hoshangabad District, in a little stream near the village Gurngaon, curious stones are found. These are exactly of the shape, size and colour of various nuts and fruits such as custard apples, betelnuts, waternuts, apricots, cocoanuts (very small ones), dates and some medicinal berries like myphal, as it is called in Marathi, and even pieces of dried ginger. On being broken the interiors are found lined and coloured like their counterparts in real life, fresh fruits and nuts.

The villagers tell a curious legend about the "stone fruits", as they call them. Though it is an ingenious explanation from the mythical point of view, it has little historical authenticity. It is said that in this part of the forest, there lived more than three hundred years ago a fakir called Sheikh Shahib. Now it happened one day that a band of Banjaras (a nomadic trading community) was passing that way, having loaded their carts with commodities like cocoanuts, almonds etc. The fakir asked them what they were carrying, to which the insolent Banjaras replied that they were carrying stones. Enraged at their impudence the fakir said, "So be it!", and to their horror the Banjaras found that all the fruits and nuts had turned into stones. Frightened, they threw their loads into the stream and these are to be seen there to this day.

Conclusion

I have given the tale of man-bull relationship and ultimately the account of the death-scene in the Bhaja Caves which is a puzzle in archaeology.

The explanation of the formation of rustless iron by the Agariyas is not just a folk-belief but an actual technological fact which needs further investigation. Dr. P. C. Ray's scrutiny of the iron pillar at Delhi is a step in this direction. But the tribal smithery should not be further neglected.

I have given these examples which have close links with folklore. The folklore relationship with ancient cave-paintings and architecture, smithery and natural transformations of vegetable products like fruits and nuts into "stones" need careful investigation. It indicates that in many branches of knowledge folklore can still be helpful.

REFERENCES

Bannerji, Chandra Shekhar. 1877. The Kaimur range. *Journal of the Asiatic society of Bengal* 46, 16-36.

Bhagvat, Durga. 1966-67. Bear in Indian culture. *Journal of the Asiatic society of Bombay*, 1966-1967, 31—93.

Id. 1974. *Asval*. Puṇe.

Burgess, James. 1883. *Buddhist cave temples*. London.

Id. (ed.). 1911. *Śatruñjayamāhātmya*. Transl. by Weber. *Indian Antiquary* 30 (1911).

Coomaraswamy, Anand. 1921. *Art in Asia and Indonesia*. New York.

Cottell, Liconard (ed.). 1961. *Concise encyclopaedia of archaeology*.

Deshpande, V. N. 1963. *Kapilāṣaṣṭhīcī dānaparvaṇī*. In: *Mahārāṣṭralokasāhityamālā*, vol. III, part I, Poona, 141ff.

Dubois, Jean Aldec. 1906. *Hindu manners and customs*. London.

Elwin, Verrier. 1936. *The Agarias*. London.

Fergusson, James. 1910. *The history of Indian and eastern architecture*. London.

Fergusson, James and and Burgess, James. 1910. *Cave temples of India*. London.

Petrie, William Matthew Flinders. 1910. *Arts and crafts of ancient Egypt.* Chicago and Edinburgh.

Govardhanacarya, A. 1911. A lacuna in the vamsha. *Indian Antiquary* 40 (1911), 58-61.

Griffith, John. 1897a. *The paintings in the Buddhist cave temples of Ajanta.* London.

1897b. *Ajanta.* London.

Hawles, Jacquetta. 1963. *The world of the past,* vol. IX. London, 112-122.

Iyengar, Venkatesh. 1954. *Popular culture of Karnataka.* Bangalore.

Jog, Viṣṇu Narasiṃha (ed.). 1956. *Śrī Saṃta Nāmadeva Mahārāja yāṃcī gāthā.* Puṇeṃ, *śake* 1853 (1930); reprint.

Joshi, V. V. 1936. *Loka-kathā and lokagīte.* Nagpur.

Lal, Rai Bahadur Hira. 1921. Human sacrifice in ancient India. *Man in India* 1, 51-61.

Merutunga, Acharya. 1901. *Prabandhacintāmaṇi.* Transl. by C. H. Tawny. Calcutta.

Mitra, Kalipad. 1932. On the Gaydana festival. *Indian Antiquary* VI.6, 1ff.

Mitra, S. C. 1910-11. A Bihari nursery story of the bargaining, animal type. *Journal of the anthropological society of Bombay,* IX (1910-1911), 163-166.

Pradhan, Ayodhya Prasad. 1968. *The Buddhist system of meditation,* vol. I. New Delhi.

Ray, Prafulla Chandra. 1932. *History of ancient Indian chemistry.* Calcutta.

Shah, Asharam Dalichand. n.d. *Gujarātī kahevat.* Mumbai.

Singh, R. C. 1968. Bhitagam brick temple. *Bulletin of museums and archaeology in Uttar Pradesh,* No. 1.

Thurston, Edgar. 1909. *Tribes and castes of southern India.* 7 volumes. Madras.

Thompson, Charles S. (Reverend). 1895. *Rudiments of the Bhili language.* Ahmedabad.

Tucci, Guiseppe. 1949. *Tibetan painted scrolls.* Rome.

Yazdani, G. 1930. *Ajanta,* vol. I. Hyderabad.

R. C. Dhere

FOLK PERCEPTION AND SAINTS' PERCEPTION

The Saints' Medium of Enlightenment

The saints rose up from the common people. They were representatives of the people in the real sense of the term and hence they used the folk medium for the enlightenment of the masses. Those to whom our new thought is to be directed so as to change their lifestyle should like to listen to us, should welcome the new thought and should have fellow-feeling for the preacher and his preaching. This is the first requirement of the work of enlightening people, and it is nowhere seen in the thought, word and practice of the preacher as it is in those of the saints. We immediately perceive that the preachers in whom it is seen are of a saintly nature. This requirement cannot be fulfilled unless there is compassion for those who are to be addressed and transformed.

The saints did not hate the classical languages of the learned, or ignore whatever was eternal and essential in them. But in order to have a dialogue with the masses they took to the language of the people, used popular metres like the *ovī* and the *abhaṅga* and expressed themselves through them. They used the way of folk-songs and created the fantastic world of *bhārūḍs* (dramatic poems), *lāvaṇīs* (erotic songs) and ballads. It is true that many times the saints adversely criticised popular beliefs and the deities related to them. But, taking into consideration the toughness of these socially degrading and time-bound beliefs, it must be said that the saints upgraded them and their manifest forms which are the folk deities. While doing this, they had to give a new form to the popular beliefs, rid them of their time-bound triviality, and fill them with fresh noble content. The universal mercy or compassion which the saints showed while achieving this is really wonderful, beyond description. In the words of Tukārām, the saints had a feeling of restlessness as they saw people drowning themselves, and, therefore, they dwelt among them, speaking their language and living the way they did. They continued to do their best to express through their deeds what they considered the ennobled ideal life. The literature of the saints is full of the marks of the bleeding agonies they suffered while transgressing the thorny hedge of the limits of time and "blood and flesh". These marks are the colourful signs of their intimate relationship with us. We can experience it in different forms and ways in the literature of the saints. For example, instead of condemning or ridiculing folk etymology, they have endowed it with a rich, new life. That makes us respect them and their way of enlightenment all the more. Before seeing how the poet-saints used folk etymology to fulfil their objective we have to understand what folk etymology means.

The Nature of Folk Etymology

All educated persons have some rough idea about etymology. It is true that in our daily life we use innumerable words from our own language without caring for their etymology. Still, many times we feel curiosity for the origin or etymology of some uncommon words and their meaning. Language is concerned not only with basic living but also with all aspects of culture, and that is why we feel curious to know the exact meaning of words and their fine semantic shades. We need to go to the roots of the words in order to convey our thoughts to others accurately and clearly by using apt words.

But an ordinary educated person does not necessarily try scientifically to satisfy this curiosity. In the case of an uneducated person, it is simply impossible. There are words which are obsolete, which have been lost semantically in the course of time along with their accompanying functions. When such words fall on our ears, or when it becomes unavoidable to struggle with their meaning because of their association with some important matter, then we try to analyse them with the help of their similarity with the words we know. It is in this way that folk etymology is born—when unfamiliar words are loaded with meaning, different from the original one, in an unscientific manner. In short, unscientific, wrong etymology is folk etymology. When the original meaning of a word is lost, attempt is made to interpret it by burdening it with a different meaning drawn from an artificial splitting of it. Our literary tradition and daily use of the language provide innumerable examples of this phenomenon. According to linguistics, folk etymology is unscientific and therefore wrong. Still, the folk perception it displays is not only interesting but also a subject of serious study, from the linguistic and social points of view. Though many times folk etymology is barren, harmless and ineffective, it can also be extremely revolutionary and bring about serious social consequences, both good and bad.

Examples of Folk Etymology

We have not as yet given serious thought to folk etymology. Naturally, we have not produced even primary studies just indicating the importance of folk etymology as a means of the study of society or social mind. In fact, we need a dictionary of folk etymology just as we have an etymological dictionary of a given language. Such a dictionary will be a great help to scholars working in the fields of linguistics, social history and folk psychology. Here I am offering just a few examples of folk etymology which can meet my limited objectives.

While studying the literature of the poet-saints I had to investigate various religious cults and their deities. Then I found that there was a tendency to explain the names of the deities and their "essential" holy places, as also the different facts connected with them, with the help of folk etymology. In the present context of "folk perception" and "saints' perception" I have selected examples from the same field, namely, that of deities, their places and their ritual practices.

There is a place called Maṅgsuḷī in Belgaum District. It is on the Miraj-Bijāpūr road and is known as a living and powerful seat of god Khaṇḍobā. There on the pinnacle of his temple is an inscription mentioning the date: "Śake 1653 (A.D. 1731) Māgha Śuddha 7". The temple was built by Basavaprabhū Desai of Vantamuri (Belgaum District) during the regime of king Alī Ādilśāh of Bijāpūr. According to oral tradition, god Khaṇḍobā of Naḷdurg came to Maṅgsuḷī because of the *bhakti* of Basavaprabhū. This means that this seat of Khaṇḍobā is a comparatively recent creation belonging to the Muslim period. With the rise of the authority of god Khaṇḍobā in Maṅgsuḷī the importance of the original ruling deity began to dwindle and there began to be a tendency to explain the place name, Maṅgsuḷī, in such a way as to stress the greatness of Khaṇḍobā. This tendency made the folk perception derive the place name, Maṅgsuḷī, from the word Malla-suḷī, meaning (the place) where the demon Malla was impaled by god Khaṇḍobā on the stake. As regards this etymology: for one thing, the village of Maṅgsuḷī was already in existence before Khaṇḍobā appeared there because of the *bhakti* of Basavaprabhu Desai; and, secondly, the (imaginary) corruption into Mallasuḷī is impossible. Therefore, the derivation of the place name Maṅgsuḷī from Mallasuḷī and its explanatory basic story of Khaṇḍobā impaling the demon Malla are just the outcome of folk etymology. According to the Sanskrit text *Mallārimāhātmya* this myth is connected not with Maṅgsuḷī but with Pembar, near Bidar, where the demon Malla was not impaled on a stake, but was killed in battle by Khaṇḍobā. Thus, the myth used to justify deriving the name Maṅgsuḷī from Mallasuḷī has nothing to do with Maṅgsuḷī. It is obvious that the folk etymology is meant to establish the new authority of Khaṇḍobā in Maṅgsuḷī and to make people either neglect or forget the original ruling deity of that place.

Actually the place name Maṅgsuḷī is made up of two words: *maṅga*, meaning goddess, and *suḷe*, meaning a prostitute, a shameless woman, a nude. Maṅgsuḷe or Maṅgsuḷī means "a goddess in the form of a nude woman". This scientific etymology of the place-name clearly points towards the goddess known as Lajjā-Gaurī (Shameful Gaurī). Even today there is in Maṅgsuḷī the seat of a goddess known as Lakṣmī in a locality called Lakṣmīvāḍī. It has a strange folk tale behind it. The devotees of the goddess did not find the nude form presentable. So one of them prayed to her: "Mother, please do not stand before us like this." The goddess agreed and stood with her face turned in the other direction. Since then the people started worshipping her back. That is what the story tells. Someone must have reversed the nude statue of the goddess, keen for coitus, or replaced it with a flat stone slab, and invented a myth to justify his action. This is the obvious interpretation of the folk story. When the goddess with whom the original meaning of the place name Maṅgsuḷī was connected became secondary or neglected, a fresh folk perception implying the importance of the new ruling god became popular. This etymology is of course wrong and far fetched in relation to the original meaning of the word. Still, it tells us about the transformation of the centre of faith in this place, and, therefore, a scholar of the history of religion will have to take it into consideration. This is an example of how serious truths are evolved from the wrong explanations given by or through folk etymology.

Reference to Khaṇḍobā in the context of Maṅgsuḷī reminds me of another example–the example of the *vāghyā* of Khaṇḍobā. The same thing has happened in the case of *vāghyā* which happened with the Kannada Maṅgsuḷī explained by the Marāṭhī Mallasuḷī. A *vāghyā* is one of the devotees of Khaṇḍobā. He is a dog of this hunter god, in the form of a human being. The Marāṭhī word *vāghyā* is derived from the Kannada word *vaggeya*, meaning a dog. But when Maharashtra forgot the original Kannada word *vaggeya* and its meaning, the term *vāghyā* was connected with *vāgh* (tiger), phonetically and morphically similar to it. The poet Sheikh Mahammad of Śrigonda mentioned the *vāghyā* as one who "barks and asks for alms" and as "a young boy who is transformed into a dog and made to bark". A number of *bhāruḍas* composed by the poet-saint mention the barking and growling of the *vāghyās*. Many times these *vāghyās* touch the ground with their hands and imitate the walking on all fours and the barking of dogs. They do this in full faith. The *Jayādrimāhātmya* (or the *Jejurīmāhātmya*) contains a story telling how the tiger was transformed into the dog. It is meant to coordinate the dogness of the *vāghyā* preserved in old literary allusions and present practices on the one hand, and the tigerness of the *vāghyā* suggested by phonetic similarities on the other. There are innumerable such examples showing the influence of folk etymology in structuring the lives of gods.

It is in the case of Khaṇḍobā that Jyotiba Phule, in his essay on "*Gulāmgirī*" ("Slavery"), has taken to folk etymology to explain the nature of folk gods. He says, "Khaṇḍobā was so proud of his fair fighting that he never attacked an enemy who turned his tail. That is why he was named 'Mār-taṇḍ' of which Mārtaṇḍ is the corruption." This is Jyotiba's explanation of the popular name Mārtaṇḍ, which is but a part of the long compound name Mallāri-Mārtaṇḍa-Bhairava which appears in the *Mallāri-māhātmya* and suggests the story of his incarnation. Jyotiba has used the myth of Khaṇḍobā with the help of folk etymology to further his own goal of enlightenment and to support his own ideas.

All these examples of folk etymology which I have cited are connected with Khaṇḍobā. But what I intend to discuss here is not the glorification of folk deities or folk religion on the part of the poet-saints, but the way in which they have achieved their aim of enlightenment with the help of folk etymology. We have to consider the work of the saints within this framework.

Standing on the Brick

The three examples given above will clearly show that folk etymology always has a story behind it. The thinking of the folk mind always takes the form of a narrative. Pure, abstract thinking does not generally come within its purview. That is why the literature of the poet-saints keeps on abstracting through narratives on the one hand, and making concrete through images and parables on the other. Not all could fulfill the folowing vow with as much competence as Jñānadev, who made it:

> As I speak,
> I will give form to the formless
> and make the senses experience that
> which is beyond them.

Still, the way of all poet-saints is the same. They are always seen giving a concrete form to abstract principles and thus bringing them within the reach of the common people. They strive hard to dress up abstract thoughts and make them stand on the pedestal of the public understanding. This method of making the abstract concrete by giving it a narrative form is suggestive of the developed understanding of the folk mind. It shows the saints' awareness of the nature of the folk mind, which can grasp abstractions only through stories.

The deity most dear to the Marāṭhī poet-saints is Viṭṭhal. They harp incessantly on the subject of his even feet standing on the brick. They envy the brick for its good fortune in having constant contact with his feet. From where did the brick come? Even after analysing the *sthala-purāṇas* and looking into the innumerable references in the literature of the poet-saints, we find it obvious that the brick has grown from the folk etymology of the most dear name, Viṭṭhal. He is Viṭṭhal who stands on the '*vīṭ*', the brick. The folk perception has split the name Viṭṭhal into two components, *vīṭ* and *ṭhal*, and has explained the name Viṭṭhal as meaning "the one who is standing on the brick". But this explanation is story-based, asking for a story to justify it. As soon as this folk etymology falls on the ears, questions arise in the mind: Whence this brick? Who planned it? And why? At whose request or call did God stand on it? Then comes the story of Puṇḍalik with answers to these questions. Viṭṭhal, this "substance of beauty", stood on the brick because of the devotee Puṇḍalik. Jñānadev has honoured the story of the brick in the following way:

> "Maybe the *brahman* lost its way,
> and came uncovered to Paṇḍharpūr.
> The devotee Puṇḍalik saw it
> and made it stand on the brick.
> That is our treasure, Viṭhobā.
> God Brahmā and others contemplate him.
> His even feet look nice on the brick."

This folk etymology of the name Viṭṭhal, the myth of Puṇḍalik arising naturally from it, the acceptance of this myth in good faith as a "divine event" by the people and the saints, and finally, the universality created out of it—all this is indescribably fantastic. For the saints, Puṇḍalik becomes a symbol of *bhāva*, loving devotion:

> "I saw Śrī Hari
> standing on the brick,
> with even feet,
> on the bank of the Bhīmā of *bhakti*."

This "brick" in the literature of the saints shows their high regard for folk etymology and the explanatory myth which gives it concrete form.

Mhāḷasā/Mohinī and Bhavānī

Just as the literature of the Marāṭhī saints is pervaded by Viṭṭhal, the thought world of Jñānadev, the fountainhead of the tradition of saints, is nourished by the fascinating Mhāḷasā of Nevase. Jñānadev composed his *Bhāvārthadīpikā* (or the *Jñāneśvarī*) at Nevase. At the end of this work he mentions the place and its deity, Mhāḷasā, in the following words:

> "There, at the most holy place in the three worlds,
> where dwells Śrī Mhāḷasā,
> who is the life-thread of the world."

The deity at Nevase is known to all as Mohinīrāj. But Jñānadev calls the deity Mhāḷasā. The *Līḷācaritra* of the Mahānubhāvas also refers to her as Mhāḷasī or Mhāḷasā. Bahirā Jātaveda, a contemporary author of Jñānadev, also calls her by the name Mhāḷasā. For Ekanāth also, who lived more than 300 years later than Jñānadev, she is still Mhāḷasā. In the '*Life of Jñānadev*' attributed to Nāmadev, Nevase is Mhāḷasāpur. It is clear from all this evidence that the ruling deity of Nevase was Mhāḷasā. Jñānadev takes her to be the life-thread of the world and glorifies the region presided over by her as "the most holy among the three worlds". Now we know that Mhāḷasā is an independent folk goddess or a goddess included in the family of Khaṇḍobā as his legal wife. The question is, how was she transformed into Mohinī at Nevase? How was she raised to the status of the "life-thread of the world"? Again there is a folk etymology to answer these questions. It is this: "Mhāḷasā is the one who intoxicates, lures." This goddess is known as Māḷaj, or Māḷcī, or Malavva in Karnatak, and as Mhāḷasā, or Mālhāisā in Maharashtra. Thus, Māl, or Mhāl, or Mālh is the common component in these regional names of the same goddess. Both the word *malai* in the name Mailār and the word *māl* in the name Mhāḷasā indicate a mountain, and both of these deities dwell on hill-tops. Then whence comes the etymology: "Mhāḷasā is the one who lures"? The verbs like *mālātaṇẽ, mālāthaṇẽ, mālhātaṇẽ,* and *mālhāthaṇẽ* from the *Jñāneśvarī* show that there was a root like *māl* or *mālh* in some native language. In the *Jñāneśvarī* this verb means "to lure", "to attract". The folk etymology of Mhāḷasā had its source in the formal similarity between the word *māḷ,* meaning "a mountain", and the root *māl,* meaning "to lure". In the post-Jñānadev period, there was a tradition of calling the area around Nevase Māḷīmoha. The word *Māḷīmoha* is a translation compound of two synonyms, *māḷī* and the Sanskrit *moha.* This place name also suggests a folk etymology of Mhāḷasā as a "luring image".

People and also the saints accepted this luring form of Mhāḷasā grown up from folk etymology. Since Mohinī was an incarnation of god Viṣṇu, people started calling him Mohinīrāj. Because of his female/male form, he got the status of Ardhanārīśvara or Ardhanārīnārāyaṇa in the Vaiṣṇava tradition. When the nectar churned out from the ocean was distributed, Mohinī was partial to the gods, and she killed the demon Rāhu. She was the family deity of Bahirā Jātaved. He accepted in good faith this new myth originating from folk etymology and, imitating Jñānādev, praised her in the following hymn:

> "On the right side the husband,
> and on the left, the universe;
> Even Brahmā and other gods cannot decide
> whether she is a man or a woman.
> The Creator says: 'O my Mother,
> you are both, the father and the mother,
> the lover and the beloved.'
> By this magic you take care of your household
> of children as big as the universe."

If Bahirā Jātaved experiences the primeval principle of the universe in her form, Jñānadev takes her as the life-thread of the world. Those who are conversant with the writings of Jñānadev will easily realise that the phraseology used by Bahirā Jātaved to describe Mhāḷasā belongs to the *Anubhavāmṛta* of Jñānadev. The concept of the "Lover and the Beloved" was already expressed by Jñānadev in his *Anubhavāmṛta* in the form of the identity between Śiva and Śakti. The very images and phrases which Jñānadev used to describe the unity of Śiva and Śakti, without any reference to Mhāḷasā, are employed by Bahirā Jātaved to describe Mhāḷasā. The meaning of all this is clear. It is this: that Jñānadev's concept of the unity of Śiva and Śakti was fed by the myth of Mohinī born from the folk etymology of the name Mhāḷasā.

Accepting the folk etymology of one more deity, the saints have enlightened the masses on still another level. This deity is the goddess Bhavānī. That she became the Great Mother, the inspiring power of Maharashtra during the times of Śivājī, is a fact supported by the writings of the saints. Bhavānī was the family deity of Śivājī and Rāmadās as she was the deity of innumerable lineages in Maharashtra. But it was Saint Ekanāth who enriched her life by adding to it an altogether new substance of power befitting his times. Ekanāth was the Lokanāth, the Folk-lord, who provided the basis for the work achieved by Śivājī and Rāmadās. The attribute *Rāmavaradāyinī* of the goddess Bhavānī, which was very dear to and repeatedly used by Rāmadās, was first mentioned by Ekanāth. Rāmadās says that he searched out Mother *Rāmavaradāyinī*. This he did from the *Bhāvārtha-Rāmāyaṇa* of Ekanāth. In the Araṇyakāṇḍa of the *Bhāvārtha-Rāmāyaṇa,* Ekanāth has included a local story about Tuḷajā-bhavānī. After Rāvaṇ had abducted Sītā, Rām started roaming about, crying, "O Sītā, O Sītā". Bhavānī was surprised to see this. She did not think it proper that Rām, whose name her husband (Śiva) contemplates constantly, should cry like this for his wife. So, with the consent of Śiva, she took on the form of Sītā in order to test Rām. Lakṣmaṇ was deceived by it, but Rām immediately came to know that it was the very Ādimāyā appearing as Sītā in order to test him.

"Śrī Rām asked her, 'Who are you?' (*tū kāi ?*)

and that very name (Tukāi) became common.
It is still in use.
She is called Tukāi Jagadamba.
Her own place in the Daṇḍakāraṇya, named after her,
is still worshipped by the people.
Tukāī! She is the Mother who gave a boon to Rām."

The very same Bhavānī whom Rām asked, "Who are you, Mother?" became famous as Tukāī. The folk etymology of Bhavānī's popular name, Tukāī, was first recognised by Ekanāth. Tukāī is Bhavānī's popular name in Maharashtra. Folk perception splits it into *tū kā āi* (meaning, "Is it you, Mother?"). But then the question arose: "Who asked this and to whom?" To answer this question, a story had to be invented—a story about the meeting of Rām and Bhavānī. When Rām passed the test, Bhavānī was pleased, and she gave him a boon that he would kill Rāvaṇ and win back Sītā. This is the explanatory myth about the folk etymology of the name Tukāī as *tū kā āi*. The poet-saints found a new attribute of Bhavānī in this myth: *Rāmavaradāyinī*, giver of a boon to Rām, which they used for public awakening. Saying, "Eh woman, open the door", they sat obstinately at the threshold in order to awaken the Rām in the folk mind and bring him the support of the spiritual power, *ātma-śakti*. Like Ekanāth, Rāmadās also accepted this myth *in toto:*

"There in the solitude of the forest,
the Virgin Goddess saw Rām,
and Rām saw the Goddess.
They had a dialogue:
'Who are you and whence do you come?
What's your name?'
'I am the very Tukāī.
Go away; I give you a boon.
Since then, she is called Mother,
the giver of a boon to Rām."

Rāmadās not only invoked the *Rāmavaradāyinī* Bhavānī, but also challenged her. On the strength of his own *bhakti* and the past evidence of her prowess at destroying evil, he enjoined her to show her valour in the present context. In this way Rāmadās tries to support the cause of the new incarnation of Rām (namely, Śivājī) in fighting against the new demons. He treats Śivājī's battles as if he were the angry god incarnate and prays to the *Rāmavaradāyinī* Bhavānī to stand behind him and give him strength. Seeking support from the story of Rām, Bhavānī appears as a very special power in the context of Śivājī and Rāmadās. Śivājī, who was a devotee of Bhavānī, keeps the ideal of Rām before him and fights against the demons of his times. These events contain evidence of myths making history, and history getting the status of divine myths. In all these happenings, the folk etymology *tū kā āi*, the myth of *Rāmavaradāyinī* arising out of it, and the insight of the poet-saints in using this myth for the enlightenment of the people are all unique. This is an example that throws light on the coordination between folk perception and the saints' perception.

Public leaders desiring to enlighten the people and change their life-style can benefit a good deal from these three examples. No enlightenment can be achieved just by entertaining utopian ideas and repeating them barrenly. When thoughts about achieving the upliftment of the Self and the people become manifest, they bind the whole of life under their spell. It is this being spellbound which translates thoughts into action. When this happens, the ground is ready to convey self-evident and merciful thoughts to the people according to their capacity to receive them. In this context, the memory of an honest Maharashtrian Marxist comes to my mind. Thinking again about religious beliefs towards the end of his life, this thinker said that humanism should be the religion of today and tomorrow, and in order that this new religion may descend into our life, beliefs like religious beliefs should be on the rise. I think this suggests the possibility of becoming folk-minded. This can be achieved through merciful thinking. If the public leaders remain unaware of this, it will be our fate to say after Vyāsa, "No one listens to me"—with this difference, that Vyāsa said it raising his arms, and we will say it beating our forehead with our hands. To avoid this, we have to remember the way of the saints again and again. It will appeal even to those who do not accept the saints and their way of thinking. In fact, even those who are keen to put an end to the seven hundred-year-old dominance of the saints on the folk-mind will have to use their methods if they want to reach the masses.

GENERAL INDEX

INDEX OF INDIC WORDS

CONTRIBUTORS

Dr. Durga Bhagwat
Rajendravihar
Guilder Lane
Bombay 400008
India

Dilip Chitre
Flat No. 2, Vijaya Apartments
Plot No. 54, Swastishree Society
Karve Nagar
Pune 411029
India

Professor M. N. Deshpande
D-25 Press Enclave
Saket
New Delhi 110 017
India

Professor M. K. Dhavalikar
Deccan College
Pune 411 006
India

Dr. R. C. Dhere
"Vidisha"
10 Abhiram Society
Tulsibhagwale Colony
Pune 411 009
India

Professor Anne Feldhaus
Department of Religious Studies
Arizona State University
Tempe, Arizona 85287-0402
USA

Professor James W. Laine
Macalester College
1600 Grand Avenue
St. Paul, Minnesota 55105-1899
USA

Professor P. B. Mande
"Mangalprabha"
109, N5 (South)
CIDCO
Aurangabad 431 003
India

Dr. Traude Pillai-Vetšchera
Lichtensteinstr. 57
A-1090 Wien
Austria

Dr. Erik Reenberg Sand
Femkanten C8
DK-2630 Taastrup
Denmark

Professor N. K. Wagle
Centre for South Asian Studies
University of Toronto
Sidney Smith Hall
100 George Street
Toronto, Ontario M5S 1A1
Canada

Professor Eleanor Zelliot
Department of History
Carleton College
Northfield, Minnesota 55057
USA

List of Illustrations to M. K. Dhavalikar's article The living past. The first farmers of Maharashtra and their successors.